Sustainability as a Global Culture

The Political Economy of the SDGs and Mispricing of the Future

Haluk Haksal

Series in Economics

VERNON PRESS

www.vernonpress.com

In the Americas:

Vernon Press
1000 N West Street, Suite 1200,
Wilmington, Delaware 19801
United States

In the rest of the world:

Vernon Press
C/Sancti Espiritu 17,
Malaga, 29006
Spain

Series in Economics

Library of Congress Control Number: 2026944442

ISBN: 979-8-2616-0075-6

Cover design by Vernon Press with elements by Magnific.

This book provides a comprehensive perspective on sustainability and environmental economics, making it a valuable resource for both teaching and research.

Professor Sevil Acar
Professor of Economics, Boğaziçi University, Istanbul, Türkiye

This is an intellectually rich book that diagnoses the global pricing system's failure to internalize ecological and social costs, and builds a credible analytical framework for correcting it. Dr. Haksal offers an original analytical architecture that shows what follows when we stop treating sustainability as a trade-off and start treating it as the frame within which economic choices are made. This book is well-suited as a textbook in ecological economics or sustainability.

Professor Murat Tarakci
Professor of Innovation Strategy, IMD Lausanne, Switzerland

Here is a book that treats sustainability from a political economy and finance perspective. It adopts a Green Keynesian approach and gives pricing and investments a key role, and thus provides a fresh perspective on sustainable investments.

Professor Rick van der Ploeg
Director of Research, Professor of Economics, University of Oxford, UK

Sustainable finance has travelled a long way, but genuine sustainability is nowhere close. With this book, Dr. Haluk Haksal provides a comprehensive overview to readers interested in the history and future of sustainable finance. You will find yourself immersed between analytical detail and appeal to sustainability as a precondition for human freedom and dignity.

Philipp Censkowsky
Faculty of Business and Economics (HEC Lausanne),
University of Lausanne, Switzerland

This book offers a compelling reframing of sustainability. Rather than treating it as a trade-off among competing objectives, Haluk Haksal presents it as a global culture that shapes how we invest, govern, and live. By tracing the path from mispriced markets through sustainable investment to macroeconomic policy, he provides both a sharp diagnosis of why current systems fall short and a coherent framework for aligning them with ecological limits and long-term human well-being. The clarity and structure of the analysis make this book particularly valuable for teaching in sustainability and environmental economics, as well as ecological economics.

Professor Karl Schmedders
Professor of Finance, IMD Lausanne, Switzerland

What distinguishes this book is its clarity on what actually changes behavior: culture, not compliance. By treating the SDGs as shared ethical coordinates rather than bureaucratic milestones, Haksal delivers an educational foundation we urgently need. The critique of GDP orthodoxy and the case for post-GDP economics are not tangential; they are overdue. Pluridisciplinary thinking has become the baseline.

Dr. Nathan Delacrétaz
Research Fellow, Center for Risk Management Lausanne (CRML)
Faculty of Business and Economics (HEC Lausanne),
University of Lausanne, Switzerland

Contents

List of Figures

List of Tables

List of Abbreviations

AI	Artificial Intelligence
ANN	Artificial Neural Networks
APEC	Asia-Pacific Economic Cooperation
ASCM	Agreement on Subsidies and Countervailing Measures
C	Consumption
CBAM	Carbon Border Adjustment Mechanism
CBDR	Common but Differentiated Responsibilities
CBOE VIX	Chicago Board Options Exchange Volatility Index
CC BY-NC	Creative Commons Attribution–Non Commercial License
CDM	Clean Development Mechanism
Carbon VIX	Carbon Volatility Index
COP	Conference of the Parties
Copernicus	Copernicus Climate Change Service
CSRD	Corporate Sustainability Reporting Directive
CTE	Committee on Trade and Environment
DICE	Dynamic Integrated Climate Economy
ECMWF	European Centre for Medium-Range Weather Forecasts
EHB	European Hydrogen Bank
ESG	Environmental, Social, and Governance
ETS	Emissions Trading System
EU	European Union
EUAs	European Union Allowances
EU ETS	European Union Emissions Trading System
EV	Electric Vehicle
FED	Federal Reserve System
G	Government Expenditure
GBM	Geometric Brownian Motion
GDI	Gender Development Index
GEI	Gender Equality Index
GII	Gender Inequality Index
GDP	Gross Domestic Product

GHG	Greenhouse Gases
GISD	Global Investors for Sustainable Development
GISTEMP	Goddard Institute for Space Studies Surface Temperature Analysis
GNI	Gross National Income
GNP	Gross National Product
GPI	Genuine Progress Indicator
HDI	Human Development Index
HPI	Happy Planet Index
I	Investment
IAMs	Integrated Assessment Models
IHDI	Inequality-Adjusted Human Development Index
IPCC	Intergovernmental Panel on Climate Change
IRR	Internal Rate of Return
ISEW	Index of Sustainable Economic Welfare
IWI	Inclusive Wealth Index
IWR	Inclusive Wealth Report
LCA	Life Cycle Assessment or Analysis
LCC	Life Cycle Costing
LCI	Life Cycle Inventory
LCIA	Life Cycle Impact Assessment
LCSA	Life Cycle Sustainability Assessment
LCT	Life Cycle Thinking
LSTM	Long Short-Term Memory
M	Import
MC	Ministerial Conference
MFA	Material Flow Analysis
MPI	Multidimensional Poverty Index
NASA	National Aeronautics and Space Administration
NBER	National Bureau of Economic Research
NDCs	Nationally Determined Contributions
NGOs	Non-Governmental Organizations
NOAA	National Oceanic and Atmospheric Administration
NPV	Net Present Value
ODA	Official Development Assistance

OECD	Organization for Economic Cooperation and Development
PCAF	Partnership for Carbon Accounting Financials
PPP	Purchasing Power Parity
R&D	Research and Development
RICE	Regional Integrated Climate Economy
RNN	Recurrent Neural Networks
ROA	Real Options Approach
SCC	Social Cost of Carbon
SDGs	Sustainable Development Goals
SEI	Stockholm Environment Institute
SFDR	Sustainable Finance Disclosure Regulation
SFSC	Short Food Supply Chain
SNN	System of National Accounts
SSF Report	Stiglitz-Sen Fitoussi Report
S-LCA	Social Life Cycle Assessment
TESSD	Trade and Environmental Sustainability Structured Discussions
TFP	Total Factor Productivity
UDHR	Universal Declaration of Human Rights
UN	United Nations
UNDP	United Nations Development Programme
UNEP	United Nations Environment Programme
UNFCCC	United Nations Framework Convention on Climate Change
UNGA	United Nations General Assembly
UNPRI	United Nations Principles for Responsible Investment
UNU	United Nations University
X	Export
WACI	Weighted Average Carbon Intensity
WMO	World Meteorological Organization
WTO	World Trade Organization

Preface

This book explores development from a political-economic perspective. Nevertheless, I wish to make the following distinction from the outset: development is often immediately associated with economics—understandably so, as economics provides powerful tools, methods, and theories for analyzing growth, investment, and efficiency. However, development is first and foremost a matter of human rights.

The very first article of the Universal Declaration of Human Rights (UDHR) affirms:

> All human beings are born free and equal in dignity and rights. They are endowed with reason and conscience and should act towards one another in a spirit of brotherhood.

This statement reflects a global consensus: every human being, regardless of place of birth, is entitled to the same fundamental rights and dignity. Yet, for a large share of the world's population, these rights remain out of reach.

While these rights are universal in principle, they are far from being universally enjoyed. For more than half of the world's population—those living in countries that have not achieved a minimum threshold of development—basic rights such as food, clean water, education, and healthcare remain inaccessible. It is in this context that the Sustainable Development Goals (SDGs) emerge as a global blueprint for turning these rights from aspirations into realities.

This book arises from an urgent concern: that our economic and financial systems, though vast in scale and influence, often fall short of enhancing what truly matters—the freedom and capability of people to live lives they have reason to value.

Human rights may be legally recognised, yet not effectively enjoyed by populations that fall below a certain development threshold. It is like being in an invisible prison—one where the walls are not physical, but structural and economic. In such a condition, people may be theoretically free, yet unable to satisfy even their most basic needs.

In this context, I recall the 2005 report by former UN Secretary-General Kofi Annan, titled *In Larger Freedom: Towards Development, Security and Human Rights for All.* Deeply influenced by Amartya Sen's capabilities approach, Annan argued that development must be understood not as the accumulation of wealth, but as the expansion of substantive freedoms. He stated that development cannot be achieved without security, nor security without development, and that neither can be sustained without respect for human rights. This vision underscores a simple but fundamental truth: development, security, and human rights are deeply interconnected and mutually reinforcing.

Two decades later, these insights remain at the core of today's global challenges.

The question, therefore, is: if sustainable development has become a global aspiration, why do our economic and financial systems continue to produce unsustainable outcomes?

The book's central diagnosis is that the global pricing system is structurally misaligned with sustainability imperatives. More precisely, prices fail to convey meaningful information about long-term welfare because ecosystems are treated as costless, social dimensions are marginalised, and the interests of future generations are systematically excluded. The path to addressing this misalignment lies in sustainable investment, examined across both microeconomic and macroeconomic perspectives. The study explores how sustainability transforms firms' cost structures and challenges macroeconomic assumptions about growth and welfare.

The analysis develops across several key themes:

- The implications of SDG-aligned finance;
- The valuation of externalities and carbon pricing;
- The role of Keynesian uncertainty in evaluating sustainable investments;
- The use of behavioural economics in promoting sustainable consumption;
- And the need for alternatives to GDP in assessing human and ecological well-being.

This book addresses researchers, graduate and undergraduate students, policymakers, and politicians—those who not only study but also influence economic, social, and environmental futures. While grounded in academic research and directed towards students and scholars, it is also written with a broader non-expert audience in mind. To this end, every chapter concludes with two complementary summaries:

- **Key Insights**: A concise, analytical synthesis intended for expert readers and academics;
- **In Simple Words**: A more globally accessible, narrative-style summary written for non-experts in the field and the general public, meant to translate complex ideas into a more relatable and intuitive form.

These sections aim to expand the book's reach and foster a broader understanding of how sustainability intersects with political economy.

The structure of the book follows a deliberate asymmetry:

Chapter 1 begins with values—introducing sustainability as a global culture grounded in human rights. It sets the conceptual foundation for the economic analysis that follows.

Chapter 6 opens with the book's central diagnosis of a misaligned global pricing system and brings together the analytical framework developed throughout the study. It then reconnects this economic analysis with a human rights perspective and a global culture of sustainability. The result is a narrative that begins with *why this matters*, develops by explaining *how the system operates*, and concludes by showing *how it can be transformed*—before returning to what ultimately defines its purpose.

While not exhaustive, I hope this book provides a coherent conceptual framework and an ethical compass for navigating the complexities of sustainable development.

Haluk Haksal
Geneva, 2026

Acknowledgments

I would like to express my sincere gratitude to **Prof. Sevil Acar** (Boğaziçi University) for her valuable and thoughtful comments on an earlier version of this manuscript. Her insights, particularly regarding the inclusion of ecological footprint analysis, significantly strengthened both the conceptual coherence and the analytical depth of the study.

I am grateful to **Prof. Mikdat Kadıoğlu** (Istanbul Technical University) and **Prof. Zafer Aslan** (Istanbul Aydın University) for their expertise on the meteorological dimensions of double materiality. Their feedback was especially helpful in refining the case study on cloud altitude trends and their operational and environmental implications for aviation.

I thank **Captain Irfan Ozan Ongun**, a senior pilot, for sharing his personal observation that inspired the case study on double materiality in aviation. His firsthand account of shifting cloud altitudes over his 25-year career helped conceptualise the link between atmospheric change and aviation fuel consumption.

My appreciation goes to **Anne-Laure Bornoz** and **Isabelle Michaud** of **Lausanne Région**, whose contributions during our interviews were instrumental in developing the case study on behavioural nudges and local sustainability strategies. Their perspective on the "Buy Local" campaign enriched the discussion of life-cycle thinking and circular-economy practices at the municipal level.

I also wish to express my appreciation to my colleagues, reviewers, and scholars with whom I exchanged ideas during the development of this work. While I cannot name everyone, their questions, critiques, and encouragement have contributed to the refinement and depth of this study.

Chapter 1
Introduction

This book begins from a critical premise: the prevailing global pricing system is structurally misaligned with the imperatives of sustainability. It traces the roots of this disconnection, showing how dominant economic paradigms have decoupled value creation from ecological thresholds, social equity, and intergenerational responsibility.

The signs of systemic overshoot are clear. Humanity is approaching ecological and planetary boundaries that can no longer be ignored. The climate crisis, biodiversity loss, and deepening inequality collectively demand a redefinition of what constitutes genuine progress.

In this context, the adoption of the Sustainable Development Goals (SDGs) represents the most comprehensive expression of a long-evolving global commitment to sustainability. Building on earlier frameworks such as the Millennium Development Goals and foundational principles articulated in key milestones—such as the 1987 Brundtland Report and the 1992 Earth Summit—the SDGs consolidate and extend these efforts, not merely as a set of international commitments, but as the manifestation of a global culture. This emerging paradigm is grounded in scientific evidence and universal ethical principles, advocating for a reorientation of value systems towards outcomes that prioritise human well-being and planetary integrity.

Defining the SDGs as a Global Culture

North (1990) conceptualised institutions as humanly devised constraints that structure human interaction, distinguishing between formal rules (such as regulations, laws, and constitutions) and informal constraints (such as codes of conduct, customs, and conventions). Building on this foundation, Denzau and North (1994) introduced the concept of mental models—the internal representations that individuals construct to interpret their environment—and defined shared mental models as a framework that guides choices and structures the evolution of political-economic systems. Based on this conceptual framework, this study defines the SDGs as a **global culture**—an evolving set of informal constraints rooted in shared mental models that function as behavioural coordinates for collective action across societies.

Although originally framed as a policy agenda for 2015–2030, the normative power reaches far beyond this temporal boundary. This global culture is not confined to the 21st century, nor limited to international development goals. It is a long-term framework for framing how societies conceive of progress, planetary responsibility, and justice.

The unifying logic of this culture lies in its dual foundation: it is scientifically grounded, drawing on empirical insights into planetary boundaries and social thresholds, and ethically anchored in the principles of the *Universal Declaration of Human Rights.*

To embrace this global culture is to align one's identity and actions with the values of sustainability as an expression of what it means to be human.

Do we recognise sustainability not merely as a constraint, but as a meaningful and permanent way of life?

Do we see ourselves as part of this global culture?

The idea of a global culture grounded in shared values raises an important question: how do these values translate into actual economic behaviour? If sustainability is to become more than a normative aspiration, it must frame not only institutions and policies, but also individual preferences and decision-making frameworks. This brings us to a deeper inquiry: how does economics conceptualise human choice, and how might this change when sustainability becomes internalised as part of collective identity?

Sustainability as an Endogenised Preference

The traditional microeconomic framework treats preferences as exogenous, meaning they are assumed to originate outside the model and are taken as given. Individuals are assumed to act rationally to satisfy these given preferences. The framework does not ask why someone prefers A over B, nor whether those preferences align with collective well-being or ecological viability.

In contrast, this book adopts a different analytical lens. By defining sustainability as a global culture, it endogenises preferences—treating them as shaped by shared mental models, with the Sustainable Development Goals (SDGs) serving as behavioural coordinates for this culture.

This perspective provides a basis for interpreting the SDGs through an economic lens, revealing their implications for decision-making, valuation, and institutional design.

At its core, this reorientation begins with a mental shift: recognizing that natural resources are central constraints that must inform economic reasoning from the outset. In this context, policymakers' preferences—and how they are shaped—become central, a theme further developed in the next section.

Sustainability as a Default Choice

According to Lionel Robbins (1932), economics examines human behaviour under conditions of scarcity, where limited means must be allocated among competing ends. This principle underpins two foundational concepts in mainstream economics: trade-offs and opportunity costs. But when sustainability is understood not as one policy option among others, but as a global culture—internalised, shared and transmitted—it is no longer subject to that logic in the same way. It becomes a default condition, a baseline of value and identity rather than something weighed against competing interests.

This section briefly recalls these two concepts to clarify why sustainability cannot be treated as part of a trade-off once it becomes a central dimension of collective identity—a global culture.

Trade-offs arise because resources are limited: choosing one use of a resource implies forgoing another. This concept, known as opportunity cost, is central to decision-making in personal finance, business strategy, and public policy alike.

For example, with a limited budget of USD 100, you may need to choose between buying a coat or a pair of jeans—but not both. Similarly, choosing between working or resting also involves forgoing one benefit in favour of another. In either case, the value of what you give up is your opportunity cost.

Opportunity cost also shapes collective outcomes, influencing decisions by governments and institutions. In all cases, evaluating the value of foregone alternatives remains central to economic reasoning.

One well-known example in public policy is the trade-off between economic growth and environmental protection. A government may pursue short-term economic gains by promoting industrial expansion—often at the cost of deforestation, higher emissions, and ecological degradation. These strategies can generate immediate benefits, such as job creation, infrastructure investment, and GDP growth, but they impose substantial long-term costs: pollution, biodiversity loss, and reduced capacity to meet climate targets. In some cases, political leaders may even withdraw from international agreements, such as the 2015 Paris Agreement under the UNFCCC, to prioritise short-term national interests. These decisions illustrate how opportunity cost plays out on a global scale: gains today versus consequences tomorrow.

Global and regional financial crises, along with escalating climate and health emergencies, have shaped the first quarter of the 21st century. As a new international economic order gradually takes form, its evolution will be shaped by complex trade-offs involving technology, trade, geopolitical realignment, and shifting development priorities. Each of these factors—and their interaction—will redefine opportunity costs for policymakers operating under uncertainty.

The future is uncertain, but one thing is clear: For those who feel they belong to the global culture of sustainability or recognise themselves in it, sustainability is not a trade-off; it is a way of being. When sustainability is perceived as a global culture, it no longer competes with other priorities. It becomes the framework within which we define how to live, govern, and care for one another. In this sense, the global culture of sustainability offers a higher-order identity—one that transcends ethnic, regional, and national boundaries. It provides a shared reference point for how we live, govern, and care for one another. As such, it forms the ethical foundation of intergenerational well-being, echoing the vision articulated in the 1987 Brundtland Report—a vision in which justice and responsibility extend across time, space, and society.

1.1. Historical Roots of the Sustainability Crisis

This section situates the study by examining how the evolution of economic thought has contributed to the current environmental crisis and to the global mispricing of nature.

The sustainability crisis we face today reveals the limitations of the economic ideas that have long guided our institutions and markets. From the Industrial Revolution onward, growth and efficiency have taken precedence, while ecological limits and social justice were treated as secondary or excluded entirely. This has created a system that generates wealth by depleting the very foundations of long-term well-being. Addressing sustainability requires a deeper shift in what our economies value, reward, and protect.

Despite historically unparalleled levels of global wealth in the 21st century, billions of people still lack access to fundamental human rights as articulated in the Universal Declaration of Human Rights. This persistent gap exposes a central paradox of modern development and raises a foundational question:

Why does economic growth so frequently fail to translate into ecological sustainability and social justice?

The Rise of Neoliberalism and the Linear Economy

The rise of the Chicago School, led by Milton Friedman, was marked by his influential 1970 essay, "*A Friedman Doctrine: The Social Responsibility of Business Is to Increase Its Profits.*" This advanced a view of corporate governance centred solely on shareholder value maximisation. Under this framework, broader social and environmental concerns were external to the core economic calculus.

The Friedman doctrine became a cornerstone of neoliberal economic thought, shaping policies that promoted deregulation, privatization, and the unrestricted expansion of markets. These ideas found operational expression in the linear economic model, characterised by:

- A focus on financial metrics while excluding ecological and social dimensions.
- The marginalisation of communities and ecosystems in investment and policy decisions.

- The systematic externalisation of environmental costs, allowing firms to pursue private gain while offloading degradation onto the public and future generations.

A flawed pricing system underpinned this model; market prices did not accurately reflect true societal costs, resulting in a divergence between individual incentives and collective well-being. As a result, market signals failed to prevent environmental overexploitation or address rising inequality.

The ecological consequences of this paradigm are now starkly visible in biodiversity loss, rising emissions, and transgressions of planetary boundaries. Notably, the rise of this neoliberal paradigm in the early 1970s coincides with the emergence of global ecological overshoot—a connection explored further in Chapter 4.

Figure 1.1: Global Temperature Anomaly Relative to Pre-Industrial Levels (1850–1900 Baseline).

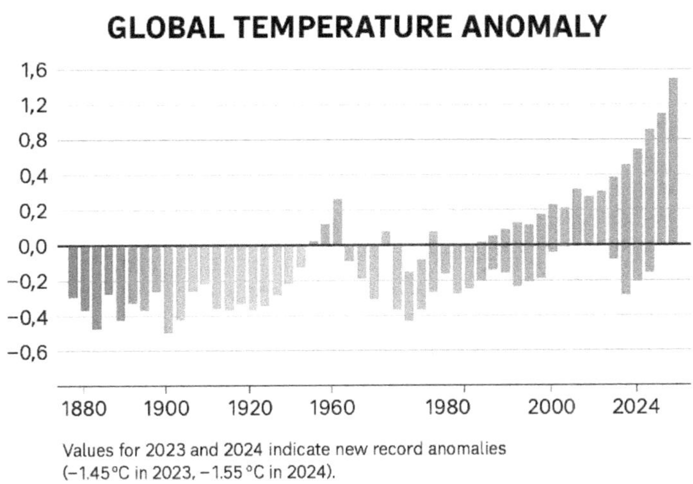

Source: Author, based on data from NASA GISTEMP (2025), NOAA (2025), WMO (2025), Copernicus / ECMWF (2025).

Note: Figure created by the author using open-access datasets. No copyright permission required.

Figure 1.1 illustrates the environmental degradation associated with this model in terms of climate change. Values for 2023 and 2024 indicate new record anomalies (~1.45 °C in 2023, ~1.55 °C in 2024). According to the World Meteorological Organization (WMO), 2023 had a global mean near-surface temperature of ≈ 1.45 °C above the 1850–1900 pre-industrial baseline. WMO confirms that 2024 is the warmest year on record and the first calendar year to reach approximately 1.55°C above the pre-industrial baseline.

Population Growth and Resource Strain

Historically, human population growth was limited by subsistence constraints, primarily the availability of food and basic resources. However, successive technological revolutions—first in agriculture and later in industrial production—unleashed exponential demographic expansion.[1]

- The global population rose from approximately 190 million in year 0 to about 8.2 billion by 2025.
- The most accelerated growth occurred post-1800, in parallel with industrialization and fossil-fuel–based development.

Thomas Malthus's classical theory, which posited that population tends to grow geometrically while food supply increases only arithmetically, anticipated systemic stress on natural resources[2]. While technological progress has postponed some of the predicted scarcities, Malthusian concerns remain relevant today. In the context of planetary boundaries, rising demographic pressure continues to amplify ecological degradation, intensify resource competition, and challenge the sustainability of current economic models. These issues are examined further in Chapter 4 through tools such as life-cycle assessment and ecological footprint accounting, which help quantify the ecological impacts of increasing demand.

However, population growth alone does not determine environmental impact. The relationship between demographic expansion and ecological degradation—particularly in terms of emissions—is shaped by deeper structural factors. To understand the true drivers of environmental pressure, we must look beyond the number of people on the planet and examine how resources are consumed, and by whom.

Emissions Inequity and Global Responsibility

Discussions around population growth must be situated within the broader context of per capita emissions and global consumption patterns. High birth rates in low-income countries are often invoked in sustainability debates, yet such arguments overlook stark disparities in carbon footprints.

- For instance, the total fertility rate in Mali is approximately 5.9 births per woman, far exceeding that of the United States, which stands at around

[1] Harper, S. (2018).

[2] Malthus, J. (1798).

1.6. Similarly, the Central African Republic has a high fertility rate—around 6.0—while Australia's is comparably low, at approximately 1.6.[3]

- Similarly, annual CO_2 emissions per capita in Mali remain extremely low—around 0.2 t—compared to approximately 13.5 t in the United States. In the Central African Republic, emissions are also minimal—about 0.1 t—while in Australia, they are among the highest globally, at roughly 14.0 t.[4]

This implies that although countries like Mali and CAR have birth rates nearly four times higher than those of the U.S. and Australia, their per capita carbon emissions are more than 75 times lower.

Such asymmetry highlights that global sustainability challenges cannot be reduced to demographic growth alone. Instead, they emphasise the importance of addressing unsustainable consumption patterns in high-income economies—a key concern of SDG 12: Responsible Consumption and Production. Effective climate responsibility demands equity-informed frameworks that acknowledge historical emissions, resource intensity, and systemic overconsumption in the Global North. This inequality between consumers and emitters will reappear in Chapter 5, where we examine how ecological degradation and wealth concentration reinforce one another.

Early Warnings and the Rise of Environmental Economics

Awareness of anthropogenic climate change predates the modern environmental movement. As early as 1912, a British newspaper article (Fig. 1.2) warned that burning coal would increase atmospheric carbon concentrations, potentially altering Earth's climate—an early recognition of the greenhouse effect.

In parallel, foundational contributions to environmental economics began to emerge. In 1920, economist Arthur Cecil Pigou introduced the concept of externalities, referring to the unpriced social or ecological costs (or benefits) of economic activities that affect third parties. Pigou advocated for corrective measures—Pigouvian taxes—to internalise negative externalities, such as pollution. By aligning private costs with social costs, this framework supported the polluter pays principle, aiming to enhance overall societal welfare. His work laid the groundwork for integrating environmental considerations into economic theory and remains central to sustainability-related policy today.

---

[3] World Bank (2025), fertility data.

[4] World Bank (2025), C02 emissions data.

Figure 1.2: Early Media Reference To Anthropogenic Climate Change (1912).

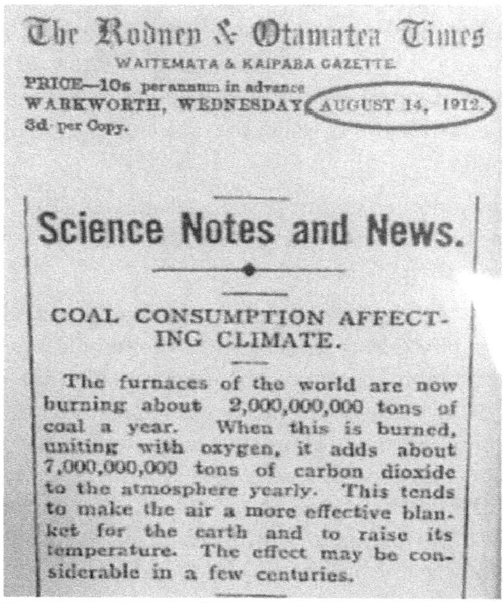

The Rodney & Otamatea Times
WAITEMATA & KAIPARA GAZETTE
PRICE—10s per annum in advance
WARKWORTH, WEDNESDAY AUGUST 14, 1912.
3d per Copy.

Science Notes and News.

COAL CONSUMPTION AFFECTING CLIMATE.

The furnaces of the world are now burning about 2,000,000,000 tons of coal a year. When this is burned, uniting with oxygen, it adds about 7,000,000,000 tons of carbon dioxide to the atmosphere yearly. This tends to make the air a more effective blanket for the earth and to raise its temperature. The effect may be considerable in a few centuries.

Source: Rodney and Otamatea Times (Waitemata and Kaipara Gazette), 14 August 1912.

«Coal consumption affecting climate change:

> 2 billion tons of coal are burned annually, uniting with oxygen, which adds about 7 billion tons of CO2 to the atmosphere each year. => Global warming!
> The effect may be considerable in a few centuries!»

In 1972, the Club of Rome[5] published *Limits to Growth*, a seminal report that modelled the long-term consequences of exponential economic and population growth on a planet with finite resources. Using the World3 model, the authors simulated global scenarios from 1900 to 2100[6] and warned that under a

[5] Club of Rome is a nonprofit organization composed of intellectuals, high-level politicians, UN administrators, diplomats, scientists, economists, and business leaders from around the globe.

[6] This computer model tracked per-capita consumption, population, industrial and agricultural production, plotted against resource depletion, cultivated land, and pollution levels, including CO2 emissions. It provided a method for studying how complex systems change over time. It also developed nonlinear relationships. For instance, as more land is made arable, what is left is drier or steeper. The cost of coping with these problems raises the cost of developing the land—a nonlinear relationship. The model's main question

"business-as-usual" trajectory, the world would face severe ecological and economic decline within the twenty-first century.[7] Their analysis emphasised that without fundamental reforms to consumption patterns, energy use, and population policies, Earth's carrying capacity would be exceeded.

These warnings have since proven strikingly prescient. The original *Limits to Growth* report included a rough estimate suggesting that, under a business-as-usual scenario, atmospheric CO_2 concentrations could reach 380 ppm by 2000. Though not a scientifically robust or empirically calibrated forecast, this projection closely matches the observed concentration at that time, which was approximately 370 ppm.[8] By early 2026, atmospheric CO_2 levels have surpassed 428 ppm—well beyond the widely cited safe threshold of 350 ppm. The timeline of this study thus coincides with the critical period foreseen in *Limits to Growth*, underscoring the enduring relevance of its insights and the urgency of systemic transformation. Figure 1.3 illustrates monthly and long-term trends in atmospheric CO_2 concentrations, including the continued increase through the mid-2020s, highlighting both seasonal variability and long-term accumulation associated with human activities.

Figure 1.3: Atmospheric CO_2 Concentration (Keeling Curve), 1960-2025.

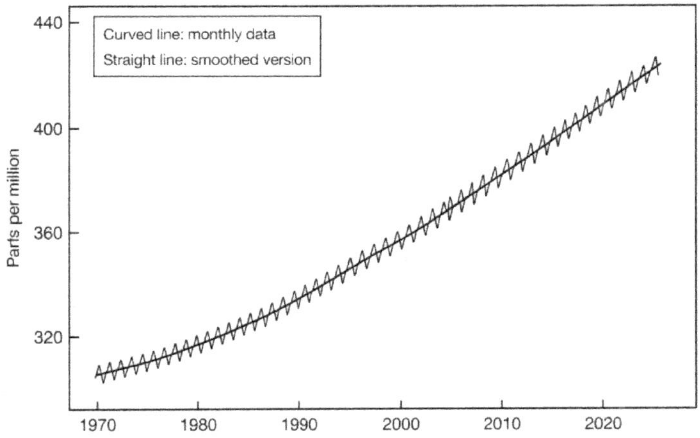

Source: Author, based on publicly available data from NOAA Global Monitoring Laboratory and Mauna Loa Observatory.

---

was: "How may the expanding global population and materials economy interact with and adapt to the earth's limited carrying capacity over time?"

[7] *Limits to Growth* identified five fundamental factors that determine—and through their interaction, constrain—growth on this planet: i) population increase, ii) food production, iii) non-renewable resource depletion, iv) industrial output, and v) pollution generation.

[8] NOAA Global Monitoring Laboratory (2025).

Table 1.1 presents decadal averages of atmospheric CO_2 concentrations, highlighting the accelerating rate of increase over time. These trends underscore the structural implications of sustained linear economic expansion and reinforce the urgency of transitioning towards circular and regenerative systems.

Table 1.1: Decadal Atmospheric CO_2 Concentration Trends.

Years	**Parts per million (ppm)**	**Annual speed of increase (approx.)**
1970s	320-330 ppm	1.3-1.4 ppm/year
1980s-1990s	340-370 ppm	1.5 ppm/year
2000s	370-400 ppm	2 ppm/year
2010s-2020s	>400-430 ppm	2.5 ppm/year

Source: Author, based on publicly available data from NOAA Global Monitoring Laboratory.

1.2. Institutional Milestones in Global Environmental Governance

This section outlines the global institutional response to the historical shortfalls in economic policy-making.

The evolution of global environmental governance has been marked by key institutional milestones that progressively integrated sustainability into international policy frameworks:

- 1972: The United Nations Conference on the Human Environment in Stockholm marked the first major global environmental summit, resulting in the establishment of the *United Nations Environment Programme (UNEP)*, a foundational step in multilateral ecological governance.
- 1987: The *Brundtland Report* (*Our Common Future*) formally introduced the concept of *sustainable development*, defining it as "meeting the needs of the present without compromising the ability of future generations to meet their own needs," thus framing sustainability as both an ethical and developmental imperative.
- 1988: The *Intergovernmental Panel on Climate Change (IPCC)* was established by UNEP and the World Meteorological Organization (WMO) to provide rigorous scientific assessments on climate change, its impacts, and response strategies, becoming the authoritative global body on climate science.
- 1992: The *Earth Summit* in Rio de Janeiro institutionalised sustainability through the adoption of the *UN Framework Convention on Climate Change (UNFCCC)*[9] and the *Convention on Biological Diversity*, embedding environmental goals within international legal instruments.

[9] The UNFCCC is a multilateral treaty that opened for signature during the Earth Summit in 1992, shortly after the first assessment report by the IPCC in 1990. It entered into force

- 1997: The *Kyoto Protocol* introduced binding greenhouse gas emissions targets for industrialised countries and established market-based mechanisms such as emissions trading and the Clean Development Mechanism (CDM), marking the first attempt at a legally binding global climate regime.
- 2015: The adoption of the Sustainable Development Goals and the Paris Agreement marked a turning point in international sustainability governance—two landmark frameworks that continue to shape global action.

The Sustainable Development Goals (SDGs)[10] were adopted at the *United Nations Sustainable Development Summit* in New York as the centerpiece of the *2030 Agenda for Sustainable Development.* Comprising 17 integrated goals, the SDGs articulate a universal vision to address interconnected global challenges—from poverty and inequality to climate change and biodiversity loss (Fig. 1.4). More than a policy agenda, they serve as a blueprint for redefining development along dimensions of equity, ecological resilience, and intergenerational justice. Their implementation is not only essential for advancing human well-being but also for ensuring the long-term viability of planetary systems.

The Paris Agreement, adopted at *COP21* in December 2015 under the auspices of the *UNFCCC,* reaffirmed global political will to confront climate change. It established a legally binding framework to limit global warming to well below 2°C, while pursuing efforts to constrain the rise in temperature to 1.5°C above pre-industrial levels. At the heart of the Agreement lies the mechanism of *Nationally Determined Contributions (NDCs)*—country-specific climate action plans subject to a five-year review cycle. This iterative structure

---

in 1994 to stabilise greenhouse gas (GHG) concentrations at a level that would prevent dangerous anthropogenic interference with the climate system. The Conference of the Parties (COP) is the supreme decision-making body of the UNFCCC. It reviews national reports submitted by Parties, assesses progress, and guides implementation. The secretariat's seat is in Bonn, where the COP would meet annually unless a Party offers to host the annual session, which is regularly the case. The COP has served as the platform for key climate agreements, including the Kyoto Protocol (1997) and the Paris Agreement (2015).

[10] The Sustainable Development Goals (SDGs) emerged from the 2012 United Nations Conference on Sustainable Development in Rio de Janeiro, with the aim of developing a universal framework to address interconnected environmental, social and economic challenges. The SDGs replaced the Millennium Development Goals (MDGs), which established measurable, globally agreed development targets for the period 2000–2015.

is designed to foster transparency, accountability, and progressively ambitious commitments over time, aligning national policies with a shared global goal.

Together, the SDGs and the Paris Agreement define the institutional backbone of the global sustainability transition, linking social, economic, and environmental priorities through a unified framework of accountability and collective action. Chapter 2 builds directly on this institutional foundation by examining how sustainability becomes operationalised through finance, disclosure, and materiality.

Figure 1.4: The Sustainable Development Goals (SDGs).

Source: United Nations (2025), Sustainable Development Goals.

A Decade of SDGs: Progress and Setbacks

Ten years after their adoption, the *Sustainable Development Report 2025* reveals a sobering picture: only 16.6 percent of SDG targets are currently on track globally. The few areas of notable progress include: mobile phone penetration and internet access (SDG 9), access to electricity (SDG 7), and reductions in under-five and neonatal mortality (SDG 3). These gains reflect longstanding investments in infrastructure and public health.

Conversely, five critical targets are experiencing widespread stagnation or regression: the obesity rate (SDG 2), press freedom (SDG 16), sustainable nitrogen management (SDG 2), the Red List Index of biodiversity loss (SDG 15), and corruption perception (SDG 16). These setbacks point to systemic challenges in governance, environmental stewardship, and public accountability.

At the broader goal level, none of the 17 SDGs is expected to be fully achieved by 2030. Particularly off track are SDG 2 (Zero Hunger), SDG 11 (Sustainable Cities), SDG 14 (Life Below Water), SDG 15 (Life on Land), and SDG 16 (Peace, Justice, and Strong Institutions)—all of which face persistent structural barriers and have shown little or no progress since 2015. These findings underscore the urgent need for renewed political commitment, systemic reform, and integrated policy responses to realign development trajectories with the goals of the 2030 Agenda.

Planetary Health and Boundaries

While the SDGs offer a roadmap for global progress, the planetary boundaries framework reveals just how far current development trajectories have strayed from ecological viability. The Planetary Health paradigm underscores the fundamental interdependence between human well-being and the integrity of Earth's ecological systems. It calls for interdisciplinary, systems-based approaches to address converging global crises, including climate change, biodiversity loss, pollution, and disruptions to food and water systems, recognizing that these challenges are not only environmental but also public health emergencies.

Complementing this perspective, the Planetary Boundaries framework identifies nine Earth system processes essential for maintaining a stable and resilient planet.[11] Each boundary has scientifically defined thresholds that, if crossed, increase the risk of abrupt and potentially irreversible environmental change. As of 2024, six out of nine boundaries have been transgressed, including climate change, land system change, freshwater change, biogeochemical flows (nitrogen and phosphorus cycles), biosphere integrity, and novel entities (e.g., chemical pollution and plastics).

This transgression underscores the growing pressure from anthropogenic activity on Earth's life-support systems and underlines the urgency for aligning policy, finance, and innovation with the principles of planetary stewardship. As illustrated in Figure 1.5, humanity's safe operating space is shrinking, necessitating transformative action grounded in scientific evidence and global cooperation.[12] These boundaries will later be translated into operational metrics in Chapter 4, where tools such as life cycle assessment, carbon accounting, and ecological footprint analysis quantify humanity's pressure on the planet.

11 Planetary Health Check (2024).

12 Potsdam Institute for Climate Impact Research (2025).

Figure 1.5: Planetary Boundaries.

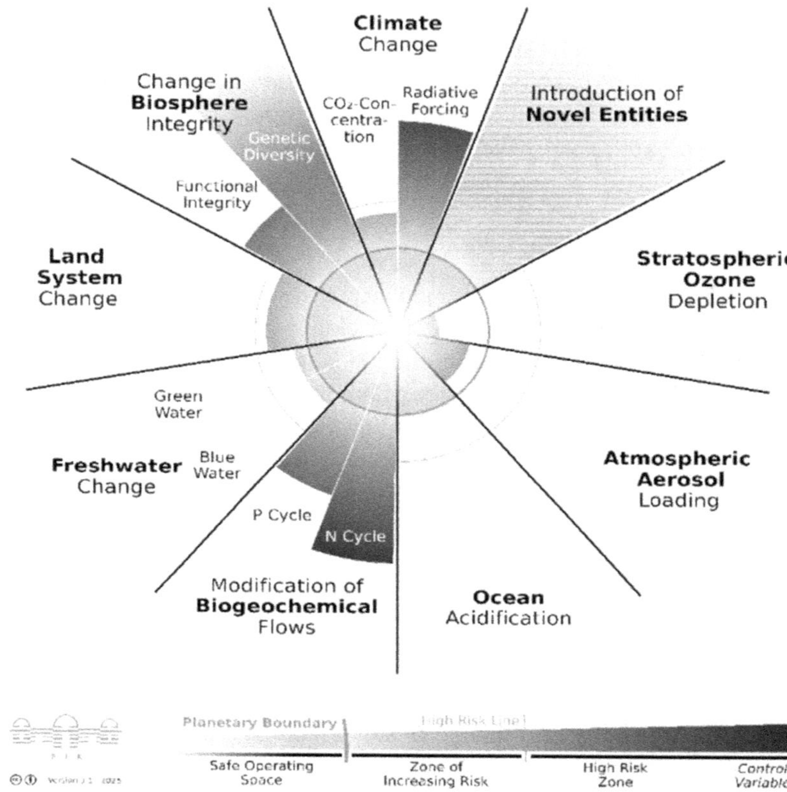

Source: Potsdam Institute for Climate Impact Research (PIK), *Planetary Boundaries* infographic, Version 3.1 (2025).

Note: Unmodified figure. Reused under the terms of the Creative Commons Attribution 4.0 International (CC BY 4.0) license, which permits commercial use with attribution—complete source listed in the bibliography.

1.3. Sustainable Investment

Having outlined the historical, institutional, and ecological context for sustainability, we now turn to the concept of sustainable investment, which operationalises these principles in financial and economic decision-making.

This book builds on recognised definitions—such as those provided by the EU Sustainable Finance Disclosure Regulation (SFDR), the Global Investors for

Sustainable Development (GISD) Alliance, and Harvard Business School[13]—which together provide a strong conceptual foundation—but develops a broader analytical framework. Based on eight core dimensions, this framework captures both the operational and normative features of sustainable investment. These include:

- Sustainable objectives and SDG alignment
- Exclusions and governance
- Double materiality (financial and impact)
- Irreversibility and flexibility tools
- Impact measurement
- Long-term and intergenerational orientation
- Regulatory and standards alignment
- ESG integration

These elements are analysed in detail throughout the study and synthesised in Table 1.2, which outlines how each dimension is treated across the chapters.

These chapters collectively establish the conceptual and operational framework for *sustainable investment.* By systematically examining each dimension of *sustainable investment* from diverse analytical perspectives, the book provides a coherent blueprint for directing capital towards sustainability, resilience, and social equity.

The following section outlines the book's structure, which is organised around the key elements presented in Table 1.2.

---

[13] **EU Sustainable Finance Disclosure Regulation (SFDR)** defines sustainable investment as any investment in an economic activity which: "contributes to an environmental or social objective," "provided that such investments do not cause significant harm to any of those objectives" ("Do No Significant Harm") and that the investee companies follow good governance practices." European Commission (2019).

Global Investors for Sustainable Development (GISD) Alliance, a UN-led initiative, defines "Sustainable development investing (SDI) as an approach in which "the positive contribution of an investment should not be outweighed by negative impacts from the same investment over the life of this investment. The contribution can be made through products, services, operations, or projects financed across asset classes and in multiple sectors or themes." Global Investors for Sustainable Development Alliance (GISD). (2020). While this book uses the broader term sustainable investment, the SDI definition provides an important ethical and impact-oriented foundation.

Harvard Business School, "Sustainable investing refers to a range of practices in which investors aim to achieve financial returns while promoting long-term environmental or social value." Harvard Business School Online (2023).

Table 1.2: Core Elements of Sustainable Investment and their Analytical Treatment across Chapters.

Sustainable Investment Element	Definition Aspect	Where It Appears
Sustainable Objective and SDG Alignment	"Contributes to an environmental or social objective."	Chapters 2 (finance evolution), 4 (LCA, carbon accounting, LCT), 5 (Green Keynesianism)
Exclusions and Governance	"Do No Significant Harm" + good governance	Chapter 2 (ethical exclusions, materiality), 3 (polluter pays, pricing externalities), 5 (subsidy phase-outs)
Double Materiality (Financial + Impact)	ESG integration into risk and impact accounting	Chapter 2 (double materiality), 4 (carbon & life cycle accounting), Chapter 5 (inequality, wealth, ecological metrics)
Irreversibility and Flexibility Tools	Real options, scenario analysis	Chapter 3.3 (EU hydrogen projects, uncertainty)
Impact Measurement	Demonstrated through LCA and SDG indicators	Chapters 4 (LCA, Carbon Footprint, LCSA), 5 (alternative metrics)
Long-Term and Intergenerational Orientation	Intergenerational equity, natural capital measurement	Chapters 3 (social cost of carbon), 5 (inclusive wealth, IWI, natural capital depletion)
Regulatory and Standards Alignment	SFDR, CSRD, UN PRI	Chapters 2 and 4 (reporting standards, ESG frameworks), Chapter 3 (governance implications), Chapter 5 (metric institutional momentum)
ESG Integration	Core to sustainable finance strategies	Chapters 2 (stages 1–3), 3 (carbon pricing governance), 4 (GHG accounting within lending), 5 (Green Keynesian investment reallocation)

Source: Developed by the author as a conceptual synthesis of sustainable investment dimensions examined throughout the book.

1.4. Structure of the Book

This study originated from a workshop I designed for doctoral students and has since evolved through years of graduate-level teaching, research, and engagement with sustainability practitioners. It is structured into six chapters that together provide a coherent analytical framework for understanding sustainable investment and its implications for economic decision-making, governance, and policy design.

The analysis progresses from conceptual foundations and financial systems to firm-level incentives, micro-level sustainability tools, and finally to the macroeconomic transformations required to align economic systems with ecological limits.

Chapter 1 establishes the book's diagnostic and conceptual foundations. It identifies a structural misalignment between the prevailing global pricing system and ecological and social realities. This divergence is traced to dominant economic paradigms that do not treat ecological and social dimensions as binding boundaries.

The chapter then introduces the book's central conceptual contribution: interpreting the Sustainable Development Goals (SDGs) as informal constraints embedded in shared mental models. In this sense, they constitute a global culture. Within this framework, ecological and social constraints are repositioned from competing objectives to boundary conditions of economic reasoning. The chapter concludes by introducing sustainable investment as the transmission mechanism through which the global culture defined in this study becomes operational within economic systems.

Chapter 2 examines how sustainability becomes embedded in financial reasoning. It traces the structural transformation of finance from a system focused primarily on shareholder value towards one in which environmental and social considerations increasingly influence capital allocation. This evolution unfolds through distinct stages, ranging from reputational risk management to the integration of sustainability-related risks into financial analysis and, ultimately, to the reorientation of capital towards long-term environmental and social objectives consistent with the Sustainable Development Goals. Central to this transformation is the concept of materiality. It defines the conditions under which sustainability issues enter corporate disclosure and financial evaluation. As materiality extends beyond investors to encompass a broader set of stakeholders, financial accountability operates across a wider temporal and societal horizon. The analysis concludes with the concept of double materiality, which integrates the inward financial effects of sustainability issues with the outward impacts of firms on society and the environment. In doing so, it establishes the conceptual link between embedding sustainability in financial reasoning and the analysis of economic incentives and cost structures presented in Chapter 3.

Chapter 3 shifts the focus from institutional and reporting frameworks to economic incentives, showing how sustainability transforms firms' cost structures and investment decisions when environmental damage is internalised.

The chapter begins by revisiting mainstream growth models to examine the omission of environmental constraints from economic reasoning, and the subsequent integration of emissions and biophysical limits in later climate–economy models.

It then examines the translation of environmental damage into prices through carbon taxes and emissions trading systems, with particular attention to the EU Emissions Trading System as a core instrument for internalising climate-related externalities in firms' costs and capital allocation decisions. Building on this, the chapter shows that carbon markets operate under different types of uncertainty—some that can be modelled with probabilities and others that cannot—and explains why this matters for investment decisions.

The chapter then demonstrates why traditional Net Present Value (NPV) techniques are inadequate for long-horizon, irreversible, and uncertainty-dominated sustainability investments, and introduces the Real Options approach as a framework that values flexibility in investment timing and design. These ideas are illustrated through an applied policy case: the EU Hydrogen Strategy, which demonstrates how public policy can embed real-options logic—such as delay, staging, and scalability—into mission-oriented clean-technology investment.

Finally, the chapter explores the role of artificial intelligence—particularly neural networks—in enhancing real-options valuation by enabling adaptive, data-driven decision-making under uncertainty. Rather than replacing economic judgment, these tools strengthen the capacity to update investment strategies as new information emerges, reinforcing flexibility as a central principle of sustainable investment.

Chapter 4 shifts the focus from firms to the practical tools and behavioural mechanisms that guide micro-level sustainability decisions. It introduces analytical methods for measuring environmental impacts across economic activities, including life-cycle approaches and carbon accounting. The chapter then examines how behavioural insights influence consumption and investment decisions, highlighting the role of choice environments in influencing sustainable behaviour. Finally, it introduces ecological footprint accounting, which evaluates whether the cumulative effects of economic activities remain within the planet's ecological limits. In this way, Chapter 4 connects micro-level decision tools with the broader ecological constraints that define the macroeconomic sustainability challenges addressed in Chapter 5.

Chapter 5 extends the analysis by situating sustainability within a macroeconomic framework. It positions the concept of sustainable investment developed in Chapters 2–4 within the Keynesian output equation, highlighting its interaction with government expenditure. This raises a central political-economic question of the chapter: the extent to which sustainability-oriented investment aligns with fiscal policy.

The chapter begins by examining the limitations of Gross Domestic Product (GDP) as the dominant measure of economic performance, showing how it excludes ecological degradation and social inequality, and thereby creates a structural misalignment between economic evaluation and the multidimensional objectives of sustainable development.

The chapter then introduces alternative metrics that incorporate environmental, social, and intergenerational dimensions, aligning measurement frameworks more closely with the Sustainable Development Goals. This shift highlights how the way progress is measured influences resource allocation, policy priorities, and long-term development trajectories.

Building on this, the chapter examines inequality as a macroeconomic constraint on sustainable development. It shows how the concentration of income and wealth influences environmental outcomes, and how inequality and ecological degradation interact through reinforcing dynamics that deepen structural imbalances across societies.

At the core of the chapter, the analysis introduces a Green Keynesian framework that embeds sustainable investment within the macroeconomic structure. By positioning sustainable investment within the Investment (I) component of the Keynesian output equation, the chapter demonstrates how its effectiveness depends on alignment with Government expenditure (G). This framework shifts the focus of macroeconomic analysis from the volume of demand to its composition, showing how misaligned public spending—particularly fossil-fuel subsidies—can offset sustainability-oriented investment by sustaining carbon-intensive economic structures.

Finally, the chapter incorporates the trade dimension to complete the macroeconomic framework. It examines how cross-border flows affect sustainability outcomes. The analysis highlights the role of trade mechanisms in extending climate policy beyond national borders.

Chapter 6 synthesises the analytical framework developed throughout the book by bringing together pricing, economic modelling, investment, and macroeconomic policy into a coherent analytical perspective on sustainable development. It begins by reaffirming the central diagnosis of a structural misalignment between the global pricing system and ecological and social realities, then traces how this misalignment is rooted in economic models that have historically excluded environmental constraints. Building on this, the chapter positions sustainable investment as the transmission mechanism through which sustainability becomes operational, linking capital allocation to long-term environmental and social objectives.

The analysis then extends to the macroeconomic level, introducing a Green Keynesian framework in which the effectiveness of sustainable investment depends on its alignment with public spending and broader fiscal policy. Within this framework, the chapter highlights the structural nexus among inequality, ecological degradation, and the climate crisis, as well as the limitations of conventional metrics, such as GDP, in capturing these dynamics. It therefore emphasises the role of alternative measurement frameworks in aligning economic evaluation with sustainability objectives.

The chapter concludes by situating sustainable development within a human rights perspective and introducing the concept of sustainability as a global culture, expressed through those who recognise themselves in it and act accordingly.

Figure 1.6 summarises the multi-level analytical framework of this study, showing how micro-level tools, meso-level ecological limits, and macroeconomic dynamics are connected.

Figure 1.6: Multi-Level Analytical Framework of the Book.

FIRMS' COST STRUCTURES AND ENVIRONMENTAL CONSTRAINTS
(Chapter 3)
Internalisation of externalities and investment under uncertainty

↓

MICRO-LEVEL SUSTAINABILITY TOOLS
(Chapter 4)
Measurement of environmental impacts
• Life Cycle Assessment (LCA)
• Carbon Accounting

Decision frameworks and governance
• Life Cycle Thinking (LCT)
• Life Cycle Sustainability Assessment (LCSA)
• ESG reporting and governance

Behavioural drivers of decisions
• Behavioural economics
• Nudges and choice architecture

↓

MESO-LEVEL ECOLOGICAL LIMITS
(Section 4.5)
Ecological Footprint → ecological demand
Biocapacity → ecological supply
Planetary boundaries → biophysical limits

↓

MACROECONOMIC TRANSFORMATION
(Chapter 5)

A Green Keynesian political-economic framework for aligning economic systems with ecological limits

↓

SYNTHESIS AND NORMATIVE FRAMEWORK
(Chapter 6)
Integration of pricing, investment, and macroeconomic policy
Sustainability as a global culture and development as a human right

Source: Author. Chapters 1 and 2 are not represented in the figure, as they establish the conceptual and financial foundations of the analysis, while the multi-level analytical framework begins with the transformation of firms' cost structures examined in Chapter 3.

1.5. Motivation and Contribution of the Study

While the Sustainable Development Goals (SDGs) are conceptually robust and globally endorsed, they often remain abstract and high-level in public discourse. My initial motivation for this book was to unpack some of their key dimensions—especially from a political economy perspective—and to make them more analytically accessible and operationally meaningful. This is particularly important given the evolving cost structures and multidimensional uncertainties of the global sustainability transition.

The study places special emphasis on two foundational anchors that have guided the integration of sustainability into national and international agendas: the Universal Declaration of Human Rights (1948) and the Sustainable Development Goals (2015). Both frameworks, while distinct in scope and historical context, represent universal commitments to equity, dignity, and intergenerational responsibility. From a political economy standpoint, this book seeks to provide the analytical tools, interpretive frameworks, and methodological approaches needed to construct viable development pathways.

This motivation is rooted in my academic and professional trajectory. With a graduate degree in economics, a master's degree in banking and finance, a PhD in economics, and a career in international economic development, I have long reflected on the persistent tensions between financial systems and inclusive growth.

Zooming out to the broader picture, the first quarter of the 21st century has been marked by cascading global crises, ranging from financial instability and public health emergencies to climate breakdown and geopolitical fragmentation. These crises have not only eroded economic security but also undermined social cohesion and human dignity for billions of people. In response, central banks implemented unprecedented monetary interventions. Take the case of the U.S. Federal Reserve: established in 1913, it created USD 900 billion in liquidity during its first 95 years. Following the collapse of Lehman Brothers in 2008 and the COVID-19 pandemic in 2020, its balance sheet expanded tenfold, reaching USD 9 trillion by 2022. Although it has since declined to approximately USD 6.7 trillion by 2025, the magnitude remains unprecedented in history (Fig. 1.7).

Figure 1.7: Balance Sheet of the U.S. Federal Reserve (2004–2024).

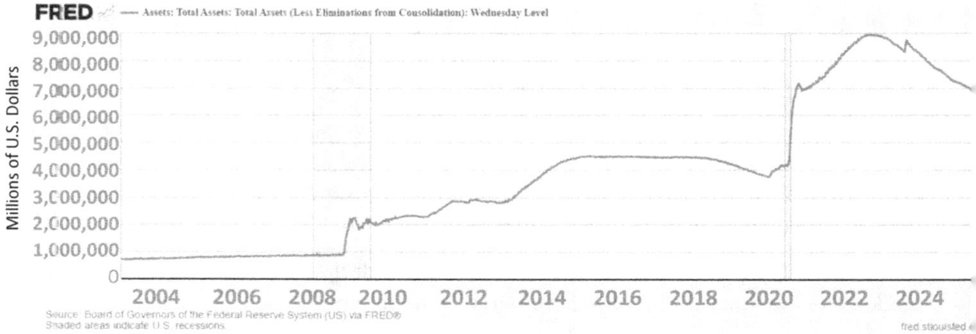

Source: Board of Governors of the Federal Reserve System (US) via FRED®, Federal Reserve Bank o Louis (2025).

Other major central banks adopted similar Keynesian-style expansionary policies. While these interventions prevented large-scale corporate collapse and mass unemployment, they also revealed structural shortcomings. Most of the liquidity bypassed marginalised populations and was not invested in strengthening their capabilities. As a result, rather than catalyzing an inclusive and transformative recovery, these responses often deepened existing inequalities.

Against this backdrop of systemic fragility and ecological overshoot, this study argues that reimagining sustainable development through the lens of finance is no longer optional—it is essential.

This book contributes conceptually by interpreting the SDGs as informal institutions—globally endorsed, ethically grounded, and capable of guiding economic behaviour through shared norms rather than legal enforcement. This interpretation draws on North's (1990) theory of institutions and Denzau and North's (1994) concept of shared mental models, distinguishing between formal rules—such as laws and regulations—and informal constraints—such as norms, conventions, and shared mental models—that underpin economic and political behaviour over time.

In this spirit, we define the SDGs as a global culture: a set of globally endorsed, non-binding norms that function as ethical guideposts and behavioural coordinates across nations. Although not legally enforceable, the SDGs have been adopted by 193 UN Member States, reflecting an unprecedented global consensus on shared values for people, the planet, and prosperity. Their power lies not in coercion but in their ability to shape expectations, mobilise behaviour, and inspire policy through normative alignment.

By interpreting the SDGs through the lens of informal institutions, this book reframes sustainability away from technical intervention and towards a durable cultural framework—grounded in science and universal human rights—that redefines long-term economic preferences, distributive outcomes, and collective responsibility.

Global Culture and Glocal Culture

While the term *glocal* highlights the interplay between global frameworks and local implementation, this book deliberately retains the term *global culture*. This choice reflects the conceptual and normative foundations of the Sustainable Development Goals (SDGs), which were adopted by all 193 UN Member States. As such, the SDGs constitute a truly global ethical framework—scientifically grounded and universally endorsed—rather than a collection of localised strategies.

Glocal dynamics certainly play an important role in how global norms are enacted across different contexts, but they remain secondary to the global normative consensus represented by the SDGs. For these reasons, the title of this book emphasises *global culture*, aligning with the idea that sustainability—understood as a shared ethical compass and institutional logic—transcends locality and defines a collective horizon for humanity.

1.6. Conclusion

Having established the book's motivation and conceptual lens, the concluding section summarises the chapter's key propositions and prepares the ground for the chapters ahead.

This chapter lays the foundations for the book and draws the big picture as follows:

1) The *Brundtland Report* (*Our Common Future*) formally introduced the concept of *sustainable development*, defining it as "meeting the needs of the present without compromising the ability of *future generations* to meet their own needs."
2) This study defines the SDGs as a new global culture—an evolving system of collectively accepted informal constraints rooted in shared mental models that functions as a lasting code of conduct.
3) If sustainability becomes a culture shared globally, whatever your ethnic origin or nationality, passed from one generation to the next, it will no longer be treated as a *trade-off* by policymakers. It will simply be a matter of how we live, resulting in *intergenerational* well-being.

In the chapters that follow, the concepts introduced here—ecological limits, institutional evolution, inequality, and natural capital—will be developed into analytical tools and policy frameworks. Together, they form the basis of a sustainable investment paradigm aligned with the values, constraints, and opportunities of the 21st century.

We can now proceed to Chapter 2, which examines why sustainability is crucial.

Key Insights — Chapter 1: Introduction

1. The Global Pricing System Structurally Fails to Internalise Ecological and Social Costs. Market prices systematically fail to incorporate environmental degradation, social harm, and intergenerational impacts, creating a persistent disconnect between private returns and collective welfare. This misalignment contributes to ecological overshoot and social inequality.

2. A Linear, Growth-Oriented Economic Model Underpins This Structural Externalisation Of Ecological And Social Costs. It embeds resource-intensive production and consumption patterns within the structure of economic activity.

3. Ecological Limits and Inequality Function as Binding Forward-Looking Economic Constraints. Climate change, biodiversity loss, and widening wealth disparities reflect unsustainable production and consumption patterns that impose material limits on economic systems.

4. This Study Conceptualises the SDGs as Informal Constraints Embedded in Shared Mental Models, Thereby Constituting a Global Culture. Consequently, sustainability begins to reshape the foundations upon which economic preferences are formed.

5. Endogenising Preferences Through the SDGs as a Global Culture Transforms Sustainability from a Trade-Off into a Default Condition of Economic Choice. In standard microeconomic analysis, preferences are treated as exogenous. When sustainability is internalised through shared mental models, preferences become endogenous, and sustainability no longer enters decision-making as a competing objective but as an integral component of the preference structure itself.

6. Sustainable Investment Constitutes the Economic Transmission Mechanism of Sustainability as a Global Culture. It aligns capital allocation with ecological limits, human rights, and intergenerational responsibility. It reshapes pricing structures (Chapter 3), informs micro-level tools and behavioural mechanisms (Chapter 4), and supports macroeconomic reallocation towards sustainable development pathways (Chapter 5).

In Simple Words — Chapter 1: Introduction

When environmental degradation and social harm are not reflected in prices, markets generate incomplete signals. Activities that damage ecosystems or increase inequality may still appear profitable because their broader costs are borne by society rather than by those who generate them.

In response to these imbalances, the international community gradually developed institutional frameworks to integrate environmental and social considerations into development policy. The most comprehensive of these is the Sustainable Development Goals (SDGs), adopted in 2015 by all UN Member States. The SDGs provide a shared framework for addressing interconnected challenges such as poverty, inequality, climate change, biodiversity loss, and others. Rather than focusing solely on economic output, they broaden the definition of progress to include ecological resilience, social well-being, and intergenerational responsibility.

This book goes one step further. It interprets the SDGs not only as policy objectives but as informal constraints embedded in shared mental models. In this sense, they function as a global culture: a system of informal constraints rooted in shared mental models informing collective behaviour.

In standard economic analysis, preferences are treated as given. Individuals are assumed to know what they want, and economic models do not question how those preferences are formed.

When the SDGs are perceived as a global culture, this assumption changes. Sustainability begins to influence how preferences are shaped. It is no longer seen merely as one objective among others but as a reference point that informs what is considered acceptable and desirable in economic decision-making.

Economics traditionally frames decision-making in terms of trade-offs, where choosing one objective implies giving up another. However, when sustainability is embedded in shared mental models, it is no longer treated as a competing objective to be balanced against short-term economic gains. Instead, it functions as a boundary condition that shapes how choices are evaluated and what is considered unacceptable in the first place. In this sense, sustainability becomes less a trade-off and more a structural baseline for economic reasoning.

This has direct implications for finance and investment. If sustainability becomes embedded in how preferences are formed and choices are evaluated, capital allocation must reflect this transformation. Sustainable investment emerges as the practical mechanism through which environmental limits, social responsibility, and long-term considerations are integrated into economic decision-making. The following chapters examine how this transformation reshapes finance, pricing, firm behaviour, and macroeconomic policy.

Chapter 2
From Sustainability to Sustainable Finance

Chapter 1 established that sustainability can be understood as a global culture embedded in shared mental models, challenging economic paradigms that fail to treat ecological and social dimensions as binding constraints. The question that follows is how this conceptual reframing becomes embedded in financial systems and investment practices.

This chapter examines how sustainability becomes operational within financial systems through the evolution of sustainable finance. It traces the transition from business-as-usual financial models towards frameworks that progressively incorporate ecological and social dimensions into financial decision-making. In doing so, it introduces the staged development of sustainable finance and analyses the concepts of materiality and double materiality as mechanisms that structure how sustainability is assessed, disclosed, and integrated into financial practice.

The analysis is situated within the institutional framework of the Sustainable Development Goals (SDGs), which provide a globally endorsed reference structure for defining sustainability objectives. Within this context, financial systems and institutions become central channels through which these objectives are translated into investment criteria, reporting standards, and capital allocation decisions.

2.1. Sustainable Development Goals-Led Finance

In 2015, the United Nations General Assembly adopted the Sustainable Development Goals (SDGs), establishing a globally endorsed framework for defining and coordinating sustainability objectives across countries and sectors. Beyond their role as a development agenda, the SDGs serve as a reference framework for assessing and aligning economic policies, corporate strategies, and financial activities.[14]

[14] The SDGs comprise 17 goals, 169 targets, and 231 indicators designed to guide and measure progress toward sustainable development by 2030. United Nations (2025). *Sustainable Development Goals.*

Within this framework, sustainable finance refers to aligning financial systems, capital flows, and investment decisions with sustainability objectives.[15] It involves directing capital towards activities that support long-term ecological and social stability while incorporating environmental and social considerations into financial analysis and risk assessment.

To understand the evolution and implications of sustainable finance, it is useful to trace the shift from a traditional linear economic model to one explicitly oriented towards sustainable development. This shift occurs in three key stages:

Business-as-Usual (Pre-Sustainable Finance)

This traditional model follows a linear "take-make-dispose" economic cycle, centred on resource extraction, production, consumption, and waste generation. Success is evaluated primarily in terms of shareholder returns and financial efficiency, assuming that natural resources are freely available, while broader environmental and social risks remain external to core financial metrics. This configuration corresponds to the neoliberal economic paradigm discussed in Chapter 1, in which ecological and social costs remain external to pricing mechanisms.

Sustainable Finance 1.0: Ethical Awareness and Exclusion Policies

The first shift towards responsibility occurs when investors begin to exclude from their portfolios certain industries or activities widely recognised as harmful, such as anti-personnel mines, child labor, environmental degradation, and wildlife exploitation. However, the focus largely remains on managing reputational risk and protecting financial returns rather than transforming the underlying economic model.

Sustainable Finance 2.0: Internalising Externalities

This stage represents a more profound shift: firms begin to internalise previously externalised environmental and social costs. Mechanisms such as carbon pricing and the incorporation of sustainability-related risks into financial calculations signal a shift in how value is defined and managed. Companies adopt tools such as Life Cycle Assessment (LCA), integrated reporting, and impact assessments to quantify and manage their broader footprint. Challenges at this stage include determining the appropriate discount rates for future damages and developing transparent, consistent methods for valuing externalities.

---

[15] United Nations Global Compact (n.d.) *Sustainable finance explained: Why it matters and how your business can lead.*

Sustainable Finance 3.0: SDG-Aligned Investment

At this mature stage, finance is explicitly oriented towards achieving the SDGs. Capital is directed towards projects and activities that advance sustainable development, such as renewable energy, green infrastructure, sustainable mobility, and circular economy systems. In this configuration, environmental and social objectives become the primary optimization criteria, subject to financial viability, rather than financial return serving as the sole objective of decision-making. Investment appraisal, therefore, shifts towards long-term ecological and social performance, consistent with a transition from a linear economic model to more circular, sustainability-oriented systems.

These stages, reflecting the transition from a linear to a circular economic model, are summarised in Table 2.1.

Table 2.1: Evolution of Sustainable Finance from Linear to Circular Economy Models.

Stage	Core value orientation	Priority structure	Decision logic	Time horizon
Business-as-usual	Shareholder value	F only	Maximisation of F	Short term
Sustainable Finance 1.0	Extended shareholder value	F dominant; E and S as constraints	Maximisation of F subject to E and S constraints	Short term
Sustainable Finance 2.0	Stakeholder value	Integrated consideration of F, E and S	Joint optimisation of F, E, and S	Medium term
Sustainable Finance 3.0	Sustainable value	E and S prioritised; F as a constraint	Optimisation of E and S subject to F	Long term

Source: Author, adapted from Schoenmaker, D. and Schramade, W. (2019).

Note: F = financial; E = environmental; S = social dimensions of sustainability.

Sustainable Finance 1.0 and 2.0 represent the stages of the current global transformation, occurring to varying degrees across segments and industries in many countries. This evolution sets the stage for the concept of *materiality*—examined in the next section—and for carbon-pricing dynamics, which we develop further in Chapter 3.

2.2. Understanding Materiality in the Context of Sustainable Finance

Sustainable Finance 1.0 and 2.0 represent stages of an ongoing transformation in which environmental and social considerations become increasingly integrated into financial decision-making. This evolution raises a central question: under what conditions do sustainability issues become financially relevant? The answer lies in the concept of materiality, which defines how environmental and social developments are identified, assessed, and translated into financially significant information.

Sustainability entered mainstream financial markets through the Environmental, Social, and Governance (ESG) framework. The term ESG was first introduced in a 2004 United Nations Global Compact report (Global Compact, 2004), developed in collaboration with the International Finance Corporation, the Swiss Government, and the then UN Secretary-General Kofi Annan. The report encouraged financial institutions to incorporate environmental, social, and governance considerations into investment analysis and was endorsed by banks, asset owners, asset managers, and rating agencies. Momentum increased in 2005 with the publication of the UN Environment Programme Finance Initiative's *Freshfields Report*, which clarified that integrating ESG factors was consistent with institutional investors' fiduciary duties.

While ESG is rooted in sustainability thinking, its practical application has increasingly shifted towards an investor-centric interpretation, focusing on how environmental and social issues affect financial returns rather than how companies impact society or the planet. This understanding explains why many ESG products and ratings emphasise risk–return implications over broader sustainability outcomes (Delgado et al., 2023).

This investor-oriented interpretation of ESG reflects the dominance of financial materiality in market practice. To understand how sustainability becomes financially relevant — and how this perspective can be expanded — it is necessary to examine the concept of materiality more closely.

2.2.1. What is Materiality?

The concept of materiality originates in financial reporting, where it refers to information whose omission or misstatement could influence the decisions of users of financial statements, primarily investors. In sustainability reporting, the concept has been broadened to consider the information needs of a wider set of stakeholders and to include an organization's most significant economic, environmental, and social impacts.

A key question for understanding materiality is: which economic, environmental, and social issues are sufficiently significant to warrant disclosure and to influence decision-making?

Materiality is a context-dependent concept that varies according to stakeholder expectations, sector-specific factors, and the organization's operating environment. It plays a central role in sustainability reporting and in the disclosure of non-financial information. These frameworks require companies to disclose their most significant impacts, thereby strengthening transparency and accountability towards stakeholders.

Sustainability reporting is the process by which companies publicly disclose their most significant impacts—economic, environmental, and social—and their contributions to sustainable development. For instance, reporting on greenhouse gas (GHG) emissions and actions taken to reduce them aligns with both the UNFCCC and the Paris Agreement. These reports enable stakeholders to assess a company's commitment and performance in relation to the Sustainable Development Goals (SDGs).

At the core of materiality lies the concept of impact, defined as any change—positive or negative, actual or potential, direct or indirect—that an organization has on the economy, environment, or people.[16] Impacts can be:

- Intended or unintended
- Short-term or long-term
- Reversible or irreversible

Impacts can include, for example:

Economic:

- Job creation or job losses
- Increased or reduced tax contributions
- Improved or deteriorated income distribution

Environmental:

- Ecosystem restoration or degradation
- Reduction or increase in pollution
- Decreased or increased greenhouse gas emissions

Social:

- Improvement or deterioration of labour conditions
- Protection or violation of human rights
- Increased or reduced social inclusion

---

[16] This understanding of impact as encompassing positive and negative, actual or potential, direct or indirect effects on the economy, environment, and people reflects a convergence across major international frameworks. Comparable formulations appear in the Global Reporting Initiative (GRI) Standards (2021), the OECD Development Assistance Committee (DAC) evaluation criteria, and definitions adopted within the United Nations system, including UNDP and UNEP guidance on development and environmental impacts. Collectively, these frameworks signal a broader shift in policy and evaluation paradigms from measuring economic performance primarily through output indicators toward assessing systemic, long-term effects on ecological and social systems.

Significantly, positive impacts do not offset negative ones. For example, a renewable energy project that displaces local communities without consent creates a non-compensable negative impact, despite its environmental benefits.

Material Topics

In determining material topics, the significance of an impact is evaluated based on its severity—defined by its scale, scope, and irremediability—and, in the case of potential impacts, its likelihood.[17] These criteria help determine which impacts are material from a sustainability perspective.

Material topics are identified through stakeholder engagement and expert consultation. Companies must assess the extent of their involvement—whether they cause, contribute to, or are linked to these impacts—and assume appropriate responsibility.

Examples of material topics may be structured across the three dimensions of sustainability:

Economic:

- Tax transparency
- Local economic value creation
- Responsible procurement practices

Environmental:

- GHG emissions
- Water use and effluents
- Biodiversity impacts

Social:

- Working conditions and occupational safety
- Human rights practices
- Anti-corruption and ethical conduct

Identifying material topics requires understanding who is affected and how, which brings the analysis to the role of stakeholders. Materiality is therefore not determined solely by internal managerial judgment, but through engagement with those who experience or influence an organization's impacts.

[17] Global Reporting Initiative (GRI) (2021) *GRI 3: Material Topics.*

Stakeholders are individuals or groups who are affected, potentially affected, or capable of affecting a company's operations.[18] They include:

- Employees
- Consumers
- Local communities
- Governments and regulators
- NGOs
- Business partners and suppliers
- Shareholders and investors

Importantly, affected stakeholders are not limited to those directly engaged with the company. Supply-chain workers, indigenous populations, and future generations—whose interests are central to the Brundtland definition of sustainable development—are also recognised as stakeholders. When direct engagement is not possible, companies may consult representative groups such as trade unions, NGOs, or academic experts.

Through stakeholder engagement, organizations identify which impacts are sufficiently significant to be considered material, thereby linking corporate activity to broader societal and environmental concerns.

Materiality frameworks are increasingly codified through international regulations and voluntary standards that shape sustainability reporting. In the European context, non-financial reporting requirements establish defined categories of sustainability-related disclosures as part of corporate transparency obligations.[19]

Among voluntary standards, the Global Reporting Initiative (GRI) Standards are the most widely used framework for publicly disclosing environmental, social, and economic impacts.[20] While GRI is closely aligned with the Sustainable

---

[18] This definition aligns with the OECD Due Diligence Guidance for Responsible Business Conduct (OECD, 2018), which distinguishes between affected stakeholders and other stakeholders with a legitimate interest in the company's activities.

[19] Under Directive 2014/95/EU, non-financial information includes, inter alia, environmental, social, and employee-related matters, respect for human rights, and anti-corruption issues (European Union, 2014).

[20] This section refers primarily to the Global Reporting Initiative (GRI) Standards, the world's most widely used sustainability reporting framework for publicly disclosing environmental, social, and economic impacts. Established in 1997 in Boston and now headquartered in Amsterdam, GRI provides internationally recognized voluntary standards

Development Goals, companies may also rely on other international or national guidelines, including ISO 26000, the UN Global Compact, the UN Guiding Principles Reporting Framework, the OECD Guidelines for Multinational Enterprises, the Task Force on Climate-related Financial Disclosures (TCFD), and the Sustainability Accounting Standards Board (SASB).

Beyond corporate reporting, several international frameworks shape how sustainability becomes embedded in financial decision-making. The Sustainable Finance Disclosure Regulation (SFDR), adopted by the European Union, requires asset managers and financial institutions to disclose how they integrate environmental, social, and governance (ESG) risks and impacts into investment processes.[21] Complementing this, the United Nations Principles for Responsible Investment (UN PRI) provide a voluntary global framework for institutional investors to incorporate ESG criteria and responsible ownership practices into investment decisions.

Together, these instruments enhance transparency, comparability, and accountability within financial markets and help align capital flows with sustainability objectives.

2.2.2. What is Double Materiality?

The previous section showed how materiality evolved from its origins in financial reporting towards a broader sustainability perspective centred on impacts and stakeholders. The concept of double materiality integrates these two dimensions by requiring companies to assess both how sustainability issues affect their financial performance and how their activities affect society and the environment.

The European Commission formally introduced the concept of double materiality in 2019 within the context of sustainability reporting.[22] It consists of two complementary dimensions:

1. **Financial Materiality:**

   Financial materiality considers how sustainability issues generate or alter risks and opportunities that affect a company's financial position, performance, or ability to generate enterprise value over time. Examples include regulatory changes, carbon-pricing exposure, supply chain disruptions, and shifts in market demand. This corresponds to the traditional understanding of materiality in financial reporting, often

---

that enable companies to report transparently on their material impacts and contributions to sustainable development (Global Reporting Initiative, n.d.).

[21] European Union (2019).

[22] European Commission (2019); Global Reporting Initiative (2021).

referred to as single materiality, which focuses on how external developments affect the company.

2. **Impact Materiality:**

   Impact materiality considers the actual or potential, positive or negative impacts that a company has on people, communities, and the environment—irrespective of whether these impacts translate into financial consequences. Impacts are assessed based on their severity and, where relevant, their likelihood. Examples include environmental impacts such as ecosystem degradation or pollution, and social impacts such as labour conditions, displacement of local communities, or effects on human rights.

These relationships may be expressed schematically as follows:

Single materiality: outside → firm
Impact materiality: firm → outside
Double materiality: bidirectional integration

Double materiality unites both perspectives. It requires firms to consider how ESG issues affect them (financial materiality) and how they affect the world around them (impact materiality). This holistic view is essential for achieving Sustainable Finance 3.0.

This bidirectional relationship is illustrated in Figure 2.1.

Figure 2.1: Double Materiality.

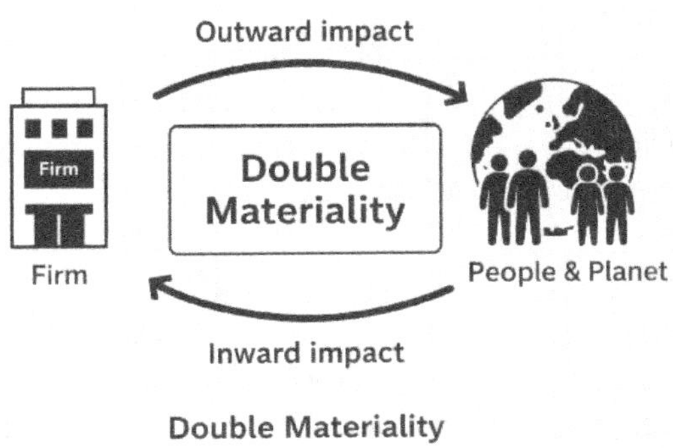

Source: Author.

A practical example of this feedback loop can be found in the aviation sector, where climate change and flight operations influence each other in both directions.

2.2.3. Case Study — Cloud Base Height and Double Materiality

The aviation sector offers a clear example of double materiality—a two-way relationship in which environmental changes, such as rising cloud heights driven by climate change, affect aviation performance by requiring higher altitudes and additional fuel use, which, in turn, contribute to environmental degradation through increased emissions.

This case study was originally inspired by a conversation with Captain Irfan Ozan Ongun, a senior pilot with over 25 years of aviation experience, including a decade in charter operations. Based on his direct observations, cloud tops that were typically encountered at around 20,000 feet in the 1990s are now frequently found at 33,000 feet. This shift forces commercial aircraft to fly at higher altitudes to stay above cloud layers—requiring more fuel and increasing emissions.

While anecdotal, his insight reflects a lived, professional perspective on the climate–aviation feedback loop and is supported by broader scientific findings. As global temperatures rise, the tropopause—the upper boundary of the troposphere—has been observed to rise, allowing convective clouds to grow taller. A study by Böhm et al. (2019) confirmed that satellite-based tracking of cloud base heights reveals regional and seasonal variations consistent with warming-induced atmospheric restructuring.

This has operational consequences: aircraft climbing to higher altitudes consume more fuel and emit more greenhouse gases, increasing operational costs and environmental impacts.

Two recent studies underscore the dynamics of this loop. Liu et al. (2025) examined how meteorological variables—such as temperature, humidity, and low visibility—significantly increase fuel consumption and CO_2 emissions in aviation. These variables, many of which are being intensified by climate change, not only reduce operational efficiency but also impose measurable financial costs.

Cui et al. (2025) add a complementary perspective by analyzing how aircraft emissions at higher altitudes—where planes increasingly cruise due to both air traffic patterns and the need to avoid elevated cloud tops—have disproportionate radiative forcing effects. Emissions at these levels contribute more intensively to ozone formation, contrail generation, and warming. As a result, the strategic decision to fly higher, often driven by a climate-affected atmospheric structure, results in greater environmental harm per unit of fuel.

Together, these studies reveal a self-reinforcing feedback loop at the heart of double materiality:

- Climate change leads to taller clouds and more erratic weather, requiring operational changes.
- These changes, such as higher climb altitudes and longer routing, cause increased fuel consumption.
- Emissions released at these altitudes are more damaging to the climate, reinforcing atmospheric change.

Figure 2.2 illustrates how rising cloud altitudes—linked to climate change—force aircraft to fly higher, increasing emissions. This operational adjustment feeds back into the climate system, exemplifying the two-way logic of double materiality: environmental shifts lead to economic consequences, which in turn exacerbate environmental stress.

This example illustrates how ecological change can function as an operational constraint rather than merely as a reputational or regulatory risk. As discussed in Chapter 1, ecological limits are not external to the economic system; they increasingly shape the conditions under which production takes place. The aviation case shows that when environmental pressures intensify, they directly alter firms' cost structures. Chapter 3 builds on this insight by examining how sustainability-related policies translate ecological constraints into pricing mechanisms and investment decisions.

Figure 2.2: Cloud Base Height Change and Double Materiality.

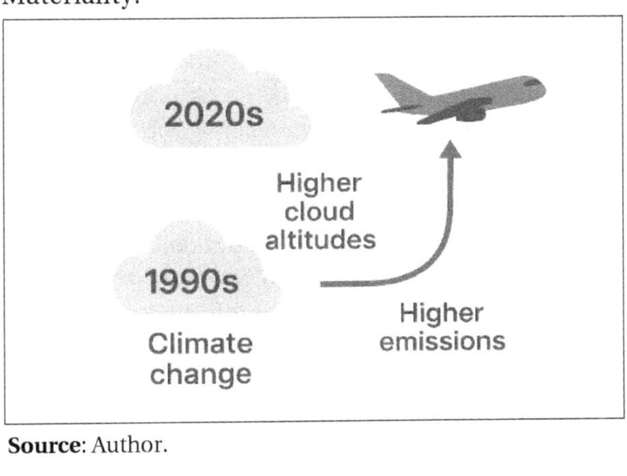

Source: Author.

Key Insights — Chapter 2: From Sustainability to Sustainable Finance

1. **Finance Structures the Allocation of Capital and Therefore Influences Economic Direction.** Financial systems determine which activities receive funding and under what conditions. When environmental and social considerations enter financial decision-making, sustainability criteria begin to shape investment flows and production patterns.
2. **Sustainable Finance Evolves Through Distinct Structural Stages.** The transformation occurs in four stages:
   - **Business-as-usual:** prioritises shareholder value while externalising ecological and social costs.
   - **Sustainable Finance 1.0:** introduces ethical exclusions and reputational risk management.
   - **Sustainable Finance 2.0:** integrates sustainability-related risks and begins internalising externalities into financial analysis.
   - **Sustainable Finance 3.0:** directs capital towards long-term environmental and social objectives consistent with the SDGs.
3. **Materiality Defines Which Sustainability Issues Matter for Decision-Making.** It identifies which environmental, social, and economic issues must be disclosed and incorporated into corporate and financial evaluations. In this way, materiality functions as a relevance filter, translating sustainability concerns into economically actionable information.
4. **The Concept of Stakeholders Expands the Scope of Accountability.** Materiality in sustainability reporting extends beyond shareholders to include employees, local communities, supply-chain actors, civil society, future generations, and other affected or potentially affected parties. This broader stakeholder perspective enlarges both the temporal horizon and the ethical scope of financial decision-making.
5. **Sustainability Becomes Institutionalised Through Reporting and Regulatory Frameworks.** International standards and regulations translate material sustainability issues into formal disclosure requirements. Through transparency and comparability, these frameworks embed environmental and social considerations into corporate governance and financial decision-making.
6. **Double Materiality Establishes a Bidirectional Accountability Framework.** Beyond assessing how sustainability issues affect firms (financial materiality), double materiality also evaluates how firms affect society and the environment (impact materiality). This two-way perspective

integrates financial performance with the ecological and social consequences of corporate activity, forming a structural foundation for Sustainable Finance 3.0.

In Simple Words — Chapter 2: From Sustainability to Sustainable Finance

Sustainability is an economic question. If markets do not reflect environmental and social costs, they send incomplete signals about what is profitable and what is sustainable. This is where finance becomes central. Financial systems determine which projects receive capital and which business models expand. When sustainability considerations enter financial decision-making, they begin to shape the direction of capital allocation itself.

The integration of sustainability into finance unfolds through distinct stages. In an initial phase, investors exclude certain harmful activities from their portfolios, primarily to manage reputational risk. In a subsequent phase, environmental and social factors are treated as financial risks that may affect long-term profitability, leading firms to incorporate sustainability-related considerations into their analyses. In its most advanced form, sustainable finance goes further: capital is directed towards activities that contribute to long-term environmental and social objectives consistent with the Sustainable Development Goals.

As sustainability entered financial decision-making, a practical question emerged: which issues actually matter? Not every environmental or social concern is equally relevant to every company. The concept of materiality helps answer this question. It identifies which sustainability issues must be considered in financial evaluations and corporate disclosures. In simple terms, materiality determines what must be considered when making decisions.

As the concept of materiality expanded, the range of relevant actors also widened. Companies are not accountable only to shareholders, but to a broader set of stakeholders — including employees, local communities, supply-chain partners, civil society, and even future generations. This broader perspective recognises that corporate activities affect many groups, often across time and geographic boundaries. As a result, financial and corporate decisions increasingly take into account not only returns to investors, but also their wider social and environmental consequences.

To support this broader perspective, sustainability considerations are increasingly embedded in reporting standards and regulatory frameworks. Companies are encouraged or required to disclose information about their environmental and social impacts, making these issues more transparent and comparable across markets. Through such disclosure systems, sustainability moves from being a voluntary concern to becoming part of formal economic governance. This institutionalisation strengthens accountability and integrates environmental and social considerations more firmly into financial practice.

Finally, the concept of double materiality recognises that sustainability operates in two directions. On the one hand, changes in the external environment — such as climate change — can affect a firm's costs, risks, and profitability. On the other hand, the activities of firms have direct consequences for ecosystems, communities, and future generations. Understanding this two-way relationship is essential for sustainable finance. It shows how economic activity both shapes and is shaped by the world around it.

Chapter 3

Sustainability and the Changing Cost Structure of Firms

To understand how sustainability reshapes firms' cost structures, we revisit Principle 16 of the 1992 Rio Declaration on Environment and Development, which articulated the "polluter pays" principle:[23]

> National authorities should endeavor to promote the internalization of environmental costs and the use of economic instruments, taking into account the approach that the polluter should, in principle, bear the cost of pollution, with due regard to the public interest and without distorting international trade and investment.

This principle marked a decisive shift: environmental damage, long treated as an externality, was to be incorporated into economic decision-making through pricing mechanisms.

The Kyoto Protocol (1997) operationalised this logic by introducing binding emission-reduction targets and market-based instruments, such as emissions trading.[24] By assigning tradable value to emission reductions, it established the foundations of international carbon markets. Carbon dioxide became a tradable and priced input within regulatory frameworks, directly affecting production costs and investment decisions.[25]

The Paris Agreement (2015) extended this framework through Nationally Determined Contributions (NDCs), requiring countries to define and periodically update their climate commitments.[26]

Together, these agreements represent a structural turning point: climate-related damages increasingly enter economic systems through regulatory and market mechanisms that affect both national policies and corporate cost structures.

---

23 United Nations (1992), *Rio Declaration on Environment and Development*, Principle 16.

24 The other mechanisms created were the Clean Development Mechanism and Joint Implementation. (UNFCCC, Kyoto Protocol).

25 United Nations Framework Convention on Climate Change (UNFCCC) (n.d.) *Emissions Trading under the Kyoto Protocol.*

26 United Nations Framework Convention on Climate Change (2015), *Paris Agreement*, Article 4; United Nations (2015).

Building on the mispricing diagnosis developed in Chapter 1, this chapter examines how the internalisation of environmental externalities reshapes firms' incentives, investment appraisal, and cost structures. It begins by revisiting mainstream growth models that abstracted from ecological constraints and then turns to contemporary mechanisms—such as carbon pricing, uncertainty modelling, and real-options analysis—that translate environmental limits into economic decisions. In doing so, the chapter bridges macro-level climate policy and firm-level investment decisions, showing how carbon pricing, uncertainty, and irreversibility jointly reconfigure the economic rationale for sustainable investment.

3.1. Growth Models and Pricing Externalities: A Brief Literature Review

3.1.1. From Cobb-Douglas to Solow and Romer: Modelling Growth Without Nature

The Cobb-Douglas production function (Cobb & Douglas, 1928) models output as a function of labor (L) and capital (K):

$$Y = A \times L^{\beta} \times K^{\alpha},$$

Where:

- Y: Output
- A: A productivity parameter capturing the overall technological and organisational conditions under which capital and labour are combined.
- L: Labor input
- K: Capital input
- α, β: Output elasticities of capital and labor, respectively.

This model, for simplicity, assumes constant returns to scale—that a proportional increase in both capital and labour leads to a proportional increase in output. It also omits natural resource and environmental costs associated with the production process. Several authors—such as Benes and Devarajan (2000), Bretschger and Smulders (2006), and Orlando (2023)—interpreted this omission as a modelling choice aimed at analytical tractability and at focusing on capital–labour dynamics.

Conversely, critics argue that this omission is not merely a simplification but a serious conceptual limitation with real consequences for understanding sustainability. From ecological economists such as Daly (1996), Daly and Farley (2011), and Diesendorf et al. (2024), to physical economists like Ayres and Warr (2005), and methodological critics like Keen (2011), scholars have noted that excluding natural and energetic inputs leads to distorted representations of economic processes and hides biophysical limits. Thermodynamic economists such as Georgescu-Roegen (1971) argued that the economic process is not a mechanical or reversible transformation, but a one-way, irreversible flow from concentrated resources—such as fossil fuels, minerals, and fertile soils—into outputs like heat, emissions, and waste that cannot be fully recovered or reused. This means that economic production inevitably degrades useful resources into dispersed forms, making full recovery physically impossible. This perspective anticipated many of the concerns later raised by ecological economics, particularly the concept of irreversibility, which has since become foundational to sustainability thinking. Irreversibility is revisited in this chapter, in section 3.3, as a key reason why sustainable investment is essential.

Whatever the reason for the omission—whether it was a simplifying assumption intended to isolate the roles of capital and labour or a deeper conceptual limitation—the crucial point is that it remained influential in mainstream economics and policy modelling well into the 1970s.

The Solow Growth Model

Solow retained the Cobb–Douglas production structure but formalised technological progress as an exogenous, time-dependent factor influencing output growth. In this framework, productivity growth—captured by the time evolution of A—became the primary driver of long-term economic expansion beyond capital accumulation. In growth accounting, this unexplained portion of output growth is referred to as the "Solow residual" and later formalised as total factor productivity (TFP), reflecting technological change as well as broader productivity-enhancing factors such as improvements in skills, organisational efficiency, and institutional frameworks (Solow, 1956; 1957).

While the model represented a major advance in growth theory, it continued to abstract from the explicit treatment of resource depletion and environmental degradation. By allowing substitution among inputs without incorporating ecological constraints, it left biophysical limits outside the core structure of economic growth analysis.

The Romer Growth Model

While Solow treated technological progress as exogenous—an external factor not explained within the model—Romer (1990) endogenised technological change by modelling it as the result of purposeful economic activity, including research and development, knowledge accumulation, and human capital investment. In Romer's framework, ideas and knowledge become central drivers of growth, and policy decisions can permanently influence long-term growth rates.

By incorporating innovation dynamics directly into the production process, Romer expanded the analytical scope of growth theory and reinforced the role of investment in knowledge creation.

However, like earlier models, the framework continued to abstract from natural resource constraints and environmental degradation. Although knowledge and technology were internalised, ecological limits remained external to the model's structure. As a result, sustained growth was treated as compatible with ongoing expansion of economic activity, without systematically integrating biophysical boundaries into the growth process.

Despite their differences, these growth models share a common structural feature: environmental degradation and resource depletion remain external to the core mechanism of output determination. This analytical separation contributed to treating environmental damage as an externality rather than as an integral component of production costs.

The next step in economic analysis, therefore, required not only modelling growth but also incorporating environmental damage into economic decision-making. The introduction of carbon pricing mechanisms marked a decisive shift: climate-related externalities began to enter firms' cost structures and the incentive systems guiding investment.

3.1.2. From Limitless Growth to Climate Constraints: The Contribution of Nordhaus

Nordhaus advanced this integration by linking economic activity to atmospheric dynamics and climate change within a unified analytical framework. Through the development of Integrated Assessment Models (IAMs), he connected emissions, carbon accumulation, temperature change, and economic output in a dynamic system (Nordhaus, 1991, 1992, 1993).

Rather than abandoning the growth framework, Nordhaus extended it by introducing climate damage functions that translate rising temperatures into measurable economic losses (Nordhaus, 1991, 1992, 1993). Environmental degradation thus entered the model as a factor affecting output and welfare, linking emissions to long-term economic performance.

His Integrated Assessment Models (IAMs) combine three core components:[27]

- Carbon circulation module – simulates how CO_2 emissions from economic activity accumulate and circulate in the atmosphere.
- Climate module – estimates global temperature changes resulting from increased atmospheric CO_2 concentrations.
- Economic module – links economic output to emissions and evaluates how temperature increases affect productivity, capital accumulation, and welfare over time.

These components are integrated into the Dynamic Integrated Climate-Economy (DICE) model, which was later extended into a regional version known as RICE. Together, these models became foundational in climate–economy modelling and are widely used in policy contexts, including IPCC assessments (Nordhaus, 2007).[28]

The Social Cost of Carbon and Internalization of Externalities

A key innovation of Integrated Assessment Models is the calculation of the Social Cost of Carbon (SCC)—defined as the present value of the incremental damage caused by emitting one additional ton of CO_2 (Nordhaus, 2017). It represents the monetary estimate of the long-term economic harm associated with a marginal increase in emissions.

This includes projected impacts on:

- Agriculture output, human health, and sea-level rise
- Ecosystem degradation and biodiversity loss
- Productivity losses and damage from extreme weather events

SCC plays a critical role in:

- Cost-benefit analyses of climate policies
- Carbon pricing mechanisms (e.g., carbon taxes, cap-and-trade)
- Project evaluation through the shadow pricing of emissions

---

[27] See Royal Swedish Academy of Science (2018), p. 23 for a summary of Nordhaus's development of IAMs and their policy relevance.

[28] The Intergovernmental Panel on Climate Change (IPCC) was co-awarded the 2007 Nobel Peace Prize for its efforts to advance scientific understanding of climate change. In 2018, William Nordhaus received the Sveriges Riksbank Prize in Economic Sciences in Memory of Alfred Nobel for integrating climate change into long-run macroeconomic analysis. See: Nobel Peace Prize (2007); Nobel Prize Committee (2018).

Challenges in SCC Estimation

1. **Choice of discount rate** – The selected discount rate strongly influences how future damages are valued relative to present costs, affecting the magnitude of the SCC.
2. **Uncertainty in damage estimation** – Climate sensitivity, economic feedback effects, and non-market impacts introduce significant uncertainty. Many ecosystem risks and tipping points remain difficult to quantify within existing models.
3. **Intergenerational equity considerations** – Divergent views on how to balance present economic activity against future welfare influence assumptions about discounting and long-term policy targets.[29]
4. **Long time horizons** – A significant share of emitted carbon remains in the atmosphere for centuries or longer, making damage projections inherently dependent on very long-run modelling assumptions.

Shadow Price of Carbon

Carbon pricing is closely linked to the Social Cost of Carbon. Within IAM frameworks, the shadow price of carbon represents the optimal marginal cost of emissions consistent with maximizing social welfare under climate constraints. In practical policy contexts, this concept informs estimates of the carbon price required to achieve specific temperature targets, including those outlined in the Paris Agreement. This is crucial for:

- Assessing whether sustainability projects yield positive Net Present Value (NPV) when emissions are properly priced[30]
- Guiding long-term investment decisions aligned with Sustainable Finance 3.0

---

[29] World Bank (2024), p. 4.

[30] Under the NPV method, the PV of a project's cash inflows is compared to the PV of the project's cash outflows. NPV is the difference between the PV of these cash flows: $NPV = -I_0 + \sum_{n=1}^{T} \frac{CF_n}{(1+r)^n}$; where:

I_0: Initial Investment; T: Lifetime of the investment; CF_n: Cash Flow in n^{th} year; r: Interest rate

If the NPV > 0, the project is acceptable as it promises a return more significant than the required rate of return.

If the NPV = 0, the project is acceptable as it promises a return equal to the required rate of return.

If the NPV < 0, the project is not acceptable as it promises a return less than the required rate of return.

3.2. Carbon Pricing Mechanism

Carbon pricing is a cornerstone of modern climate policy and represents the primary mechanism through which climate externalities are translated into economic costs. As outlined in Article 17 of the Kyoto Protocol, countries may sell unused emissions allowances if they remain below their emissions targets to others that exceed their targets.[31] Similarly, Article 6 of the Paris Agreement encourages voluntary cooperation through international carbon markets, reinforcing the principle of cost-efficient cross-border emissions reductions.[32]

Placing a value on carbon serves both as a climate policy instrument and as a long-horizon financial valuation mechanism guiding decarbonization. Carbon pricing translates projected climate damages—from rising sea levels, agricultural losses, and increased extreme weather events—into a direct financial cost for emitters. In doing so, it reallocates climate-related costs from society at large to emitting agents and creates an incentive structure that favours low-carbon technologies and innovation.

There are two primary carbon pricing instruments:[33]

- Carbon Taxes, which establish a fixed price per unit of emissions.
- Emissions Trading System (ETS), which establishes a fixed quantity (cap) of allowable emissions, where the carbon price emerges through market trading.

Under a carbon tax, policymakers fix the price of emissions while total emissions adjust. Under an ETS, policymakers fix the quantity of emissions, and the market determines the carbon price based on supply and demand for allowances.

Prices are typically denominated in USD per metric ton of CO_2-equivalent (tCO_2e), though actual implementation varies by country and may involve conversion to the local currency.[34]

---

[31] UNFCCC, Emission trading.

[32] World Bank (2023).

[33] Emission trading systems, carbon taxes, and the carbon crediting mechanism, typically involving voluntary transactions, are categorised under Direct Carbon Pricing. In contrast, practices such as fuel reforms and fuel excise taxes are examples of Indirect Carbon Pricing. We consider only emissions trading systems and carbon taxes, as we focus on the conceptual framework linked to the SDGs; other forms fall beyond the scope of this study. See World Bank Research Observer (2023) for details.

[34] The most commonly used measure of greenhouse gas (GHG) emissions is carbon dioxide equivalent (CO2e). While CO_2 is the most abundant long-lived anthropogenic

Carbon pricing directly affects firms' cost structures by increasing the marginal cost of carbon-intensive production. Firms with higher emissions per unit of output face higher operating costs, while firms that invest in cleaner technologies reduce their exposure to carbon expenses. As a result, carbon pricing alters relative production costs across sectors, influences investment appraisal through adjusted cash-flow projections, and reshapes competitive dynamics.

3.2.1. Carbon Tax (Pigouvian Tax)

First formalised by Pigou (1920), a carbon tax addresses activities that generate negative externalities by imposing a price on pollution. In the context of carbon, it sets a fixed cost per ton of CO_2 emitted, thereby increasing the price of carbon-intensive goods and services. As illustrated in Figure 3.1, the tax shifts the supply curve upward, raising the market price from P_0 to P_1 and reducing the equilibrium quantity from Q_0 to Q_1.

3.2.2. The EU Emissions Trading System (ETS)

The EU Emission Trading System (EU ETS) is the world's first and largest carbon market. Launched in 2005, coinciding with the entry into force of the Kyoto Protocol, it operates as a market-based cap-and-trade mechanism for regulating greenhouse gas (GHG) emissions.[35] A cap is set on total allowable emissions, allowances are distributed or auctioned, and firms may trade these permits. Each allowance entitles the holder to emit 1 ton of CO_2e. Firms that emit below their allocated allowances may sell surplus permits, while those that exceed their allocation must purchase additional allowances. The carbon price under the EU ETS is therefore determined by market forces—specifically, the interaction between the demand for and supply of emission allowances.

In the second part of Figure 3.1, the cap-and-trade system is represented by a vertical supply curve, illustrating that the regulator fixes the total number of

---

greenhouse gas, other gases, such as methane (CH_4) and nitrous oxide (N_2O), also have significant impacts. According to the IPCC Fifth Assessment Report (AR5), methane has a global warming potential over a 100-year time horizon (GWP100) of 28 relative to CO_2 (GWP100 = 1), while nitrous oxide has a GWP100 of 265. The 100-year horizon is the standard metric used in most climate policy and carbon market accounting. Over shorter horizons, methane's relative impact is substantially higher (GWP20 ≈ 84 in AR5), reflecting its strong but shorter-lived atmospheric effect. See Thompson, S. (2025).

[35] The EU ETS covers electricity, heat generation, energy-intensive industrial manufacturing, aviation, and maritime transport sectors. It operates across EU Member States as well as Iceland, Norway, and Liechtenstein, and is linked to the Swiss ETS.

emission allowances—in this case, the EU authorities. This fixed supply indicates that the emissions cap is established independently of market demand. As the EU gradually tightens the cap to align with its climate targets, the supply of allowances diminishes, creating greater market scarcity. This reduction in supply raises carbon prices, thereby reinforcing the economic incentive for companies to reduce their emissions. Recent reforms introduced more aggressive annual reduction rates (European Commission, 2025):

- "1.74% annually (2013–2020)"
- "2.2% (2021–2023)"
- "4.3% (2024–2027) and 4.4% (2028–2030)"

Figure 3.1: Carbon Tax and Cap-and-Trade Approach Pricing Dynamics.

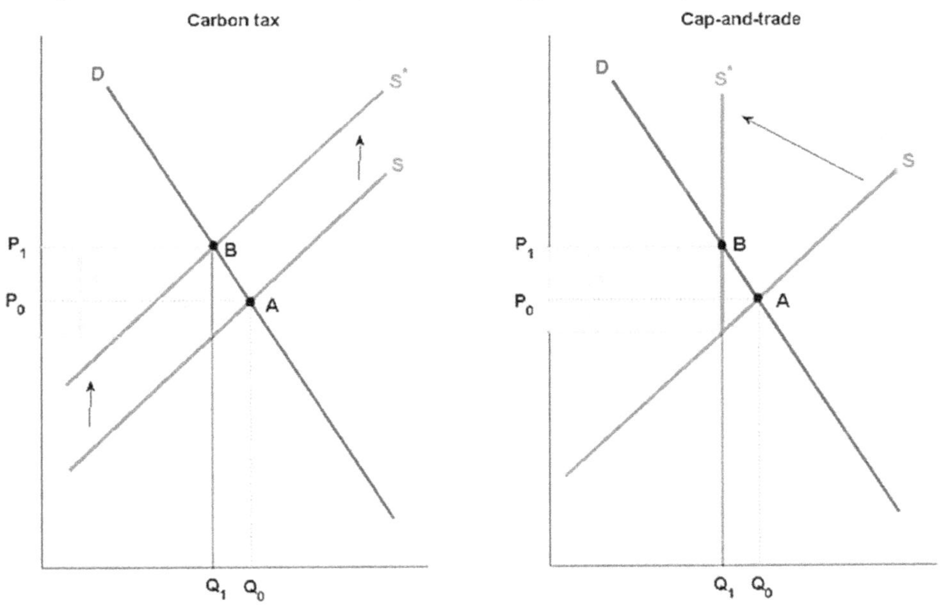

Source: Whitehead, J. (2008).

Note: Reproduced with permission from the author. Full source listed in the bibliography.

Figure 3.2 provides a conceptual overview of how the cap-and-trade system functions, illustrating the direction of allowance flows in market transactions.

Figure 3.2: Emissions Trading System (ETS) or Cap-and-Trade Approach.

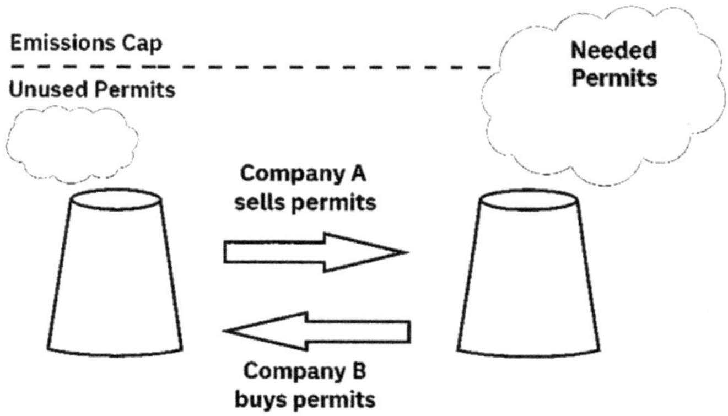

Source: Author's own schematic illustration of allowance trading under a cap-and-trade system.

Figure 3.3 illustrates the trend in carbon prices (in euros) from 2008 to 2025, highlighting the impact of EU climate policy measures on market dynamics. Over this period, the gradual reduction in the number of emission allowances, as part of the EU's cap-setting strategy, has played a significant role in driving up carbon prices, reflecting increased scarcity and stronger climate ambitions.

Figure 3.3: Carbon Price Trends in the EU ETS (2008–2025), in Euros.

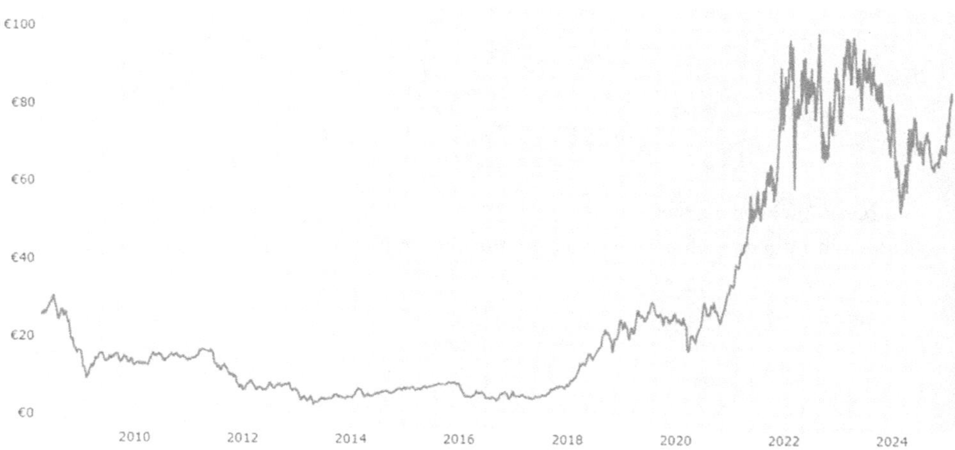

Source: Sandbag (2025). Reproduced with permission from the Sandbag EU ETS Carbon Price Viewer.

Globally, most emissions trading systems (ETSs) and carbon taxes remain concentrated in high- and middle-income economies, with the EU, the United States, and China operating some of the largest schemes.[36] However, developing and least developed countries (LDCs) are increasingly entering the carbon pricing landscape, despite economic, legal, and institutional constraints that complicate implementation.

The EU Carbon Border Adjustment Mechanism (CBAM), which took effect in 2026, extends emissions accountability to third-country exporters by incentivizing the adoption of equivalent carbon-pricing systems or by applying a border charge based on the embedded emissions of imported goods.

Although methodologies for estimating the monetary value of carbon continue to evolve, the overall trend indicates a rising carbon price. This shift strengthens the economic case for decarbonization, as each ton of GHG emissions carries an increasing cost, raising the relative price of carbon-intensive products. These dynamics are examined further in the following section, which discusses the sources and implications of carbon price volatility.

3.3. Keynesian Uncertainty and Carbon Price Dynamics

This section examines the relevance of Keynesian uncertainty for understanding the complex and non-linear behaviour of carbon markets, particularly the EU Emissions Trading System (EU ETS).

3.3.1. Conceptual Insight: Keynes's Distinction Between Calculable and Non-Calculable Uncertainty

In climate economics, uncertainty plays a fundamental role in shaping expectations, policy design, and market dynamics. Keynes's distinction between calculable and non-calculable uncertainty provides a powerful analytical lens for interpreting carbon market behaviour. In his own words:

> By “uncertain” knowledge, let me explain, I do not mean merely distinguishing what is known for sure from what is only probable. The game of roulette is not subject, in this sense, to uncertainty;[37] nor is the prospect of a Victory bond being drawn. Or, again, the expectation of life

[36] World Bank (2023).

[37] We note that Keynes does not qualify the game of roulette as uncertain, though this is the most common example of uncertainty cited traditionally. Keynes finds that statistical quantification is inadequate for examining uncertainty, as human decisions affecting the future don't depend on strict mathematical expectations. Keynes argued that the analysis of behaviour under uncertainty differs from that of risk, which involves a well-defined probability distribution with a set of possible future outcomes.

> is only slightly uncertain. Even the weather is only moderately uncertain. The sense in which I am using the term is that in which the prospect of a European war is uncertain, or the price of copper and the rate of interest twenty years hence, or the obsolescence of a new invention, or the position of private wealth owners in the social system in 1970. About these matters, there is no scientific basis on which to form any calculable probability whatever. We simply do not know. (Keynes, 1937).

Keynes distinguishes between calculable uncertainty—such as in roulette, where outcomes follow known or estimable probability distributions—and deeper, non-calculable uncertainty—such as future innovations, where no reliable statistical basis exists for assigning probabilities to future events.

3.3.1.1. Epistemic and Ontological Uncertainty

In interpreting Keynes's framework, uncertainty may be analytically distinguished into two dimensions: epistemic and ontological.

1. Epistemic Uncertainty:

Epistemic uncertainty arises from incomplete knowledge or insufficient data about the current or future state of the world.[38] In principle, it can be reduced through improved information, models, and data.

- Example 1: Weather forecasts are uncertain, but not unknowable. The limitations come from imperfect data and model precision—this is a knowledge-based, or epistemic, limitation.
- Example 2: Forecasting carbon prices in the EU ETS over the next year relies on known inputs—such as policy frameworks and historical data—yet uncertainty remains regarding firm behaviour, macroeconomic conditions, and energy demand fluctuations.

These are epistemic uncertainties—'known unknowns'—that are still amenable to probabilistic modelling and scenario analysis.

2. Ontological Uncertainty:

- Ontological uncertainty arises not from data gaps or model imperfections, but from the inherent unpredictability of complex, evolving systems. Keynes articulates this view in *A Treatise on Probability* (1921):[39]
- "States of the universe, identical in every particular, may never occur."

[38] Reuver, M. et al. (2020).

[39] Keynes, J.M. (1921), p. 286.

This implies that economic and social systems are non-ergodic and historically contingent, since future states are not drawn from a stable and repeatable probability distribution.

Example 1: A breakthrough climate technology, such as scalable fusion energy, cannot be confidently predicted before it emerges. No probability distribution can be assigned, as the event may not yet be imaginable.

Example 2: Unanticipated societal shifts—such as the impact of social media on climate activism or radical policy realignments—are likewise beyond probabilistic representation.[40]

In these cases, the space of future possibilities itself is unknown, making standard models inadequate. Ontological uncertainty cannot be addressed through more data or better estimation—it lies beyond the reach of statistical tools.

Table 3.1 summarises the conceptual differences between epistemic and ontological uncertainty, highlighting their distinct implications for decision-making in sustainability-related markets.

Table 3.1: Keynesian Distinction Between Epistemic and Ontological Uncertainty in Climate Markets.

Type of Uncertainty	Source	Example
Epistemic	Lack of knowledge or data	Forecasting carbon prices with limited market information
Ontological	Structural unpredictability of evolving systems	Radical policy shift or breakthrough technology

Source: Developed by the author as a conceptual synthesis based on the discussion above.

Note: Epistemic uncertainty is often addressed through probabilistic models, such as Bayesian methods, including stochastic processes and scenario analysis. Ontological uncertainty reflects the fundamental unpredictability of complex systems and cannot be captured by statistical modelling.

In practice, both types co-exist and interact—particularly in climate and energy markets, where decisions must be made under incomplete knowledge and evolving system conditions.

3.3.2. The EU ETS Carbon Pricing Mechanism

Carbon prices in the European Union Emissions Trading System (EU ETS) do not evolve smoothly or predictably. They reflect the dynamic interplay of regulatory policy adjustments, energy market fluctuations, investor sentiment

---

40 Reuver, M. et al. (2020).

macroeconomic conditions, and geopolitical shocks. In response, several modelling approaches have emerged in climate finance.

One of the most widely used is the Geometric Brownian Motion (GBM) model, which assumes that prices follow a continuous random walk around a long-term trend. However, carbon markets often exhibit behaviours—such as sudden spikes, volatility clustering, and abrupt regime changes—that the GBM framework cannot fully capture. To address these complexities, more advanced models have gained traction in both academic research and financial practice. These include GARCH models, which account for time-varying volatility (Paolella & Taschini, 2008), mean-reverting models, which reflect the corrective influence of policy signals and market expectations (Chevallier, 2011), jump-diffusion processes, which incorporate sharp price movements driven by structural shocks (Zhou et al., 2019), and regime-switching frameworks, which allow for shifts between distinct market states characterised by different volatility or trend dynamics (Benz & Truck, 2009).

Each model captures different dimensions of uncertainty. For sustainable investors, selecting the right model reflects how uncertainty is perceived and how flexibility is valued in long-term climate investments. Different models embed different assumptions about how carbon prices respond to uncertainty dynamics. The modelling approach influences carbon price forecasts, cost trajectories, and ultimately the valuation of low-carbon investment opportunities.

Among the available modelling approaches, Geometric Brownian Motion (GBM) remains a useful benchmark because of its analytical clarity and compatibility with investment valuation techniques. While it does not capture all structural features of carbon markets, it provides a tractable representation of calculable uncertainty. The GBM framework models carbon prices as a stochastic process combining a deterministic trend and random fluctuations, formally expressed through the following stochastic differential equation (SDE):

$$dC_t = \overbrace{\mu C_t dt}^{\text{drift}} + \underbrace{\sigma C_t dW_t}_{\text{uncertainty}} \tag{1}$$

where:

- μ : drift parameter (expected rate of price increase)
- C_t: the carbon price at time t, i.e., the price for an emission allowance per ton of CO2 in the EU ETS
- dt: infinitesimal time increment;
- σ (sigma): volatility parameter, measuring the dispersion (magnitude) of short-term price fluctuations

- dW_t: increment of a Wiener process (Brownian motion), representing a random shock with mean zero and variance dt

In the equation above, the change in the carbon price dC_tconsists of two components:

1. **Drift** — the systematic part of the process, represented by $\mu C_t dt$. This term captures the expected proportional change in the carbon price over time. In applied settings, it may reflect structural forces such as regulatory tightening, evolving allowance scarcity, or broader macroeconomic conditions.
2. **Uncertainty** — the variable component, represented by $\sigma C_t dW_t$. The volatility parameter σdetermines the magnitude (standard deviation) of price fluctuations around the expected path, while dW_tintroduces the random shock at each instant. This term captures calculable (epistemic) uncertainty—the component of uncertainty that can be represented probabilistically and quantified through volatility, reflecting continuous market adjustments such as energy price movements or evolving expectations. However, abrupt structural breaks or regime shifts fall outside this framework. In this sense, GBM provides a tractable representation of the uncertainty embedded in carbon prices that can be modelled statistically. Uncertainty that cannot be expressed through probability distributions — that is, ontological uncertainty — lies outside the scope of this framework.

Figure 3.4 below provides a stylised visualization of how drift and volatility operate in a Geometric Brownian Motion framework, illustrating the interplay between deterministic trends and stochastic fluctuations in carbon pricing.

Figure 3.4: Illustration of a Random Walk Showing Mean Drift and Volatility.

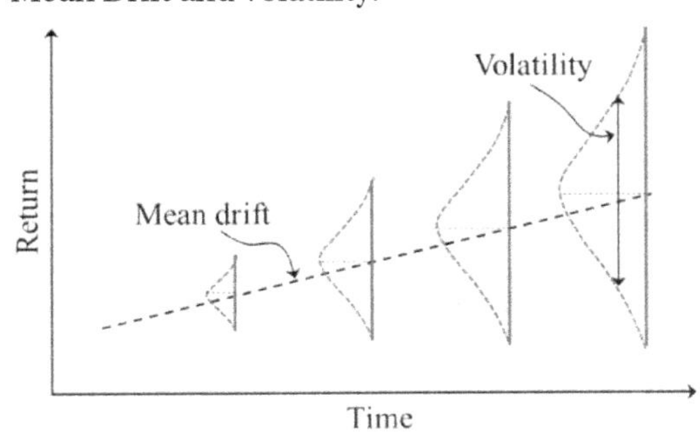

Source: Lee, G. G. & Ham, S.-W. (2023), reproduced under CC BY 4.0.

In this formulation, GBM provides a tractable representation of calculable (epistemic) uncertainty embedded in carbon prices. It assumes that price movements occur within a stable probabilistic structure. However, structural breaks, regime shifts, and fundamentally unforeseeable events — forms of ontological uncertainty — lie outside this framework. This limitation is not merely technical: policymakers must recognise that such "unknown unknowns" and the associated structural trade-offs may emerge at any time, affecting both carbon markets and long-term climate investment strategies (Gillingham et al., 2018).

Table 3.2: GBM and the Limits of Probabilistic Carbon Price Modelling.

Model Feature	GBM	Beyond GBM but still probabilistic	Outside probabilistic frameworks
Continuous price dynamics with constant volatility	Yes	-	-
Time-varying volatility (volatility clustering)	No	GARCH model	-
Discrete price jumps	No	Jump-diffusion models	-
Regime shifts between probabilistic states	No	Regime-switching models	-
Ontological uncertainty	No	No	Yes

Source: Developed by the author based on Paolella & Taschini (2008); Benz & Truck (2009); Chevallier (2011); Zhou et al. (2019); and the conceptual discussion in Section 3.3.

These modelling boundaries have direct implications for sustainable investment decision-making. If a substantial share of carbon price dynamics is driven by uncertainty that probabilistic models cannot fully capture, valuation approaches that rely exclusively on expected price paths become inherently fragile. For investors and policymakers, this shifts the focus from forecasting precise price trajectories to designing investment strategies that remain robust across a wide range of possible futures. In this context, the central challenge is not to eliminate uncertainty but to build flexibility into investment decisions—an issue addressed in Section 3.3.3 through the lens of real options and strategic adaptability.

Before turning to this flexibility-oriented perspective, the next subsection examines the real-world application of GBM-led probabilistic approaches in the EU ETS, with particular attention to how carbon price volatility is measured and interpreted.

3.3.2.1. Carbon Price Volatility in Context

Relevance for Sustainable Investment and the SDGs

At first glance, short-term volatility in carbon markets may primarily concern traders and regulators. However, carbon price instability directly affects sustainable investment decisions and long-term capital planning.

The risk profile of carbon markets can be assessed by comparing the volatility of carbon prices with that of other major asset classes. Table 3.3 presents the annualised volatility of EU Allowance (EUA) spot prices alongside selected asset classes, including agricultural commodities (e.g., wheat, corn), currencies (e.g., EUR/USD, JPY/USD), and energy benchmarks.

According to the Joint Research Centre (JRC) of the European Commission (2023), over the period 2011 to 2022, carbon prices exhibited higher volatility than most agricultural commodities and major currency pairs, and in certain periods exceeded the volatility of selected energy benchmarks such as Brent crude oil.

Managing carbon market volatility is therefore important for aligning financial flows with the Sustainable Development Goals (SDGs), particularly those related to climate action, innovation, and sustainable infrastructure. Greater price stability improves the predictability of investment returns and reduces uncertainty premiums, thereby supporting capital allocation consistent with Paris Agreement objectives.

Table 3.3: Comparative Volatility of EUAs and Other Asset Classes (2011–2023).

Asset Class	**Daily Volatility (%)**
EUAs (Carbon Prices)	**~0.46 – 2.9**
Brent Crude (Energy)	~0.30
Arabica Coffee	~0.32
Agricultural Commodities	~0.20 – 0.24
Gold	~0.15
Aluminum	~0.14
Equities (e.g., Exxon, Nestlé)	~0.15 – 0.23
Major Currencies (EUR, JPY, GBP)	~0.05 – 0.14

Source: European Commission, Joint Research Centre (2023).

Implications for Modelling and Risk Management

The high volatility of carbon markets justifies the use of stochastic models such as Geometric Brownian Motion (GBM) to represent probabilistic price dynamics. However, as discussed above, such models cannot fully capture structural or regime uncertainty arising from policy shifts and systemic change.

3.3.2.2. The Carbon Volatility Index (Carbon VIX) and Policy Uncertainty in the EU ETS

Carbon price uncertainty is a central feature of the EU Emissions Trading System (EU ETS) and a key determinant of how firms hedge and manage climate-related risks over time, since allowance prices respond to regulatory adjustments, macroeconomic conditions, and geopolitical developments that shift both the supply and demand for EUAs.

This uncertainty has been identified as a barrier to decarbonisation investments, particularly in capital-intensive industries that depend on long-term planning horizons (Canadian Climate Institute, 2022).

Carbon VIX: A Market-Based Measure of Forward-Looking Uncertainty

The Carbon Volatility Index (Carbon VIX)—inspired by the well-known CBOE VIX—is derived from EUA option prices and serves as a real-time indicator of market-perceived future carbon price volatility.

Unlike backward-looking statistical measures, Carbon VIX integrates:

1. Dispersed information from market participants, aggregated through option pricing.
2. A forward-looking perspective that is not anchored to historical price patterns.

Key Features:

- EUA option premiums rise with increasing expected volatility; higher Carbon VIX values therefore indicate greater carbon price uncertainty.
- The metric reflects changes in both policy anticipation (e.g., EU climate reforms) and market shocks (e.g., energy crises).

Historical Drivers of Carbon VIX

Figure 3.5 depicts historical spikes in the Carbon VIX corresponding to significant policy changes and macroeconomic shocks, illustrating how both regulatory and demand-side events shape forward-looking volatility in carbon markets.[41]

[41] Fuchs et al., 2024.

Figure 3.5: Carbon Volatility Index (Carbon VIX).

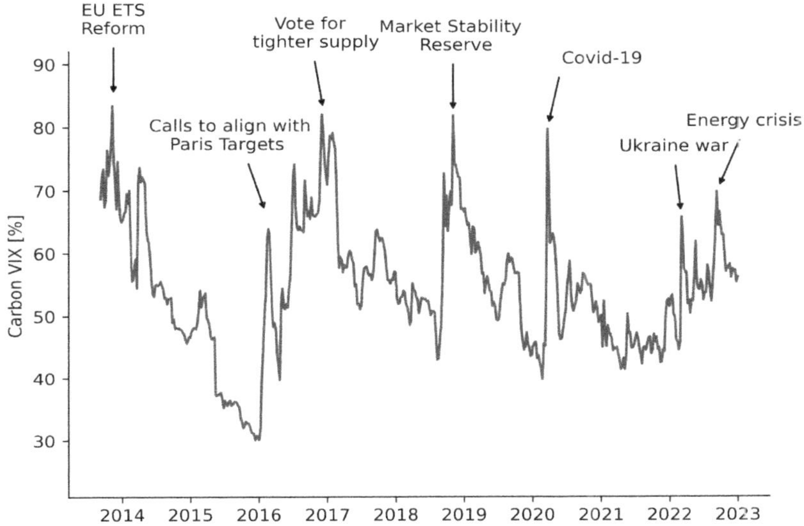

Source: Fuchs et al. (2024). Reproduced with permission from the authors.

Table 3.4 complements Figure 3.5 by translating the visual pattern of volatility spikes into structured analysis, classifying each episode as supply-side or demand-side, and highlighting its impact on market expectations.

Table 3.4: Historical Drivers of Carbon VIX Spikes and their Policy Classification.

Spike Event	Type	Impact on Carbon VIX
2013 EU ETS Reform Proposal	Supply-side	First major spike
Paris Agreement (2015)	Supply-side	Policy-driven rise
Market Stability Reserve (2018)	Supply-side	Initial uncertainty spike
COVID-19 Pandemic (2020)	Demand-side	Sharp increase
Russia–Ukraine War (2022)	Demand-side	High uncertainty
Energy Crisis (2022–2023)	Demand-side	Sustained elevated levels

Source: Developed by the author based on data and events discussed in Fuchs et al. (2024).

These illustrate the dual role of policy shifts and macroeconomic shocks in shaping EUA market expectations.

Governance implications: Integrating ESG frameworks and carbon market mechanisms

Effective carbon pricing does not operate in isolation but is increasingly intertwined with evolving ESG (Environmental, Social, and Governance) frameworks. Mechanisms such as the EU ETS must be supported by transparent institutions, credible emissions accounting, and socially responsive regulation in order to be fully effective.

For example, signatories to the UN Principles for Responsible Investment (UN PRI) commit to integrating ESG factors into decision-making, including through active engagement in carbon-intensive sectors. This introduces a layer of accountability within financial markets, reinforcing the expectation that climate-related risks and environmental performance are financially material.[42]

Ultimately, robust carbon pricing must be supported by governance structures that ensure transparency, participation, and long-term credibility, making it a central tool not only for emissions reduction but also for sustainable development governance.

3.3.3. Why Real Options Are Needed: Linking Uncertainty to Investment Flexibility

The volatility observed in carbon markets complicates long-term investment valuation, particularly in sectors characterised by high capital intensity and irreversibility. In this context, the distinction between epistemic and ontological uncertainty becomes operational rather than merely conceptual: while price dynamics may be modelled probabilistically, policy regimes, technological transitions, and geopolitical shocks introduce forms of uncertainty that lie outside stable probability distributions.

Under epistemic uncertainty—where future outcomes can be modelled probabilistically—real options add value by preserving flexibility in the face of volatile price dynamics. The option to wait, stage, expand, or abandon an investment becomes economically meaningful when capital commitments are largely irreversible, and future price paths remain uncertain (González-Muñoz et al., 2024; Kemala and Hakam, 2025). In such settings, real options provide a more robust decision framework than traditional Net Present Value (NPV), as they incorporate the value of learning before committing resources.

Ontological uncertainty, by contrast, arises from unpredictability that lies outside known probability spaces. It is non-ex-ante calculable, reflecting future states of the world that cannot be reliably anticipated using probabilistic models (Keynes, 1937; Haas et al., 2023; Lempert et al., 2024). Unlike epistemic uncertainty, it cannot be reduced through improved data or refined modelling techniques. It reinforces the need for flexible investment tools. Approaches that maintain optionality—such as staged infrastructure deployment or contingent policy triggers—enable decision-makers to remain responsive to evolving conditions. In these contexts, real options do not eliminate ontological

[42] UNPRI (2023).

uncertainty or assign it a precise price; rather, they provide a decision framework for navigating irreversible commitments in an evolving economic environment.

In sustainability-related investments, both types of uncertainty coexist and interact. Irreversibility amplifies the cost of error in both forms: once investments are committed, many costs cannot be recovered, and early commitments under misguided assumptions can lock firms or economies into suboptimal pathways. Therefore, real options serve not only as a valuation tool but also as a strategic logic—making them essential in low-carbon, long-horizon, and uncertainty-dominated sectors.

Table 3.5 summarises the key distinctions between epistemic and ontological uncertainty and clarifies their implications for modelling and investment strategy.

Table 3.5: Real Options under Epistemic and Ontological Uncertainty.

Dimension	Epistemic Uncertainty	Ontological Uncertainty
Nature	Incomplete knowledge; probabilistic; "known unknowns"	Fundamental unpredictability; non-ex ante calculable; "unknown unknowns"
Modelability	Can be represented with probability distributions (e.g., Bayesian, GBM)	Probability-distribution-based modelling is not adequate because future states cannot be specified ex-ante.
Example	EU ETS carbon price	Breakthrough climate technologies; radical policy shifts; systemic disruptions
Role of Real Options	Add measurable value by waiting, adapting, or scaling amid volatility	Preserve flexibility under irreversible commitment when future states cannot be probabilistically specified

Source: Developed by the author based on referenced literature and Section 3.3.3.

The following subsections operationalise this framework by first presenting the Real Options approach (3.3.3.1), then examining its application in the EU hydrogen strategy (3.3.3.2), and finally discussing recent advances in adaptive valuation using artificial intelligence (3.3.3.3).

3.3.3.1. Expanding the Net Present Value (NPV) Framework: the Real Options Analysis

The Real Options approach extends traditional NPV analysis by recognising that investment opportunities under uncertainty resemble financial options.

Sustainable investment decisions are typically undertaken under conditions of uncertainty and irreversibility. While volatility refers to short-term fluctuations around a long-term mean, uncertainty reflects the deeper difficulty of forecasting long-term outcomes, including their expected values and probability distributions.[43]

The limitations of the traditional Net Present Value (NPV) rule become particularly salient in this context. Standard NPV analysis evaluates investment projects as if they were now-or-never decisions and therefore does not account for the value of managerial flexibility when investment timing can be adjusted. Yet most sustainability-related investments are at least partially irreversible. Clean energy infrastructure, industrial decarbonisation projects, and large-scale adaptation measures require substantial upfront capital expenditures that cannot be fully recovered once committed.

Irreversibility operates at multiple levels. Financial irreversibility arises because many sustainable projects, such as renewable energy infrastructure, require substantial upfront capital and involve sunk costs that cannot be recovered once incurred. If such investments prove unviable due to policy changes or market shifts, these losses cannot easily be recovered. Social and intergenerational irreversibility is even more consequential: investment and policy choices made today may permanently alter environmental conditions, public health outcomes, and the resource base available to future generations, linking sustainable investment directly to intergenerational justice. In such contexts, the timing of investment becomes economically meaningful. These features expose a structural limitation of conventional NPV analysis. When uncertainty is significant and capital commitments are irreversible, the option to wait, revise, expand, or abandon a project carries independent economic value—value that static discounted cash-flow techniques fail to capture.

This insight is central to real-options theory: under uncertainty and irreversibility, delaying an investment can itself create economic value because waiting allows decision-makers to learn from future information before committing irreversible capital (Dixit and Pindyck, 1994).

As a result, the NPV method exhibits several critical limitations when applied to sustainable investment decisions.

The traditional NPV rule relies on two implicit assumptions that are often unrealistic in practice. First, the NPV rule implicitly assumes that the investment is *reversible*, i.e., costs can at least partially be recovered if the investment is less profitable than expected. Uncertainty does not influence the decision to make reversible investments: if the investment results in a loss due to unexpected changes, the expenditures can still be recovered. Second, the NPV rule is only

[43] Sahalia, Y, A. et al. (2024).

valid for an *irreversible* investment if you have to decide now whether or not to invest because you will not be able to invest in the future. Most sustainable investments are irreversible to some extent and need to have the possibility of delaying the investment. The analogy with financial options clarifies why the NPV rule fails in this case (Dixit and Pindyck, 1994).

These assumptions translate into several practical limitations when the NPV method is applied to sustainability-related investment decisions.

1. **Inflexibility in Handling Uncertainty**

   Traditional NPV analysis relies on expected cash-flow projections and does not explicitly incorporate the value of flexibility under uncertainty, such as fluctuations in carbon and energy prices or technological advancement rates. These variables are not just volatile but also structurally uncertain over long time horizons.

2. **Assumption of Immediate Investment**

   The method evaluates investment as a one-time decision taken in the present, and does not assign value to the option of waiting for additional information. This is often unrealistic in sustainability contexts, where waiting can provide strategic advantages, enabling firms to gather additional information, observe market developments, or monitor policy shifts—strategies particularly valuable in dynamic, uncertain environments.

3. **Intertemporal Mispricing of Risk**

   In standard applications, NPV analysis applies a single discount rate across all future cash flows, regardless of project maturity or intergenerational considerations. This can misrepresent the intertemporal risk structure of sustainability projects, in which long-term risks are often more significant and uncertain than short-term risks.[44]

These limitations become even more pronounced when uncertainty extends beyond calculable risk, as discussed above.

To address these limitations, real-options analysis incorporates the value of managerial flexibility under uncertainty. Building on the seminal work of Avinash

[44] The selection of the discount rate is often a politically sensitive issue. For instance, under the Obama administration, the U.S. applied a 3% rate for SCC calculations. In contrast, the Trump administration used a 7% rate, resulting in substantially lower present values for future climate damages. This illustrates how policy-driven discount rates can dramatically shift the valuation of carbon-intensive investments.

Dixit and Robert Pindyck (1994), the approach recognises that many investment opportunities resemble financial options whose value depends on the ability to adjust decisions as new information becomes available. In this framework, investment opportunities resemble financial options that allow decision-makers to delay investment, expand successful projects, contract operations when conditions deteriorate, or abandon projects if they become economically unviable. Rather than treating investment as a fixed "now-or-never" decision, Real Options analysis evaluates the strategic value of waiting and adapting decisions over time. Such flexibility is particularly valuable in sustainability-related investments, where technological change, policy evolution, and carbon price dynamics create highly uncertain long-term environments.

Transition to Real Options under Uncertainty

Real Options analysis provides a more suitable valuation approach.[45] By conceptualizing investments as *options*—such as the right, but not the obligation, to expand, delay, scale down, or abandon a project—real options frameworks enable adaptive, stage-gated decision-making in the face of ontological uncertainty. This is particularly relevant for sustainable infrastructure, where long-time horizons, evolving technologies, and regulatory volatility dominate the landscape.

Yet, traditional real options techniques (e.g., binomial trees, Black-Scholes-type models) often rely on unrealistic assumptions—such as constant volatility or perfect market knowledge—that rarely hold in climate-sensitive or ESG-integrated investment environments.

However, even real options analysis—though more flexible than traditional NPV—primarily addresses epistemic uncertainty, in which future scenarios are unknown but can still be approximated using models and data. In contrast, the literature on deep and ontological uncertainty emphasises that some future states are fundamentally non-ex ante calculable and lie outside any stable probability space (Keynes, 1937; Haas et al., 2023; Lempert et al., 2024). Under such conditions, probabilistic valuation within real options models becomes less reliable. Nevertheless, real options remain valuable as a framework for structuring flexible and adaptive decision-making.

Building on this logic of adaptive flexibility, recent advances in artificial intelligence and machine learning aim to expand the analytical tools available for investment decision-making under complex uncertainty.

[45] See Annex for an overview of the *Real Options* approach.

3.3.3.2. Real Options in the EU Hydrogen Strategy

To meet its 2030 climate and decarbonisation targets, the European Union must deploy climate-compatible technologies while maintaining the competitiveness of its industrial base. Among these technologies, renewable hydrogen has emerged as a strategic solution, particularly for sectors where direct electrification is technologically difficult or economically inefficient (European Commission, 2020).

However, the hydrogen market faces considerable uncertainty, including fluctuating carbon prices, evolving production technologies, underdeveloped infrastructure, and uncertain end-user demand. These challenges necessitate an investment strategy that acknowledges uncertainty and values flexibility in decision-making.

This subsection illustrates how real options logic is embedded in EU hydrogen policy by examining the policy framework governing hydrogen investment in the EU. As of 2022, only 2% of the EU's energy consumption came from hydrogen, and this was primarily produced from natural gas—a source associated with high CO_2 emissions.[46] To support both its 2030 climate objectives and its longer-term decarbonisation pathway, the EU has introduced a comprehensive Hydrogen Strategy, aiming to have renewable hydrogen meet 10% of the EU's energy demand by 2050.

A central element of this strategy is the establishment of the European Hydrogen Bank (EHB) in 2022.[47] Its mandate is to mobilise private investment across the hydrogen value chain—both within and beyond the EU—by mitigating market risk and managing investment uncertainty.

Table 3.6 illustrates how the EU Hydrogen Strategy incorporates different types of real options. These include the option to wait, scale, stage, switch technologies, or abandon projects in response to evolving market and policy conditions. These mechanisms illustrate how public policy can deliberately incorporate real-options logic by preserving flexibility in investment timing, scale, and technological pathways.

---

[46] European Commission (n.d.) *Hydrogen – EU energy system.*

[47] European Commission (n.d.) *European Hydrogen Bank.*

Table 3.6: Application of Real Options in the EU Hydrogen Strategy.

Real Option Type	EU Implementation
Option to Wait[48]	Firms can defer investment for up to five years post-auction
Option to Scale	Projects can expand or contract based on infrastructure development and market conditions.
Option to Stage	Staged investments are enabled by phased access to subsidies and evolving regulations.
Option to Switch	Infrastructure and production pathways can adapt as technologies evolve (e.g., transition from fossil-based hydrogen to renewable hydrogen production).
Option to Abandon	Firms are not obligated to invest even if they win subsidies, thereby preserving downside risk.
Market-Based Flexibility	Premium levels can be adjusted over time to calibrate investment incentives.

Source: Author, adapted from Wolf, A. (2025).

While the EU Hydrogen Strategy illustrates how real options logic can be embedded in policy design, recent advances in artificial intelligence extend this logic by providing new computational tools for valuing flexible investment strategies under uncertainty.

3.3.3.3. Neural Networks and Adaptive Real Options Valuation

Artificial Intelligence (AI) and other digital technologies associated with the Fourth Industrial Revolution increasingly support the implementation of the Sustainable Development Goals (SDGs) by enabling large-scale data analysis and adaptive decision-making.[49] In this section, we first provide an overview of neural networks and then examine how these models can support the evaluation of sustainable investment projects.

Recent advances in machine learning—particularly Artificial Neural Networks (ANNs)—offer new tools to relax some of the restrictive assumptions embedded in traditional real options models.[50] Neural networks are computational architectures inspired by biological neurons, composed of layered, interconnected units that learn statistical patterns from data.[51] Unlike closed-form analytical models, neural networks can approximate complex nonlinear relationships and learn adaptively from new information.[52]

---

[48] In the context of auction-based allocation, the option to wait highlights the relevance of a real options perspective for managing uncertainty. It provides firms with flexibility in investment timing, thereby accelerating capacity building in the hydrogen market.

[49] Sachs, J. D., Mazzucato, M. et al. (2019).

[50] Yang, Z. (2014).

[51] Hardesty, L. (2017).

[52] Gachechiladze, M. (2022).

Neural networks do not replace this forward-looking logic; rather, they enhance the ability to approximate and update option values as new information emerges. In this setting, neural networks present three key capabilities:

1. Learning from Data, Not Assumptions

Neural networks can approximate real option values (e.g., the value of delaying or expanding a project) by learning from simulated or historical data, thereby reducing reliance on predefined volatility or distributional assumptions. This is particularly useful in modelling investment responses to carbon price fluctuations, regulatory transitions (e.g., phaseouts of fossil fuel subsidies), and evolving ESG ratings or disclosure standards.

2. Optimal Timing and Path-Dependent Flexibility

Recurrent Neural Networks (RNNs) and Long Short-Term Memory (LSTM) models are especially suited to multi-stage, path-dependent investment decisions. They can learn sequential investment policies that map evolving project states into actions, which can then be interpreted in real options terms as decisions to expand, wait, or abandon a project, without requiring an ex-ante closed-form valuation formula.

3. Integration of Financial and Non-Financial Indicators

Sustainable investment decisions often combine financial performance (e.g., IRR, volatility) with non-financial metrics (e.g., SDG alignment, social impact, biodiversity preservation). Neural networks can integrate these heterogeneous data sources within a single modelling framework, enabling multi-dimensional project evaluation consistent with ESG principles and SDG-oriented investment objectives.

Applied Example: Deep Real Options for Mobility Infrastructure

Brunner and Bakhshi (2022) provide an empirical illustration of this approach through a "Deep Real Options" framework applied to sustainable mobility infrastructure. Using RNN-based models, they analyse multi-stage investment decisions in projects such as electric vehicle charging networks. The model learns adaptive investment strategies in scenarios of regulatory change, market adoption variability, and cost uncertainty—conditions under which traditional binomial or Monte Carlo methods become computationally burdensome or insufficiently flexible.

This approach allows for:

- **Endogenous scenario generation based on evolving policy regimes:** The model simulates a range of future policy, demand, and cost configurations that are highly uncertain in sustainability-related sectors, addressing the limitations of rigid scenario structures in traditional models, such as binomial trees.

- **Optimal timing of investment actions:** Neural networks learn sequential policies indicating when to invest, wait, expand, or abandon at each stage—reflecting core real options logic without requiring an explicit valuation formula.
- **Strategic flexibility in response to climate-driven uncertainties:** Particularly relevant for investments exposed to **policy volatility**, **technological disruption**, or behavioural shifts (such as electric vehicle adoption rates[53] or carbon tax adjustments).

By integrating real options logic with data-driven pattern recognition, neural network–enhanced approaches provide a flexible framework for evaluating long-term irreversible investments under conditions of epistemic uncertainty, while also supporting strategic adaptability in the presence of ontological uncertainty in sustainability-oriented investment contexts.

While these computational approaches enhance investment valuation under uncertainty, sustainable decision-making also requires systematic measurement of environmental impacts at the project level. The next chapter, therefore, examines micro-level analytical tools—such as life-cycle assessment, carbon accounting, and behavioural policy instruments—that support sustainability-oriented decision-making within firms.

Key Insights — Chapter 3: Sustainability and the Changing Cost Structure of Firms

1. **Early Growth Models Largely Omitted Environmental Constraints and Focused Primarily on Capital and Labour.** Later contributions—most notably Nordhaus's climate–economy models—explicitly integrated emissions, resource limits, and long-term climate impacts, laying the groundwork for sustainability-oriented economic analysis.
2. **Internalising Environmental Costs Reshapes Firms' Cost Structures.** Carbon pricing mechanisms translate climate damages into financial obligations for emitters. This integration moves environmental harm from the periphery of economic analysis into the core of corporate cost structures, capital allocation, and strategic decision-making.
3. **Carbon Markets Operate Under Both Epistemic and Ontological Uncertainty.** Carbon markets such as the EU ETS are exposed to both

[53] How quickly and widely people, companies, or governments are switching from gasoline or diesel vehicles to electric ones.

epistemic and ontological uncertainty. While probabilistic models can represent volatility and expectations under epistemic uncertainty, unexpected policy shifts, technological breakthroughs, or geopolitical events introduce ontological uncertainty that manifests as sudden market shocks.

4. **Real Options Analysis Provides the Needed Flexibility Under Both Epistemic and Ontological Uncertainty.** In the case of epistemic uncertainty—where future outcomes are probabilistic and modelable—real options allow firms to wait, stage, adapt, or abandon projects as new information emerges. In the case of ontological uncertainty, unexpected events can arise at any time, and real options provide a strategic decision framework that preserves flexibility in fundamentally new situations. In sustainable investment, where uncertainty and irreversibility coexist, flexibility itself becomes a core source of economic value.

5. **The Traditional Net Present Value (NPV) Method is Insufficient for Sustainable Investment.** NPV assumes stable conditions, immediate investment, and a constant discount rate. It does not incorporate the value of waiting or adapting under uncertainty and therefore underestimates the strategic importance of flexibility. Long-horizon sustainable investments require valuation frameworks that move beyond static discounting towards methods—such as real options—that explicitly account for uncertainty and flexibility under irreversible investment conditions.

6. **EU Hydrogen Policy Illustrates the Application of Real Options in Practice.** In pursuing its 2030 climate and decarbonisation targets, the European Union has identified renewable hydrogen as a strategic solution for hard-to-abate sectors. Nevertheless, the hydrogen market is characterised by significant uncertainty related to carbon prices, technologies, infrastructure development, and future demand. The European Hydrogen Bank applies a real options approach, demonstrating how public policy can institutionalise flexibility in emerging clean technology markets and support SDG-aligned investment.

7. **Neural Networks Learn Adaptively from New Information, Enhance the Performance of Real Options, and Support SDG Implementation.** Neural networks improve the approximation of option values and strengthen flexible investment strategies under epistemic uncertainty, while also reinforcing adaptive decision-making when ontological uncertainty involves unpredictable change. In doing so, they enhance the role of real options in guiding SDG-aligned sustainable investment.

In Simple Words: Chapter 3 – Sustainability and the Changing Cost Structure of Firms

For much of the 20th century, economic models focused on capital and labour as the main drivers of growth. Nature — including resource depletion and pollution — was often absent from these simplified frameworks. Policymakers considered these models as if they fully reflected economic reality. As a result, environmental costs were not taken into account in economic decisions. In recent decades, both economic modelling and policymaking have begun to shift, as climate costs are increasingly integrated into analytical frameworks and into real-world instruments such as carbon pricing systems.

The basic idea is simple: polluters should bear the cost of the harm they cause. One key tool for estimating this cost is the Social Cost of Carbon (SCC), which seeks to quantify the economic damage from emitting one additional ton of carbon dioxide, including rising sea levels, health problems, and crop losses.

To put this idea into practice, there are two main approaches:

- **Carbon Taxes** — charge a fixed amount for each ton of CO_2 emissions.
- **Cap-and-Trade Systems** — set a limit on total emissions and let companies trade emission permits.

The EU Emissions Trading System (EU ETS) is the most prominent example of a cap-and-trade program. Companies that pollute less can sell their unused allowances to those that pollute more. The EU has gradually reduced — and remains committed to reducing — the number of available permits through 2030. This increases the scarcity of emission allowances, raising the carbon price and accelerating the transition to a low-carbon economy. In addition to the shrinking supply of permits, other factors also influence carbon prices. On this point, a distinction made by economist John Maynard Keynes is helpful:

- **Epistemic uncertainties** arise from factors we don't yet know but could estimate with updated data — like next year's energy demand or how a new carbon tax might affect electricity prices.
- **Ontological uncertainties** are truly unknowable — such as the next pandemic, a radical policy shift, or a breakthrough in fusion energy. These cannot be assigned probabilities because we do not even know the range of possible outcomes.

Most sustainable investments — such as wind farms, electric mobility networks, or hydrogen infrastructure — are expensive and difficult to reverse. Often, decisions must be made before the full picture is clear.

That's where real options come in. They help investors remain flexible. Instead of making all decisions upfront, real options allow investors to wait, scale, or adapt as new information emerges. This is more practical than traditional tools like Net Present Value (NPV), which assume a stable world with precise numbers.

Today, neural networks — a type of Artificial Intelligence — make this approach even more powerful. Unlike fixed formulas, they learn from complex, real-world data and help navigate uncertainty in carbon markets, infrastructure planning, and green finance.

Whether uncertainty is epistemic or ontological, both challenge traditional investment thinking. In these conditions, sustainable investments benefit from approaches that prioritise adaptability — allowing decisions to evolve over time in response to new information, shifting costs, or unexpected developments.

Chapter 4
Sustainability at the Micro Level

This chapter explores how sustainability principles—particularly the Sustainable Development Goals (SDGs)—are applied at the micro level, namely, within firms, product systems, and individual behaviours. It focuses on tools and methods for quantitative and qualitative environmental assessment, circular-economy strategies, and behavioural insights that promote more sustainable choices. Together with the macroeconomic analysis developed in Chapter 5 and the meso-level ecological accounting tools introduced later in this chapter, these approaches form part of a multi-level sustainability framework that links micro-level decisions to ecological constraints and broader macroeconomic outcomes.

This chapter is structured into five sections:

- **4.1:** Life Cycle Assessment (LCA) and Circularity Tools
- **4.2:** Carbon and Greenhouse Gas (GHG) Accounting
- **4.3:** Life Cycle Thinking (LCT)
- **4.4:** Behavioural Economics and Nudge Theory
- **4.5:** Ecological Footprint (EF) Accounting and Biocapacity

Note on SDG Ordering in Tables:

In tables presenting linkages between the analysed topics and the Sustainable Development Goals (SDGs), the goals are listed according to their conceptual relevance rather than in numerical order. This approach highlights the SDGs most directly related to the methods and frameworks discussed in each section.

4.1. Life Cycle Assessment (LCA) and Circularity Tools

Life Cycle Assessment (LCA) is directly relevant to several Sustainable Development Goals (SDGs), particularly those related to resource efficiency, climate action, sustainable production, and environmental impact reduction.

The key Sustainable Development Goals (SDGs) associated with Life Cycle Assessment (LCA) are presented in Table 4.1.

Table 4.1: SDGs associated with Life Cycle Assessment (LCA) and Circularity Tools.

SDG	Goal Title	Relevance to Life Cycle Assessment (LCA) and Circularity Tools
SDG 12	Responsible Consumption and Production	Supports LCA, Material Flow Analysis (MFA), and circularity indicators by reducing material waste and promoting more sustainable products and processes.
SDG 13	Climate Action	Addresses through carbon footprint analysis and GHG reduction strategies derived from Life Cycle Impact Assessment (LCIA) results.
SDG 9	Industry, Innovation, and Infrastructure	Encourages sustainable industrialization and product design innovation through LCA and circular economy tools.
SDG 15	Life on Land	Informs decisions to reduce land degradation and biodiversity loss through land-use and material footprint indicators.
SDG 6	Clean Water and Sanitation	Links through water use and pollution indicators assessed in LCA and MFA.
SDG 8	Decent Work and Economic Growth	Supports green growth that enhances economic output while minimising ecological footprints.
SDG 11	Sustainable Cities and Communities	Helps assess the environmental impacts of products and infrastructure in urban systems.

Source: Author's analysis based on the SDG framework (United Nations, 2025).

Before introducing Life Cycle Assessment, it is useful to consider the concept of the circular economy, which contrasts with the traditional linear economic model. According to the European Union, a circular economy is a production and consumption model that maximises the value of products, materials, and resources by reusing, repairing, remanufacturing, and recycling them. Other definitions emphasise replacing the end-of-life concept with a regenerative system that aims for environmental quality, economic prosperity, and social equity—core tenets of sustainable development.[54]

One of the primary analytical tools for assessing environmental impacts within this framework is Life Cycle Assessment (LCA).

What is Life Cycle Assessment (LCA)?

LCA is a standardised and systematic method used to evaluate the environmental impacts associated with all stages of a product's life cycle, from *cradle to grave*:

- Raw Material Extraction (Cradle)
- Manufacturing and Processing
- Distribution and Transportation
- Use Phase
- End-of-Life Treatment (Grave)

[54] Kirchherr, J. et al. (2017).

LCA enables decision-makers to identify environmental hotspots, compare alternatives, and support more sustainable design, procurement, and policy development. It has become one of the most widely applied tools in sustainability science, with relevance across domains such as industry, policy, and research. This is particularly valuable for technology developers, as it supports informed choices—for example, selecting materials or processes with a lower environmental footprint.

Although LCA is most commonly applied at the micro level, such as assessing the footprint of a specific product or process, it is increasingly used at the meso- and macro levels. For example, sector-level LCAs are used to evaluate entire supply chains or industries, and Environmentally Extended Input-Output (EEIO) LCAs can capture national or global resource and emission flows. This broader scope demonstrates how LCA acts not only as a product-level tool but also as a bridge to system-level sustainability planning and policy evaluation.

A critical distinction in LCA practice lies in the use of two methodological approaches:

- **Attributional LCA (ALCA)** describes the average environmental burdens associated with the life cycle of a product or service, using data from existing supply chains. It is typically used for environmental reporting or product comparisons.
- **Consequential LCA (CLCA)** focuses on capturing the system-wide effects of a change in the system—such as a policy intervention or market shift—by modelling broader economic consequences and marginal changes.

Understanding the differences between ALCA and CLCA is crucial, as they serve complementary yet distinct purposes in sustainability assessments.

LCA follows the standards outlined in ISO 14040 and ISO 14044, encompassing four main phases:[55]

1. Goal and Scope Definition

The first step defines the study's purpose. Companies may conduct an LCA to:

- Comply with regulations (e.g., EU environmental declarations),

---

55 Although often presented sequentially, the four phases of Life Cycle Assessment defined in ISO 14040 are not strictly linear. In practice, the process is iterative, with feedback loops between stages as data and assumptions are refined. See: International Organization for Standardization (ISO) (2006).

- Satisfy market or consumer demands, or
- Improve product sustainability—for example, by reducing emissions in the textile sector.[56]

2. Life Cycle Inventory (LCI)

This phase involves collecting data on inputs (raw materials, energy, and water) and outputs (waste and emissions). It is the most data-intensive phase. Data can be primary (collected directly from the processes under study, such as company records, measurements, or surveys) or secondary (derived from databases, industry averages, or published sources).

Given its data intensity, this phase is often the most time-consuming. Software tools are typically used to support quantitative analysis, while questionnaires may be used to collect additional process data from suppliers or production facilities.

Example: For a pair of trousers, the inventory data would quantify the amounts of cotton, water, electricity, and natural gas required for production.

3. Life Cycle Impact Assessment (LCIA)

In this phase, all interactions that a product system has with the environment—known as elementary flows—are translated into indicators of environmental impact.[57] These flows include emissions to air, water, and soil, as well as resource extraction and land use. For example, in the production of a pair of trousers, cotton harvesting consumes water and land, and often relies on machinery that emits CO_2 and other pollutants.[58] The manufacture and transport of materials also contribute to emissions and resource depletion.

---

[56] For example, Environmental Product Declarations (EPDs) are widely used in the European Union to communicate the life-cycle environmental impacts of construction materials and building products. Similar lifecycle-based approaches are increasingly applied to other product categories, where environmental impacts must be assessed and disclosed using standardised LCA methodologies.

[57] LCIA includes a range of environmental impact categories that vary depending on the methodological framework used. For example, the TRACI method commonly applied in North America includes indicators such as global warming potential (kg CO_2-eq), acidification, eutrophication, smog formation, and human health impacts. The ReCiPe method, widely used in Europe, includes impact categories related to ecosystem quality, resource depletion, and broader effects on human health. The choice of LCIA method therefore influences which environmental issues are emphasised in the assessment.

[58] LCA is typically implemented using specialised software tools and life cycle databases. Commonly used software includes SimaPro, openLCA, and GaBi, while databases such

4. Interpretation

The results of the LCI and LCIA phases are evaluated to identify key findings, draw conclusions, and formulate recommendations consistent with the initial goal and scope of the study.

Figure 4.1 illustrates the four iterative phases of Life Cycle Assessment (LCA), as defined in ISO 14040 and ISO 14044.

Figure 4.1: The Four Iterative Phases of Life Cycle Assessment (LCA).

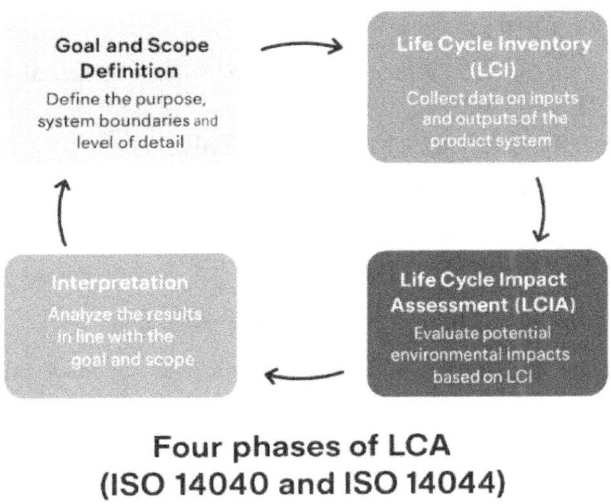

Source: Author, based on ISO 14040 and ISO 14044 standards.

As discussed in the next section, LCA also underpins the development of circularity indicators, which rely on accurate data on material and energy flows throughout the life cycle.

4.1.1. Circularity Indicators

As discussed in Section 4.1, Life Cycle Assessment (LCA) provides a robust method for quantifying the environmental impacts of products, services, or systems. However, to obtain a more comprehensive assessment of sustainability

---

as ecoinvent and national inventories (e.g., USLCI) provide standardised background data on materials, energy use, and emissions. These tools support the consistent application of LCA methods and improve the comparability and transparency of environmental assessments.

performance—particularly in relation to resource efficiency—LCA results can be complemented by circularity indicators. These indicators help assess how effectively materials are retained, reused, or recovered within the economic system, and are increasingly used to support transitions from linear to circular models across product life cycles and supply chains.

The following indicators illustrate some of the most widely used circularity measures that complement LCA in practice.

Key Circularity Indicators in Sustainability Assessment

1. Linear Flow Index (LFI) – *Micro-level*

The Linear Flow Index (LFI) measures the proportion of materials that become waste at the end of a product's life:

- LFI = 0: Fully circular (all materials reused or recycled).
- LFI = 1: Fully linear (all materials disposed of as waste).

This indicator helps quantify waste generation and reveals opportunities for material recovery and eco-design improvements.

2. Material Circularity Indicator (MCI) – *Micro-level*

Developed by the Ellen MacArthur Foundation, the Material Circularity Indicator (MCI) builds on the Linear Flow Index (LFI) and assesses:[59]

- the extent to which materials remain in the economic cycle through reuse and recycling
- the degree to which product design and product lifetime support more circular resource use

The MCI ranges from 0 to 1, with higher values indicating greater circularity.

3. Carbon Footprint Indicator – *Micro to Macro*

This indicator quantifies the total greenhouse gas emissions—expressed in carbon dioxide equivalents (CO_2e)—associated with a product, process, or activity.[60]

- derived from Life Cycle Assessment (LCA), focusing specifically on the climate change impacts;
- accounts for greenhouse gases such as CO_2, CH_4, and N_2O, expressed in CO_2-equivalent units, whereas a full LCA covers multiple environmental impact categories.

---

[59] Ellen MacArthur Foundation (2021).

[60] IPCC (2022), Annex II: Glossary.

4. Material Flow Analysis (MFA) – *Macro-level*

Material Flow Analysis (MFA) is a system-based method used to map the flow of materials within an economic system, such as a company, supply chain, sector, or entire economy. It identifies:

- the type, volume, and origin of materials entering and leaving the system;
- waste generation and resource inefficiencies across production and consumption processes;
- opportunities for improving resource efficiency and supporting circular economy strategies.

MFA is widely used for policy planning and resource assessments at national and sectoral levels. Tracing the movement of materials throughout the economy helps connect production and consumption patterns with their associated environmental impacts.

5. Material Footprint (MF) – *Macro-level*

Material Footprint (MF) measures the total raw material demand required to satisfy a nation's or sector's consumption. It captures the amount of global raw materials extracted to produce the goods and services consumed within an economy. Key variants include:

- MF per capita: reflects the resource intensity of individual consumption.
- MF per GDP: assesses the material efficiency of economic output.

Material Footprint highlights the scale of a country's or region's resource demand and provides evidence for resource decoupling strategies—that is, achieving economic growth without proportional increases in material use.

While circularity indicators help assess how efficiently materials are used and retained within economic systems, comprehensive sustainability assessment also requires the direct measurement of greenhouse gas emissions. The next section, therefore, turns to carbon accounting as a complementary tool for evaluating climate-related impacts.

4.2. Carbon (or GHG) Accounting

Greenhouse gas emissions are among the most important environmental indicators in Life Cycle Assessment (LCA) because of their direct contribution to global climate change. Building on the LCA framework introduced in Section 4.1, this section examines how organisations can measure and manage their carbon impacts through standardised greenhouse gas (GHG) accounting systems. These carbon accounting frameworks align closely with global climate objectives, particularly those outlined in the Paris Agreement and the Sustainable Development Goals (SDGs).

The key Sustainable Development Goals (SDGs) associated with Carbon (or GHG) Accounting are presented in Table 4.2.

Table 4.2: SDGs associated with Carbon (or GHG) Accounting.

SDG	Goal Title	Relevance to Carbon (GHG) Accounting
SDG 13	Climate Action	Supports the reduction and management of GHG emissions through accurate measurement and disclosure.
SDG 12	Responsible Consumption and Production	Encourages emissions reductions across production processes, supply chains, and business operations.
SDG 7	Affordable and Clean Energy	Supports the energy transition by tracking Scope 2 emissions from purchased electricity and Scope 3 emissions across supply chains.

Source: Author's analysis based on the SDG framework (United Nations, 2025).

Greenhouse Gas Protocol

The Greenhouse Gas (GHG) Protocol[61] is the most widely adopted framework for carbon accounting. It standardises the measurement and reporting of greenhouse gas emissions and expresses them in carbon dioxide equivalents (CO_2-eq) using Global Warming Potential (GWP) factors, which allow comparisons of climate impacts over a specified time horizon.

The Kyoto Protocol[62] identifies several key greenhouse gases whose emissions are typically included in carbon accounting frameworks:

- Carbon dioxide (CO_2)
- Methane (CH_4)
- Nitrous oxide (N_2O)
- Fluorinated gases[63]

By converting emissions of these gases into CO_2-equivalent units, organisations can aggregate and compare their overall climate impact across different emission sources.

---

61 World Resources Institute (WRI) and World Business Council for Sustainable Development (WBCSD) (2004).

62 United Nations (1997).

63 Fluorinated gases include hydrofluorocarbons (HFCs), perfluorocarbons (PFCs), sulphur hexafluoride (SF_6), and nitrogen trifluoride (NF_3). These synthetic greenhouse gases are widely used in sectors such as refrigeration, electronics, and semiconductor manufacturing. While typically emitted in smaller quantities than CO_2 or CH_4, they have very high global warming potentials.

GHG Emission Scopes

Greenhouse gas emissions are commonly categorised into three scopes under the GHG Protocol framework:

- Scope 1: Direct emissions from sources owned or controlled by the organisation (e.g., company vehicles, on-site combustion)
- Scope 2: Indirect emissions from the generation of purchased energy consumed by the organisation, such as electricity, steam, heat, or cooling.
- Scope 3: All other indirect emissions occurring across the organisation's value chain, including activities such as business travel, transportation and logistics, purchased goods and services, and the use of sold products.

This categorization helps organisations account for the full climate impact of their operations and supply chains.

Beyond the Basics: Standards and Frameworks in Practice

To promote transparency and comparability in environmental reporting, several widely used standards and reporting frameworks have been developed based on Life Cycle Assessment (LCA) methodologies and greenhouse gas accounting principles:

- **Environmental Product Declarations (EPDs):** Standardised documents that disclose the environmental impact of products, including carbon emissions, typically based on Life Cycle Assessment.
- **Product Carbon Footprints (PCFs):** Assess the greenhouse gas emissions associated with a product throughout its life cycle.
- **Product Category Rules (PCRs):** Define how to conduct Life Cycle Assessments for specific product categories, ensuring methodological consistency across studies.
- **Product Environmental Footprint (PEF):** A European Commission initiative that aims to standardise environmental performance measurement across the European Union.

These frameworks help firms comply with regulatory requirements, demonstrate environmental performance, and respond to growing consumer and investor demand for more sustainable products.

The Role of the Financial Sector: PCAF

Established in 2019, the Partnership for Carbon Accounting Financials (PCAF) helps financial institutions measure and disclose emissions associated with their lending and investment portfolios. Built on the principles of the

Greenhouse Gas Protocol, PCAF's Financed Emissions Standard enables banks and asset managers to:

- quantify portfolio emissions
- manage transition risk and climate exposure
- align portfolios with science-based climate targets

These practices are particularly relevant under regulatory frameworks such as the EU Taxonomy and the Task Force on Climate-related Financial Disclosures (TCFD).

Carbon Intensity Metrics

Carbon intensity metrics express greenhouse gas emissions relative to a unit of economic activity or output, enabling comparisons across time, sectors, and countries. Table 4.3 presents two widely used metrics—Emission Intensity and Weighted Average Carbon Intensity (WACI)—that inform both public policy analysis and corporate sustainability assessment.

Table 4.3: Key Carbon Intensity Metrics.

Metric	Definition	Purpose
Emission Intensity	National GHG emissions per unit of GDP (tonnes CO -eq / USD GDP)	Measures the extent to which emissions are decoupled from economic growth
Weighted Average Carbon Intensity (WACI)	Corporate GHG emissions per unit of revenue (tonnes CO -eq / USD revenue)	Evaluates corporate performance and supports ESG investing

Source: Adapted from Climate Council (2025).

Higher carbon-intensity values indicate more emissions-intensive production or operations. Financial institutions increasingly use these metrics to benchmark companies, identify lower-carbon investment opportunities, and assess exposure to carbon-pricing and transition risks.

Although carbon accounting and Life Cycle Assessment provide important tools for measuring environmental impacts, sustainability strategies also require a broader perspective that considers how products, services, and economic activities affect the environment throughout their life cycles.

4.3. Life Cycle Thinking (LCT)

While Life Cycle Assessment (LCA) provides a *quantitative* method for evaluating environmental impacts, it is grounded in a broader conceptual perspective known as Life Cycle Thinking (LCT). Life Cycle Thinking encourages decision-makers to consider the full environmental, social, and economic implications of products and services throughout their life cycles—from raw material extraction to end-of-life management.

The key Sustainable Development Goals (SDGs) associated with Life Cycle Thinking (LCT) are presented in Table 4.4.

Table 4.4: SDGs associated with Life Cycle Thinking (LCT).

SDG	Goal Title	Relevance to Life Cycle Thinking
SDG 12	Responsible Consumption and Production	Supports life cycle management and sustainable product design.
SDG 13	Climate Action	Reduces life-cycle GHG emissions and supports the internalisation of carbon costs.
SDG 9	Industry, Innovation and Infrastructure	Promotes sustainable product innovation and eco-design principles.
SDG 8	Decent Work and Economic Growth	Ensures labour rights and fair practices in supply chains through Social Life Cycle Assessment (S-LCA).
SDG 10	Reduced Inequalities	Supports social equity across value chains and geographies (via S-LCA).
SDG 1	No Poverty	Highlights social impacts in global production chains (via S-LCA).
SDG 3	Good Health and Well-Being	Encourages safer product design and minimises exposure to harmful materials.

Source: Author's analysis based on the SDG framework (United Nations, 2025).

These SDGs illustrate how Life Cycle Thinking extends sustainability analysis beyond individual products, linking production and consumption decisions to broader environmental, social, and economic outcomes across value chains.

In practice, Life Cycle Thinking has increasingly been incorporated into public policy, corporate sustainability strategies, and product design frameworks. In particular, several regulatory initiatives—especially within the European Union—now explicitly integrate life-cycle principles to guide sustainable production, consumption, and waste management.

From Life Cycle Assessment to Life Cycle Thinking: A Shift from Measurement to a Sustainability Mindset

Life Cycle Thinking aims to:

- reduce the environmental impacts of products and production processes across their life cycle;
- improve social and economic outcomes throughout global value chains;
- promote systems thinking in product design, consumption, and end-of-life management.

LCT represents the mindset that guides sustainable choices across government, business, and individual levels. Table 4.5 presents key EU policy and regulatory frameworks that incorporate Life Cycle Thinking principles.

Table 4.5: EU Policy and Regulatory Frameworks Incorporating Life Cycle Thinking (LCT).

Policy / Initiative	Purpose and Role of Life Cycle Thinking (LCT)
Sustainable Consumption and Production & Industrial Policy Action Plan	Introduced by the European Commission in 2008 to improve the energy and environmental performance of products across their life cycle.
Eco-design for Sustainable Products Regulation	Adopted in 2024, extending eco-design requirements to a broader range of products and introducing life-cycle-based sustainability criteria.
EU Eco-label Scheme (ISO 14024)	Certifies products and services with reduced environmental impact throughout their life cycle.
European Waste Framework Directive (2008)	Adopted in 2008, establishing a waste hierarchy—prevention, reuse, recycling, recovery, and disposal—that reflects life-cycle thinking in waste management policy.

Source: Adapted from Parvathy, P. et al. (2024); European Commission (2008, 2022); European Parliament and Council (2008, 2010); and Nelen et al. (2013).

While these policy frameworks institutionalise Life Cycle Thinking at the regulatory level, its practical relevance becomes clearer when examining the application of these principles in real-world contexts. Table 4.6 presents examples of how different stakeholder groups apply Life Cycle Thinking principles in practice.

Table 4.6: Examples of Life Cycle Thinking (LCT) Applied Across Stakeholder Groups.

Stakeholder	Application of Life Cycle Thinking (LCT)
Government	Public procurement policies that favour sustainable goods and services based on life-cycle criteria.
Business	Designing products for recyclability, reducing material toxicity, and minimising life-cycle costs.
Individuals	Choosing recycled products, considering product composition, and evaluating end-of-life impacts.

Source: Adapted from Nelen, D. et al. (2013).

1. Government: Local authorities can play a key role in transforming food systems by applying Life Cycle Thinking (LCT) to inform sustainable policymaking. Evaluating the entire life cycle of food—how and where it is produced, processed, and distributed—enables more informed decisions that reduce environmental impact and promote circular practices.

   One example is the *Lausanne Région* in Switzerland, which supports direct producer-to-consumer relationships. This shortens supply chains and strengthens local economies by reducing transportation needs and associated emissions.

2. Businesses: Private enterprises also play a pivotal role in applying Life Cycle Thinking. Magic Tomato, a Geneva-based company, illustrates this approach

by delivering fresh, locally sourced food using a 100% electric vehicle fleet, helping reduce transport-related emissions. The company also minimises packaging through reusable bags and reduces food waste through close coordination with local producers and a just-in-time delivery system. These practices demonstrate how businesses can apply life-cycle principles to reduce environmental pressures while strengthening regional food systems.

3. Supply Chain Actors (Businesses and Individuals): Short food supply chains (SFSCs) represent a practical application of Life Cycle Thinking by reducing the number of intermediaries between producers and consumers.[64] This can reduce emissions from logistics, storage, and packaging throughout the food supply chain. Businesses engaged in SFSCs often respond to consumer preferences for organic production, reduced plastic use, and seasonal food choices—objectives that align closely with the principles of Life Cycle Thinking.

Table 4.7 compares the sustainability characteristics of "buy local" initiatives and short food supply chains (SFSCs), highlighting both their shared environmental benefits and their differences in terms of supply chain structure and local economic engagement.

Table 4.7: Comparative Overview of "Buy Local" and Short Food Supply Chains (SFSCs).

Dimension	**Buy Local Initiatives**	**Short Food Supply Chains (SFSCs)**
Transport distance	Very short transport distances between producers and consumers, often resulting in low or near-zero transport-related emissions	Reduced transport distances compared with conventional supply chains, lowering logistics-related emissions
Production practices	Often associated with small-scale or traditional production methods, sometimes involving reduced pesticide use	Frequently linked to environmentally friendly or organic farming practices
Product freshness and preservation	Products are consumed close to the point of origin, reducing the need for preservatives and long storage periods	Shorter distribution chains allow fresher products and reduced storage and packaging requirements
Local economic impact	Strengthens local economies by supporting small-scale, often family-operated enterprises	Strengthens regional food networks by reducing intermediaries and improving producer–consumer connections

Source: Adapted from Evola, R.S. et al. (2022).

64 Evola, R.S. et al. (2022).

While both approaches share similar environmental benefits—such as reduced transport distances and fresher products—their main distinction lies in their underlying logic: "buy local" initiatives emphasise geographic proximity, whereas short food supply chains focus on reducing the number of intermediaries between producers and consumers.

4. Individuals: At the individual level, Life Cycle Thinking can guide more sustainable food choices. "Buy local" initiatives, for example, encourage consumers to consider the environmental impacts of their purchasing decisions.[65] Consumers are often motivated by factors such as product freshness, reduced use of synthetic inputs, and shorter supply chains that lower transport-related emissions. These preferences reflect core principles of Life Cycle Thinking, including environmental awareness, local engagement, and responsible consumption.

This perspective is illustrated by local-level strategies that apply LCT principles to community-based sustainability efforts. The following case from the *Lausanne Région* illustrates how municipalities can integrate these principles into public initiatives by combining circular-economy goals with behavioural nudges—a theme further explored in Section 4.4—to promote more sustainable consumption patterns.

4.3.1. Case Study: Local Behavioural Nudges and Life Cycle Thinking in *Lausanne Région* (Switzerland)

In February 2025, the Municipality of Pully — in collaboration with the municipalities of Paudex and Belmont-sur-Lausanne — launched a local version of the campaign *Ça bouge, je consomme local* ("Things are moving — I shop local"). The initiative formed part of a broader programme coordinated by Lausanne Région to encourage local consumption through behavioural nudges and civic engagement.[66]

---

[65] Capelli, L. et al. (2022).

[66] The campaign evolved through three main phases:

- 2021–2023: In response to the socioeconomic disruptions caused by the COVID-19 pandemic, *Lausanne Région* and its member communes launched several awareness campaigns to support small businesses and encourage more localised consumption patterns.
- 2023: A region-wide initiative titled "*Je vis ici, je consomme local*" was introduced across multiple communes with a unified visual identity and messaging.

This campaign illustrates the principles of Life Cycle Thinking (LCT) in practice by promoting more sustainable production, distribution, and consumption patterns:

- reduced transport-related emissions through shorter distribution routes;
- stronger local supply chains, which reduce packaging needs and energy use;
- community engagement in sustainable economic practices that support local producers;
- greater public awareness of sustainable consumption behaviours.

The initiative also aligns with several Sustainable Development Goals (SDGs), including:

- SDG 11 – Sustainable Cities and Communities
- SDG 12 – Responsible Consumption and Production
- SDG 13 – Climate Action

Implementation and Behaviour Change

Coordinated by Anne-Laure Bornoz, project manager at Lausanne Région (Promotion économique), the campaign employed a range of visual and behavioural nudges—including posters, banners, animated displays on public buses, social media campaigns (Facebook, LinkedIn), and radio broadcasts. The messaging was intentionally simple: support the local economy, reduce environmental impacts, and strengthen community resilience.

In a research interview conducted in September 2025, Anne-Laure Bornoz explained that the campaign pursued two main behavioural objectives: first, to challenge the widespread perception that buying local is inherently more expensive; and second, to remind residents that many essential goods and services are readily available within their own commune. This communication strategy draws on socio-psychological insights—particularly regarding perceived cost, convenience, and habit formation—and reflects a non-coercive, behaviourally informed intervention that encourages more sustainable consumption patterns.

- 2025: The most recent version, "*Ça bouge, je consomme local*", was launched in Pully and neighboring communes with communication strategies adapted to local mobility patterns and community needs.

This timeline is based on information provided during a research interview with representatives of Lausanne Région (2025).

The campaign addressed not only the retail and food services sectors but also the artisanal and technical sectors. For example, residents were encouraged to choose local electricians or repair professionals rather than service providers located outside the region—thereby reducing travel distances and associated carbon emissions. In this way, the initiative extended Life Cycle Thinking to everyday service decisions, making sustainability more visible, tangible, and locally embedded.

The initiative exemplifies a practical application of behavioural insights—discussed further in Section 4.4—by influencing everyday decisions through subtle, non-coercive prompts aligned with sustainability objectives.

Although no statistical tools were in place to measure behavioural change directly, Bornoz noted that website traffic data indicated significant public exposure to the campaign. Assessing its concrete impact on consumer decision-making, however, remains an open challenge.

Local Sustainability Infrastructure

Lausanne Région supports this approach through institutional mechanisms that complement Life Cycle Thinking (LCT):

- a local enterprise support desk (*Guichet des entreprises*), which provides free advisory services to small businesses and local entrepreneurs;
- the *Prix Entreprendre Lausanne Région* (PERL), an award that recognises innovative and sustainability-oriented projects in sectors such as agriculture, mobility, and circular economy initiatives.

Together, these initiatives demonstrate how local governments can combine Life Cycle Thinking in economic policy with behavioural nudges in communication strategies to advance systems-level sustainability.

Figure 4.2 presents an example of campaign visuals deployed in Pully, Paudex, and Belmont-sur-Lausanne in 2025. The initiative builds on earlier region-wide campaigns coordinated by Lausanne Région between 2021 and 2023.

Figure 4.2: Visual from the *Ça bouge, je consomme local* Campaign Promoting Local Consumption in the Lausanne Région (2025).

Source: Lausanne Région (2025). Image reproduced with permission from Lausanne Région.

The Lausanne campaign reflects a broader interest in applying behavioural principles to sustainability challenges at the local level. This case illustrates how simple, non-coercive interventions can shape everyday decisions in ways that align with Life Cycle Thinking and sustainable consumption objectives. The increasing use of such approaches in policy and development contexts highlights the growing relevance of behavioural tools in sustainability governance—a theme explored further in the following section.

Life Cycle Thinking, therefore, extends beyond measuring environmental impacts and encourages decision-makers to consider sustainability implications across the entire life cycle of products and services.

In this context, it is useful to distinguish three closely related concepts: Life Cycle Assessment (LCA) provides quantitative indicators of environmental impacts across a product's life cycle. Life Cycle Thinking (LCT) encourages decision-makers to consider these impacts when designing products, policies, or consumption choices. Life Cycle Sustainability Assessment (LCSA) extends this perspective by integrating environmental, social, and economic dimensions into a comprehensive sustainability evaluation.

4.3.2. Towards Life Cycle Sustainability Assessment (LCSA)

Life Cycle Thinking extends beyond environmental concerns to a holistic sustainability framework known as Life Cycle Sustainability Assessment (LCSA), which integrates three complementary approaches:[67]

- Life Cycle Assessment (LCA) – focuses on environmental impacts
- Social Life Cycle Assessment (S-LCA) – evaluates social impacts
- Life Cycle Costing (LCC) – measures economic performance

This integrated framework is often expressed conceptually as:

LCSA = LCA (Environmental) + S-LCA (Social) + LCC (Economic)[68]

The "+" symbol does not imply a mathematical aggregation of results. Rather, it indicates the integration of environmental, social, and economic perspectives within a unified sustainability assessment framework.

Each component contributes to the overall sustainability profile of a product or system:

- **LCA (Life Cycle Assessment)** evaluates environmental impacts across the product life cycle, including indicators such as greenhouse gas emissions, resource use, land use, and pollution.
- **S-LCA (Social Life Cycle Assessment)** evaluates social impacts across the value chain, focusing on issues such as:
    - Child labour
    - Fair wages
    - Working hours
    - Health and safety
    - Indigenous rights
- **LCC (Life Cycle Costing)** estimates the total economic cost over the product or service life cycle. It includes:
    - Expected taxes (e.g., carbon tax)
    - Labour subsidies or sustainability incentives
    - Future expenditures, discounted to their present value

[67] Life Cycle Initiative (2025).

[68] Klöpffer, W. (2008).

Together, these approaches enable triple-bottom-line thinking, allowing environmental, social, and economic outcomes to be assessed within a single, decision-relevant sustainability framework.

Figure 4.3: Life Cycle Sustainability Assessment framework.

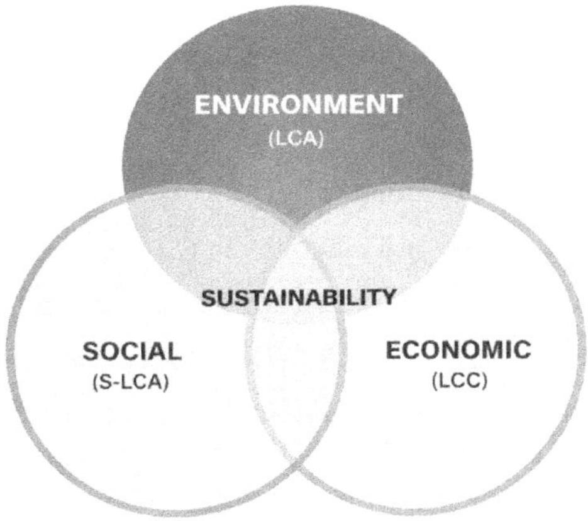

Source: Author. The diagram illustrates the integration of environmental (LCA), social (S-LCA), and economic (LCC) dimensions within a unified sustainability assessment framework.

Figure 4.4: Conceptual Hierarchy of Life Cycle Approaches in Sustainability Assessment.

Operational tools → Conceptual framework → Integrated sustainability assessment → Governance and reporting

ESG Governance and Reporting
(CSRD, SFDR, ESG metrics)

▲
|

Life Cycle Sustainability Assessment (LCSA)
Environmental + Social + Economic evaluation

▲
|

Life Cycle Thinking (LCT)
Systems perspective guiding decisions

▲
|

Life Cycle Assessment (LCA)
Environmental measurement tool

Source: Author.

4.3.3. ESG Reporting and Accounting Tools

In Europe, Environmental, Social, and Governance (ESG) reporting has become a central pillar of corporate sustainability regulation. Under the Corporate Sustainability Reporting Directive (CSRD), large companies are required to publish standardised and independently audited sustainability disclosures.[69]

This regulatory framework works in tandem with the Sustainable Finance Disclosure Regulation (SFDR), which imposes transparency obligations on financial institutions regarding the sustainability characteristics and risks of investment products.

Together, CSRD and SFDR aim to:

- ensure comparability and reliability in ESG reporting;
- align corporate disclosures with sustainable finance frameworks;
- reinforce the integration of life cycle–based performance metrics.

These frameworks promote not only environmental accountability but also greater transparency across value chains by encouraging firms to adopt life cycle methodologies such as Life Cycle Assessment (LCA), Social Life Cycle Assessment (S-LCA), and Life Cycle Costing (LCC).

In this way, Life Cycle Thinking serves as an operational bridge among regulatory compliance, corporate strategy, and the investment community—supporting sustainability-oriented decision-making aligned with the Sustainable Development Goals (SDGs).

While regulatory frameworks and life-cycle methodologies provide essential tools for measuring and governing sustainability performance, achieving meaningful progress also depends on how individuals and organisations make everyday decisions. The next section, therefore, turns to behavioural economics to explore how psychological insights and choice architecture can influence sustainable consumption and decision-making.

4.4. Behavioural Economics and Nudge Theory in Promoting Sustainable Consumption

While Life Cycle Thinking (LCT) helps align production and investment decisions with sustainability goals, achieving systemic change also depends on how individuals make decisions and respond to information. Consumer decisions are influenced not only by rational analysis but also by habits, emotions, and social norms. Behavioural science, therefore, plays a key role in understanding and shaping sustainable consumption patterns.

---

[69] European Union (2022).

The previous section illustrated how Life Cycle Thinking (LCT) can support sustainable behaviour through initiatives such as municipal "buy local" campaigns and short food supply chains. These examples highlight that transforming production systems alone is not sufficient: sustainability also depends on how individuals make everyday choices. Behavioural economics provides analytical tools to examine how people respond to information, framing, incentives, and social context. These insights offer practical guidance for advancing SDG 12: Responsible Consumption and Production.

Behavioural approaches can also contribute to several other Sustainable Development Goals by influencing consumption patterns, climate-related behaviour, and public policy design.

Key Sustainable Development Goals (SDGs) associated with behavioural economics and nudge theory are presented in Table 4.8.

Table 4.8: SDGs associated with Behavioural Economics and Nudge Theory.

SDG	Goal Title	Relevance to Behavioural Economics and Nudge Theory
SDG 12	Responsible Consumption and Production	Encourages sustainable consumption habits through behavioural insights and nudging strategies.
SDG 13	Climate Action	Promotes low-emission behaviours through behavioural interventions such as nudges, feedback mechanisms, and choice architecture.
SDG 11	Sustainable Cities and Communities	Supports behavioural interventions at the local level that promote eco-conscious urban lifestyles.
SDG 3	Good Health and Well-Being	Encourages healthier consumption patterns through behaviourally informed public policies.

Source: Author's analysis based on the SDG framework (United Nations, 2025).

One of the most promising applications of behavioural economics in sustainability policy is nudge theory. Coined by Thaler and Sunstein (2008), a *nudge* refers to a subtle policy intervention that encourages individuals to make decisions aligned with their self-interest without restricting freedom of choice. In sustainability contexts, nudges can guide individuals towards more environmentally responsible behaviour in a non-coercive manner.

Behavioural insights have increasingly shaped public policy and sustainability strategies. Thaler and Sunstein (2008) introduced the concept of nudging as a non-coercive means of influencing decision-making, laying the foundation for behavioural public policy. Kahneman (2011) provided key psychological insights through his analysis of dual-system thinking, explaining why individuals often rely on intuitive rather than deliberative reasoning. Building on these behavioural foundations, Benartzi and Thaler (2013) demonstrated how behavioural tools can influence long-term choices such as retirement planning—insights that are also relevant for sustainability-related investment and consumption behaviour. Sunstein (2014) expanded this work by examining the broader political implications of behavioural interventions. Within environmental economics, Schubert (2017) critically examined the ethical and empirical implications of green nudges.

More recently, these approaches have been increasingly adopted within public institutions and international policy frameworks: The OECD (2017) documents the growing use of behavioural insights across public sectors worldwide, while the United Nations Secretary-General's Guidance on Behavioural Science (UN, 2021) encourages governments to integrate behavioural tools into SDG-aligned policies. More recently, Naik et al. (2024) identify more than 200 behavioural interventions across the UN system, showing that nudges and behavioural insights have already delivered measurable results in advancing SDG outcomes.

4.4.1. Introduction to Behavioural Economics

Traditional economic models often rest on the assumption of *homo economicus*—a rational agent who consistently makes decisions to maximise utility. However, behavioural economics challenges this notion, recognising that cognitive biases, heuristics, social norms, and emotional factors often influence individual decision-making. These insights are particularly relevant for sustainability, as choices around consumption, resource use, and lifestyle are often driven more by habit, peer behaviour, and context than by rational assessments of environmental impact.

Understanding these behavioural drivers enables the development of more effective policies that align with how people make decisions—an approach especially relevant when tackling SDG 12: Responsible Consumption and Production.

Table 4.9 highlights key differences between neoclassical and behavioural economics across three analytical dimensions: assumptions about rationality, the nature of decision-making processes, and the modelling approaches used to predict behaviour.

Table 4.9: Contrasting Assumptions of Neoclassical and Behavioural Economics.

Feature	Neoclassical Economics	Behavioural Economics
Assumption of Rationality	Fully rational agents maximising utility or profit	Bounded rationality, influenced by cognitive biases and psychological factors
Decision-making process	Optimising and internally consistent	Influenced by heuristics, biases, and context
Predictive model	Optimisation-based theoretical models	Models informed by empirical and experimental evidence

Source: Author's analysis based on behavioural economics literature.

The Role of the State in Shaping Sustainable Behaviour

Shifting societal consumption patterns requires more than individual awareness; it depends on supportive institutional environments that reshape norms, habits, and incentives. The state may play a pivotal role in structuring choice environments that facilitate more sustainable choices.

Governments can catalyse this behavioural transformation through several strategies:

- **Behavioural Incentives and Penalties**: Tax incentives for low-emission vehicles, plastic bag charges, or carbon pricing—all designed to elicit behavioural responses.
- **Institutionalised Nudges**: Integrating default green options in public procurement, infrastructure design (e.g., green mobility), and public service menus.
- **Eco-Regulation with Behavioural Instruments**: Moving beyond top-down mandates by embedding soft governance tools like *choice architecture* and real-time feedback into regulatory frameworks.

By adopting a behavioural lens, policymakers can design adaptive, human-centred public policies that steer behaviour towards sustainability through non-coercive, choice-preserving interventions. Understanding why such behavioural interventions are necessary requires examining how individuals actually make decisions.

Are Humans Always Rational?

No—human decision-making is characterised by bounded rationality. We often:

- Overestimate our abilities (overconfidence),
- Prefer immediate rewards (present bias),
- Avoid losses more than we seek gains (loss aversion),
- Follow others' behaviour (social proof), sometimes leading to *herd behaviour* in financial markets,
- Stick to default options or habits (status quo bias).

These cognitive patterns significantly influence choices, making behavioural economics a more accurate lens for policy-making, marketing, and sustainability policy.

Historical Foundations of Behavioural Thinking

Some of the earliest insights into behavioural economics can be traced back to classical economic thinkers, who recognised that economic decisions are also influenced by psychological and social factors.

Adam Smith (1776) was an early voice in behavioural thinking. He offered key observations that prefigured behavioural insights:

- Loss aversion: "We suffer more when we fall from a better to a worse situation than we ever enjoy when we rise from a worse to a better".
- Overconfidence: "The overweening conceit which the greater part of men have of their own abilities is an ancient evil...".
- Self-control: "The pleasure which we are to enjoy ten years hence interests us so little in comparison with that which we may enjoy today...".

Vilfredo Pareto (1906) explicitly emphasised the role of psychology in the foundations of economic analysis. He wrote: "*The foundation of political economy and, in general, of every social science, is psychology.*"

Later, **John Maynard Keynes (1937)** further challenged the purely rational view of economic decision-making through his concept of **animal spirits**, which emphasises the role of emotion and instinct, particularly in financial markets.

- *Spontaneous action: "Spontaneous urge to action rather than inaction"* describes the emotional momentum in investing decisions.
- *Emotional overreaction*: He observed that markets are often shaped more by emotion than by fundamentals: "Day to day fluctuations in the profits of existing investments... tend to have an altogether excessive, and even absurd influence on the market."

Together, these early insights reveal that economic behaviour is not governed by rational calculation alone, but also by psychology, emotion, and social context. This perspective forms an important intellectual foundation for modern behavioural economics and its applications in sustainability and public policy.

4.4.2. Drivers of Human Behaviour

Three major strands of behavioural economics help explain why individuals deviate from the rational-agent model: *bounded rationality, prospect theory, and dual-system thinking.*

1. Bounded Rationality

The concept of bounded rationality, introduced by Herbert A. Simon (1955), suggests that human rationality is limited due to:

- Finite cognitive abilities
- Incomplete information
- Time constraints

Decision-making often deviates from the purely rational model because, rather than optimising, individuals tend to 'satisfice'—that is, they choose the first option that is acceptable rather than searching for the best possible alternative. In real-world conditions—such as time pressure, information overload, or uncertainty—individuals rely on simplified decision rules that reduce the cognitive effort required to make choices.

In sustainability contexts, bounded rationality helps explain why consumers may fail to choose environmentally superior products, even when these offer lower life-cycle impacts or long-term cost savings. Evaluating sustainability attributes often requires comparing complex information—such as environmental labels, life-cycle impacts, or long-term resource efficiency—which can impose significant cognitive demands on decision-makers. Faced with such complexity, consumers may rely on simple, habitual choices rather than systematically evaluating more sustainable alternatives.

2. Prospect Theory

Prospect Theory, developed by Daniel Kahneman and Amos Tversky (1979), explains how individuals evaluate outcomes as gains and losses relative to a reference point rather than in terms of final wealth. The theory highlights several behavioural regularities in decision-making under risk:

- **Reference dependence:** Outcomes are evaluated relative to a reference point rather than according to final wealth levels.

  Example: If a person expects a bonus of €1,000 but receives €800, the outcome is perceived as a loss, even though their income still increases. The evaluation depends on the expectation (reference point), not only on the final amount.

- **Loss aversion:** Losses are felt more strongly than gains of the same magnitude.

  Example: Losing €100 typically feels more painful than the satisfaction gained from winning €100. Because losses weigh more heavily than gains, individuals may become risk-seeking when trying to avoid losses.

- **Diminishing sensitivity:** The perceived impact of changes becomes weaker as gains or losses increase.

Example: The difference between €100 and €200 feels more significant than the difference between €1,100 and €1,200, even though the monetary change is identical.

Prospect Theory also explains framing effects in decision-making, showing that individuals respond differently depending on how information about gains or losses is presented. For example, energy-efficiency programmes often observe stronger responses under loss-framed messages than equivalent gain-framed ones:

- *Gain frame:* "If you upgrade your home insulation, you will save CHF 250 per year."
- *Loss frame:* "If you do not upgrade your insulation, you will lose CHF 250 per year."

Given people's loss aversion, the loss-framed messages often lead to higher adoption rates for insulation upgrades and other efficiency measures—a pattern documented in behavioural field experiments on energy conservation (Allcott & Rogers, 2014).

3. Dual-System Theory of Thinking

Dual-System Theory explains decision-making by distinguishing between two modes of cognitive processing that operate simultaneously in the human mind (Kahneman, 2011). These two modes of thinking are:

- **System 1: Automatic system**
  - Fast, intuitive, and automatic
  - Requires little cognitive effort
  - Often governs day-to-day decisions
- **System 2: Reflective system**
  - Slow, deliberate, and logical
  - Requires conscious effort
  - Used in complex decision-making tasks

Because System 1 frequently drives everyday choices, individuals may be vulnerable to systematic errors in judgment—especially in situations involving patience, self-control, or long-term thinking. Dual-System Theory helps explain systematic departures from rationality—especially in time-inconsistent behaviours, where people overvalue immediate rewards at the expense of long-term benefits. For example, even when individuals recognise the importance of retirement savings—a System 2 insight—they may fail to follow through, as System 1 impulses favour immediate consumption.

This directly challenges the neoclassical economic model, which assumes that individuals have time-consistent preferences and always act to maximise utility over time. Findings from behavioural economics show that this assumption is unrealistic—especially in areas requiring delayed gratification and long-term planning.

Policy Implications

Understanding these cognitive dynamics supports the design of behaviourally informed public policies. Examples include automatic enrolment in retirement plans and commitment devices that encourage long-term saving behaviour, both of which rely on behavioural nudges that structure the choice environment and help individuals align their decisions with long-term goals.

Such interventions help bridge the gap between **System 1 and System 2**, improving policy effectiveness while preserving individual choice. This idea is central to the concept of libertarian paternalism discussed below.

Libertarian Paternalism: A Behavioural Framework for Public Policy

Libertarian paternalism, introduced by Richard Thaler and Cass Sunstein in *Nudge* (2008), is a policy approach that preserves individual choice while gently guiding people towards decisions that promote outcomes such as healthier lifestyles, financial security, or sustainable consumption.[70]

The central idea is that because people are systematically influenced by cognitive biases and choice environments, it is both legitimate and effective for institutions to design those environments in ways that help individuals make better decisions as *they themselves* would judge them.

"Choices are not blocked or restricted—but the environment is shaped to help people make better decisions." — Thaler & Sunstein (2008)

In practice, libertarian paternalism combines two principles:

- **Libertarian:** Individuals retain complete freedom to choose or opt out.
- **Paternalism:** Institutions design choice environments to promote long-term well-being—as judged by individuals themselves—in areas such as health, financial security, and environmental sustainability.

This framework underpins many sustainability-oriented nudges because it allows policymakers to influence behaviour without imposing mandates or heavy-handed regulation.[71] Examples include carbon-footprint labelling on

---

[70] The concept was first introduced in Thaler and Sunstein (2003), "Libertarian Paternalism." It was later widely popularised in the book Nudge (Thaler & Sunstein, 2008).

[71] Kaushiva, A. (2017).

restaurant menus, default green energy options in electricity contracts, and real-time feedback tools that inform households about their energy consumption.

These interventions work by restructuring defaults or simplifying complex decisions—core elements of what behavioural economists describe as choice architecture. By shaping how options are presented, policymakers can guide behaviour while preserving individual autonomy.

4.4.3. Choice Architecture and Nudges

Choice architecture refers to the way options are organised and presented in the environment where individuals make decisions. Because human decisions are influenced by cognitive biases, heuristics, and contextual cues, the design of this choice environment can significantly affect behaviour. Within this framework, a nudge is a subtle modification to the way choices are organised, presented, or framed that predictably influences behaviour without restricting options or altering economic incentives.

Nudges, therefore, represent one practical application of behavioural insights in real-world settings. In public policy and sustainability contexts, well-designed nudges can encourage more desirable outcomes in areas such as health, finance, energy use, and environmental behaviour—without relying on coercive measures or limiting individual freedom of choice.

Table 4.10: Principles of Choice Architecture.

Principle	Explanation	Example
1. Expecting error	Systems should assume people will make mistakes and be designed to minimise the consequences.	ATMs that return the card before dispensing cash reduce the likelihood that cards will be forgotten.
2. Default rules	People tend to stick with default options, so defaults should favour beneficial outcomes.	Opt-out organ donation systems increase participation; automatic enrolment boosts retirement savings.
3. Provide feedback	Real-time feedback enables individuals to monitor and adjust their behaviour.	Battery alerts or camera previews help users take corrective action.
4. Incentives	Understand who bears the cost and who benefits, and align incentives with desired behaviours.	Free workplace lunches may lead employees to choose more expensive meals.
5. Mapping	Help individuals understand the relationship between options and outcomes.	Choosing a mobile phone plan or evaluating mortgage terms involves multiple variables that must be clearly understood.
6. Structure complex choices clearly	In highly complex decisions, simplify the process by providing support.	An expat choosing where to live may need guidance on location, cost, contract terms, and environment.

Source: Adapted from Thaler & Sunstein, 2008.

Thaler and Sunstein (2008) identify six core principles for designing effective choice environments. These are summarised in Table 4.10 and provide the conceptual foundation for applying nudges in behavioural policy.

Governments have also institutionalised the use of behavioural insights in public policy. Examples include:

- UK Behavioural Insights Team (2010), established under Prime Minister David Cameron
- US Social and Behavioural Sciences Team (2015), established under President Barack Obama

4.4.4. Nudges and the Sustainable Development Goals (SDGs)

The Sustainable Development Goals (SDGs), adopted by the United Nations in 2015, comprise 17 global objectives designed to address interconnected social, environmental, and economic challenges by 2030. The SDGs provide high-level normative signals that influence how governments, firms, and citizens frame decisions and define desirable outcomes.

Although they are non-binding, the SDGs influence national policies, corporate strategies, and civil society initiatives. This raises an important question:

How can behavioural nudges encourage individuals to support the SDGs in their everyday decisions?

Because many sustainability challenges depend on everyday choices—such as consumption patterns and energy use—behavioural interventions can play an important role in translating global sustainability goals into concrete individual actions.

As noted at the beginning of Section 4.4, the United Nations Secretary-General has encouraged governments and institutions to integrate behavioural insights—including nudges—into policies that support the implementation of the Sustainable Development Goals (SDGs) (UN, 2021). Nudges, when carefully designed, can guide individuals and communities towards more sustainable choices without restricting freedom of choice or imposing financial penalties.

Local initiatives that promote sustainable consumption provide useful examples of how behavioural approaches can support the implementation of the SDGs in practice. The Lausanne Région "Buy Local" campaign discussed in Section 4.3 offers such an example. Beyond its role in promoting local supply chains, the campaign illustrates how communication strategies and choice framing can influence consumer behaviour through subtle behavioural nudges.

Case Study: The Municipality of Pully's 2025 Buy-Local Campaign as a Behavioural Nudge

In February 2025, the Municipality of Pully—supported by Lausanne Région—launched a "Buy Local" campaign to encourage residents to shop at local businesses and support the regional economy. While seemingly a traditional promotional effort, this initiative can be interpreted through the lens of behavioural economics—specifically, as a nudge. According to Thaler and Sunstein (2008), a nudge is any aspect of the choice architecture that alters behaviour in a predictable way without forbidding options or significantly changing economic incentives. The Pully campaign fits this model for several reasons:

1. **Increasing salience and visibility:** The campaign utilises posters, social media content, and public communications to increase the visibility of local businesses. By making local shopping more salient in everyday environments, these communication tools draw consumer attention towards nearby options and encourage behavioural change without imposing mandates.
2. **Leveraging cognitive and social biases:** By emphasising the economic, environmental, and community benefits of buying local, the campaign taps into social motivations, such as community pride and support for neighbours. These social cues reinforce norms of responsible consumption within the local community.
3. **Preserving freedom of choice:** No restrictions are placed on consumer options. Residents remain entirely free to shop wherever they choose. The campaign organises the choice environment to make local shopping more salient and socially desirable—hallmarks of libertarian paternalism.
4. **Framing effects within choice architecture:** The framing of 'buy local' as a socially responsible and community-supporting action increases the salience of local businesses in everyday decision contexts. Rather than relying solely on deliberate reasoning, the campaign makes local shopping more cognitively accessible, increasing the likelihood that consumers choose nearby businesses.

Public Policy Implications

This initiative shows how local governments can act as designers of behaviourally informed policies by using low-cost, non-intrusive tools to influence sustainable consumption. By incorporating behavioural insights into public communications and local policy design, municipalities like Pully strengthen local economic resilience, reduce transport-related emissions, and encourage more conscious and community-oriented consumption patterns. In this way, behavioural interventions at the municipal level can contribute to the practical implementation of SDG 12: Responsible Consumption and Production.

At the same time, this case illustrates how global sustainability frameworks can be operationalised through behavioural interventions. Campaigns like the Buy-Local campaign translate high-level sustainability goals into concrete, context-specific actions that influence everyday behaviour. The Pully Buy-Local campaign thus demonstrates how municipalities can transform broad sustainability objectives into practical, choice-architectural interventions that nudge citizens towards socially and environmentally beneficial decisions while preserving full autonomy.

The following examples illustrate how nudge-based interventions can support SDG implementation in diverse policy contexts:

1. **Bike Infrastructure (SDG 11)**: Well-designed bike lanes and cycling infrastructure nudge people to choose cycling over car use by increasing safety, visibility, and convenience.
2. **Default Plant-Based Meal Options (SDG 12)**: Making plant-based meals the default option nudges consumers towards more sustainable eating habits.
3. **Carbon-Labelled Restaurant Menus (SDG 13)**: Displaying carbon emissions on menus nudges consumers to choose lower-emission meals (Fig. 4.5).

Figure 4.5: Carbon Footprint Labelling as a Behavioural Nudge (Restaurant Menu Example).

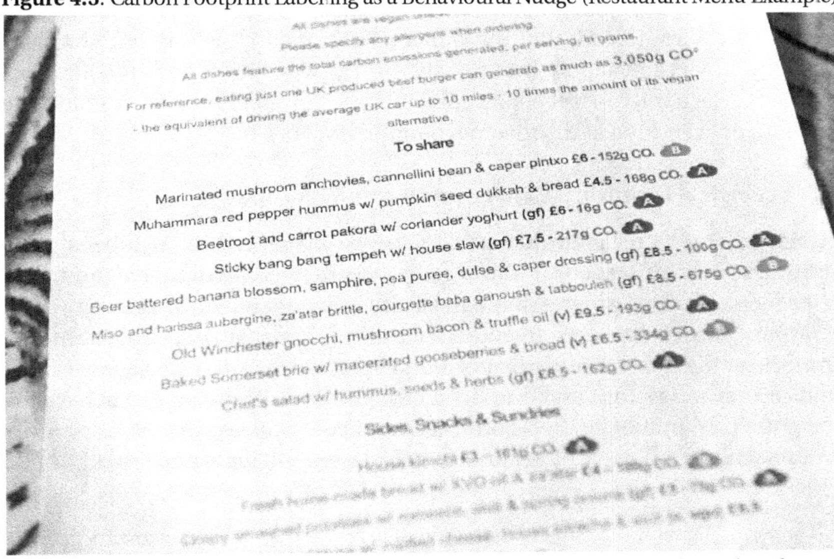

Source: Cherwell Collective (2025). Image reproduced with permission from the Cherwell Collective.

4. **Digital Carbon-Footprint Feedback Tools (SDG 12)**: The Climate Credit Card's real-time feedback nudges users to choose lower-emission products and services.

A practical example of this approach is the Corner Bank/South Pole Climate Credit Card—a behaviourally informed digital tool designed to promote more sustainable consumption habits. It functions by:

- Automatically calculating CO_2 emissions associated with each purchase
- Providing monthly and annual environmental impact summaries
- Delivering real-time feedback via mobile banking applications

By linking everyday spending to its carbon footprint, the card increases user awareness and gently nudges individuals towards lower-emission choices. It supports the goals of SDG 12 without restricting options—an effective digital nudge[72] that influences behaviour through timely, personalised feedback while preserving full autonomy.

Taken together, these examples demonstrate how SDG-aligned policies can influence behaviour not through mandates, but through subtle, non-coercive design that preserves individual autonomy. While behavioural tools help steer individual choices in more sustainable directions, their cumulative impact must ultimately be evaluated against ecological limits. Individual consumption patterns—no matter how well guided—aggregate into system-wide environmental pressures.

The following section, therefore, introduces Ecological Footprint accounting, a meso-level framework that measures how human consumption compares with the planet's available biocapacity. In this way, it provides a conceptual bridge between micro-level behavioural interventions and broader sustainability challenges examined at the macroeconomic level in Chapter 5.

4.5. Ecological Footprint (EF) Accounting and Biocapacity

Having explored how individual choices can be influenced through behavioural interventions, this section shifts focus to their collective environmental consequences. This progression reflects the broader analytical structure of the chapter. Earlier sections introduced tools for measuring environmental impacts at the product and organisational level, such as Life Cycle Assessment and carbon accounting, and examined how Life Cycle Thinking and behavioural insights can influence decision-making. Ecological Footprint accounting extends this perspective by evaluating how these individual and organisational

---

[72] The term "digital nudge" refers to the use of user-interface design elements in digital environments to steer behaviour in predictable ways without restricting options. See Weinmann, M., Schneider, C., & vom Brocke, J. (2016).

choices accumulate at the societal level and whether they remain compatible with the planet's ecological limits. This meso-level perspective also prepares the way for the transition to Chapter 5, where ecological constraints are examined from a macroeconomic perspective.

EF accounting provides a meso-level framework for assessing whether the combined resource demand of communities, cities, or nations remains within planetary biocapacity. It measures the biologically productive land and sea area required to supply the resources a population consumes and to absorb the waste it generates, given prevailing technology and resource management practices.

This territorial perspective makes EF a valuable complement to product-based tools such as LCA and carbon accounting. By aggregating data across sectors and translating it into biophysical terms, EF enables decision-makers to evaluate whether sustainability strategies align with planetary boundaries—not only in theory, but in quantifiable practice (Rockström et al., 2009; Steffen et al., 2015).

While EF accounting measures the ecological demand generated by human activities, the planetary boundaries framework identifies critical Earth-system thresholds that should not be crossed in order to maintain a stable and resilient planet. The two approaches are therefore complementary: EF accounting quantifies human demand on ecosystems, while planetary boundaries define the ecological limits within which that demand must remain.

A central concept in EF accounting is the comparison between ecological demand and ecological supply. The Ecological Footprint measures the area required to sustain human consumption (ecological demand), while biocapacity represents the biologically productive land and sea area available to generate renewable resources and absorb waste (ecological supply).

When a population's ecological footprint exceeds its available biocapacity, it runs an ecological deficit, meaning that its demand for natural resources and ecosystem services surpasses the capacity of local ecosystems. Conversely, when biocapacity exceeds the ecological footprint, a region maintains an ecological reserve, indicating that ecosystems can regenerate resources faster than they are consumed.

Persistent ecological deficits can generate long-term economic and social consequences, including resource scarcity, environmental degradation, and growing inequalities in access to natural resources—issues examined more closely in Chapter 5.

Key Sustainable Development Goals (SDGs) associated with Ecological Footprint (EF) accounting and biocapacity are presented in Table 4.11.

Table 4.11: SDGs associated with Ecological Footprint (EF) Accounting and Biocapacity.

SDG	Goal Title	Relevance to EF Accounting and Biocapacity
SDG 12	Responsible Consumption and Production	Measures the ecological pressure generated by consumption patterns and resource demand.
SDG 13	Climate Action	Carbon emissions represent the largest component of the global ecological footprint.
SDG 14	Life Below Water	Marine ecosystems contribute to global biocapacity through fisheries and ocean-based ecological resources.
SDG 15	Life on Land	Biocapacity depends on terrestrial ecosystems such as forests, cropland, and grazing land.
SDG 11	Sustainable Cities and Communities	Urban consumption patterns strongly influence ecological footprint levels.

Source: Author's analysis based on the SDG framework (United Nations, 2025).

To connect these goals with ecological realities, sustainability analysis requires tools that measure environmental pressure beyond individual products or firms—such as Ecological Footprint accounting.

While tools such as Life Cycle Assessment (LCA), Material Flow Analysis (MFA), and carbon accounting quantify the specific impacts of products, firms, or activities, there is also a need to understand how these micro-level actions accumulate—and whether their combined effects remain within the planet's ecological carrying capacity. Ecological Footprint accounting addresses this challenge by providing a framework to evaluate whether aggregated human activities exceed ecological limits.

Ecological Footprint accounting, originally developed by Wackernagel and Rees (1996), quantifies the biologically productive land and sea area required to produce the resources a population consumes and to assimilate its waste, particularly CO_2. This ecological demand is then compared with biocapacity—the capacity of ecosystems to regenerate these resources and absorb waste. When demand exceeds supply, an ecological overshoot occurs. This framework transforms the abstract concept of environmental sustainability into a measurable and actionable model.

In essence, Ecological Footprint accounting provides a means to track the depletion of natural capital—the stock of ecological assets, including forests, water bodies, fertile soils, and biodiversity, that underpin all human and economic activity. By comparing ecological demand with the regenerative capacity of ecosystems, EF accounting indicates whether an activity or economy operates within sustainable limits. When ecological footprints exceed biocapacity, this signals a drawdown of natural capital and structural depletion.

The Ecological Footprint captures multiple dimensions of resource demand, including cropland use, forest products, fisheries, built-up land, and carbon sequestration. Unlike carbon accounting, which focuses on emissions, EF provides a composite measure of human pressure on natural systems. It is therefore well-suited to linking micro-level activities to macro-scale ecological limits.

Significantly, EF accounting can be applied across multiple spatial scales and provides insights that link household or organisational choices to regional, national, and planetary outcomes. It is neither confined to individual products nor abstracted to global aggregates alone. This meso-level perspective is critical in building coherence between intent and impact—linking sustainability strategies at the city, company, or policy level with broader ecological constraints.

Recent empirical studies highlight the urgency of this perspective. Espinosa and Koh (2024) forecast Ecological Footprint and biocapacity trajectories for the G20 through 2050. Their results are sobering: only a small number of countries are on track to achieve ecological balance. Most—including several advanced economies—remain in ecological deficit, indicating that their production and consumption patterns continue to exceed sustainable limits.

As discussed in Chapter 1, the rise of neoliberal economic thought in the early 1970s—associated with Milton Friedman's 1970 'Friedman Doctrine', which prioritised shareholder value above broader social and environmental considerations—reinforced a linear economic model that systematically externalised ecological costs. The timing is notable: the emergence of global ecological overshoot broadly coincides with the rise of economic paradigms that prioritised shareholder value and market efficiency over environmental externalities.

The Global Footprint Network's annual Earth Overshoot Day provides a widely used indicator of global ecological overshoot.[73] Figure 4.6 shows that in 1972 humanity was still living within the planet's biocapacity.

By 2024, Overshoot Day had shifted to August 1st—meaning that humanity had consumed all the Earth's renewable ecological resources for the year by that date. The gap between ecological demand and biocapacity continues to widen, and this overshoot is reflected in accelerating biodiversity loss, land degradation, and the accumulation of atmospheric carbon.

Cities such as Geneva[74] and Copenhagen[75] have integrated Ecological Footprint analysis into procurement policies, food system planning, and energy infrastructure decisions, demonstrating how local authorities can operationalise ecological limits in practice. By situating sustainability assessments within a territorial and biophysical context, EF enhances the policy relevance of tools

---

[73] Global Footprint Network (2025).

[74] City of Geneva (2022).

[75] City of Copenhagen (2013).

such as Life Cycle Assessment and carbon accounting, enabling them to inform regional planning and sustainability strategies. It also allows local authorities to assess whether development trajectories remain compatible with biocapacity constraints, making it an important complement to life-cycle–based sustainability tools.

Figure 4.6: Earth Overshoot Day, 1971–2025.

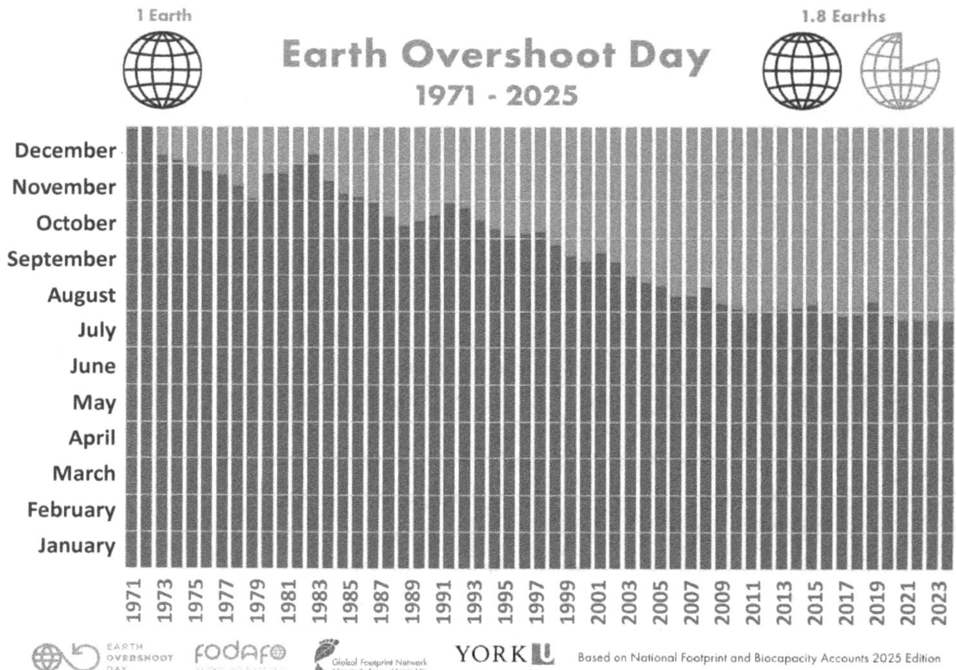

Source: Global Footprint Network (2025). Reproduced from the Earth Overshoot Day infographic with attribution.

This section also builds on the discussion of materiality and disclosure introduced in Chapter 2, showing how EF accounting provides important contextual information—particularly on regional resource pressures and biocapacity—that can inform the environmental aspects of materiality assessments. It thereby reinforces that chapter's central argument: sustainability requires identifying, measuring, and disclosing what truly matters.

The analytical perspective now broadens from micro- and meso-level sustainability assessment to the macroeconomic dimensions of sustainable development. In the next chapter, Section 5.1 revisits the limitations of GDP and introduces broader well-being indicators, while Section 5.2 focuses on natural capital—a concept first introduced in Chapter 1 and further developed here through EF accounting—and its macro-level consequences, including implications for inequality. Section 5.3 then presents a Green Keynesian framework, in which these constraints—expressed through biocapacity, ecological thresholds, and natural capital stocks—inform investment priorities and fiscal strategy.

Within this context, EF accounting serves as a conceptual bridge—linking regional and sectoral sustainability assessments to the macroeconomic transformation framework presented in Chapter 5.

Key Insights — Chapter 4: Sustainability at the Micro Level

1. **Measurement of Environmental Impacts**. Economic activity must first be measured in terms of environmental pressures. Effective sustainability strategies, therefore, require reliable methods to assess the environmental impacts of economic activity. Analytical methods allow decision-makers to evaluate how resources are extracted, transformed, used, and disposed of across production and consumption systems. These approaches translate environmental pressures into measurable indicators, support evidence-based decision-making, and help identify opportunities to reduce resource use, emissions, and waste. Measurement thus represents the first essential step towards improving environmental performance and aligning economic activity with sustainability objectives.

2. **Climate Accounting.** Among environmental pressures, greenhouse gas emissions require specific accounting because they drive climate change. Managing climate change requires accounting of greenhouse gas emissions associated with energy use, production processes, and supply chains. Carbon accounting enables organizations to identify major sources of emissions and track progress towards decarbonization targets. It also strengthens transparency in corporate reporting by allowing investors and regulators to assess climate-related risks and transition pathways. In this way, carbon accounting provides a critical foundation for aligning economic activity with global climate objectives.

3. **Life-Cycle Perspective.** Sustainability assessment must also consider entire value chains, integrating environmental, social, and economic impacts. While Life Cycle Assessment (LCA) provides a quantitative method for assessing environmental impacts, it is embedded within a broader conceptual perspective known as Life Cycle Thinking (LCT). Life Cycle Thinking represents the mindset that guides sustainability-oriented decisions across government, business, and individual levels. Building on this perspective, Life

Cycle Sustainability Assessment (LCSA) integrates environmental, social, and economic evaluation within a unified sustainability framework. These approaches increasingly support sustainability governance and reporting systems, including ESG disclosure frameworks and regulatory standards. Conceptually, these approaches form a continuum:

LCA → environmental measurement tool
LCT → systems perspective guiding decisions
LCSA → integrated sustainability assessment
ESG → sustainability governance and reporting

4. Behavioural Drivers. Even with robust analytical tools, sustainability outcomes ultimately depend on how individuals make decisions. Behavioural economics shows that economic choices are often influenced by cognitive biases, social norms, and contextual factors rather than purely rational calculation. Understanding these behavioural drivers enables policymakers and organizations to design interventions that encourage more responsible patterns of consumption and resource use. Behavioural insights, therefore, complement analytical sustainability tools by addressing the human dimension of environmental decision-making.

5. Ecological Limits and Natural Capital Constraints. The aggregate effects of economic decisions must ultimately be evaluated against the ecological limits of the planet. While analytical tools, decision frameworks, and behavioural insights influence production and consumption choices, these decisions collectively contribute to system-wide environmental pressures. Ecological Footprint accounting provides a meso-level perspective by comparing the ecological demand generated by human activities with the Earth's biocapacity, revealing whether societies operate within sustainable limits.

Two complementary analytical relationships help clarify this framework:

Within the Ecological Footprint framework
Ecological Footprint → ecological demand
Biocapacity → ecological supply
Comparing these indicators reveals ecological balance or overshoot:
EF > biocapacity → ecological deficit
EF < biocapacity → ecological reserve

Across Sustainability Frameworks
Ecological Footprint → human pressure on ecosystems
Planetary boundaries → Earth-system limits that should not be exceeded

Together, these perspectives link everyday economic decisions with the ecological limits that sustain human well-being and provide a bridge from micro-level sustainability tools to the macroeconomic transformation discussed in Chapter 5.

Schematically:

Micro-level sustainability tools (Sections 4.1-4.4)
↓
meso-level ecological limits (Section 4.5)
↓
macroeconomic transformation (Chapter 5)

This progression highlights how sustainability analysis moves from measuring individual environmental impacts to evaluating systemic ecological constraints, thereby preparing the macroeconomic perspective developed in Chapter 5.

In Simple Words — Chapter 4: Sustainability at the Micro Level

Addressing sustainability challenges begins with understanding how everyday economic activities affect the environment. Every product we buy, every service we use, and every investment we make involves the use of energy, materials, and natural resources. These activities generate environmental pressures, such as pollution, waste, and greenhouse gas emissions. If economic activity is to become more sustainable, we need practical ways to identify where these impacts occur and how they can be reduced.

This is why sustainability requires measurement tools. By examining how resources are extracted, transformed, transported, used, and eventually discarded, analysts can identify where the largest environmental pressures arise. Measuring these impacts helps governments, firms, and consumers make better decisions about production processes, product design, and resource use. Without such measurement, environmental problems remain largely invisible in economic decision-making.

Many environmental impacts can be measured, but greenhouse gas emissions require particular attention because they are the main driver of climate change. For this reason, specific methods have been developed to track the amounts of carbon dioxide and other greenhouse gases produced by economic activities. These approaches make it possible to identify where emissions occur within production processes, energy use, and supply chains. By making emissions visible and measurable, carbon accounting helps companies, investors, and policymakers understand where reductions are needed and track progress towards climate targets.

To understand the environmental consequences of economic activity, analysts also use methods that examine the entire life cycle of products and services—from the extraction of raw materials to production, use, and final disposal. Life Cycle Assessment (LCA) is a quantitative method that measures environmental impacts across these stages. It is incorporated within a broader conceptual framework known as Life Cycle Thinking (LCT), a mindset that encourages sustainability-oriented decision-making. A further step, Life Cycle Sustainability Assessment (LCSA), integrates environmental, social, and economic considerations within a single framework for evaluating sustainability. These perspectives increasingly inform corporate reporting and governance systems, helping investors, regulators, and society assess how economic activities affect both the environment and social well-being.

However, sustainability outcomes do not depend only on measurement tools and analytical frameworks. They also depend on how people make decisions in everyday situations. Research in behavioural economics shows that individuals do not always act through careful calculation. Habits, social norms, convenience, and the way choices are presented can strongly influence behaviour. Understanding these patterns allows policymakers and organisations to design decision environments that encourage more sustainable choices, helping individuals align their actions with long-term environmental goals.

Even when decisions become more informed and responsible, their combined effects must still be evaluated against the ecological limits of the planet. Human activities require land, water, energy, and natural resources, while ecosystems have a limited capacity to regenerate these resources and absorb waste. When the demand generated by human activities exceeds this capacity, environmental pressures accumulate. Tools such as ecological footprint analysis help reveal whether societies are operating within these limits. Understanding these limits is essential for ensuring that economic activity remains compatible with the long-term stability of natural systems.

Chapter 5
Sustainability at the Macro Level

While Chapters 2–4 examined how sustainability can be operationalised at the micro and meso levels, this chapter turns to the macroeconomic and political-economic foundations of sustainable development, situating these mechanisms within the structures that ultimately determine whether sustainability transitions succeed. At this level, sustainability becomes a question of political economy, centred on how investment, production, and distribution are organised within ecological limits. Macroeconomic indicators, inequality dynamics, and fiscal policy frameworks therefore play a decisive role in structuring sustainability transitions. This chapter is structured into three sections:

- **Section 5.1:** Gross Domestic Product (GDP) and alternative metrics
- **Section 5.2:** Inequality
- **Section 5.3:** Green Keynesianism

Together, these sections address three central dimensions of sustainability: how economic progress is measured, how its benefits and costs are distributed, and how macroeconomic policy can steer economies towards socially inclusive and ecologically sustainable development.

Note on SDG Ordering in Tables:

In tables presenting linkages between the analysed topics and the Sustainable Development Goals (SDGs), the goals are listed according to their conceptual relevance rather than in numerical order. This approach highlights the SDGs most directly related to the methods and frameworks discussed in each section.

5.1. Gross Domestic Product (GDP) and Alternative Metrics

Gross Domestic Product (GDP) measures the total market value of all final goods and services produced within a country over a given period and has long served as the dominant indicator of economic performance. Yet it fails to account for critical dimensions such as environmental degradation, social inequality, and well-being, rendering it an incomplete measure of progress in the context of the SDGs.

Alternative metrics such as the Human Development Index (HDI) and the Genuine Progress Indicator (GPI) offer more holistic frameworks. By incorporating social and environmental dimensions alongside economic output, they align more closely with the multi-dimensional objectives of the 2030 Agenda for Sustainable Development.

The key Sustainable Development Goals (SDGs) associated with alternative metrics to GDP are presented in Table 5.1.

Table 5.1: SDGs associated with Alternative Metrics beyond GDP.

SDG	Goal Title	Relevance to alternative metrics beyond GDP
SDG 17	Partnerships for the Goals	Serves as the institutional and measurement framework for post-GDP transition, especially through Target 17.19, which calls for new indicators to complement GDP.
SDG 8	Decent Work and Economic Growth	Reframes economic performance by shifting the focus from output growth to inclusive and sustainable prosperity, a core objective of post-GDP metrics such as the GPI.
SDG 10	Reduced Inequalities	Addresses the distributional dimension of development outcomes, central to both HDI and GPI, and views inequality as a macroeconomic constraint rather than a residual outcome.
SDG 12	Responsible Consumption and Production	Establishes structural limits to growth by internalising environmental externalities, challenging GDP's assumption that all consumption contributes positively to economic performance.
SDG 13	Climate Action	Integrates climate impacts into economic performance assessments, reinforcing the role of ecological constraints in redefining progress beyond GDP.
SDG 15	Life on Land	Accounts for the incorporation of natural capital depletion and biodiversity loss into macroeconomic accounting frameworks such as the GPI.
SDG 3	Good Health and Well-being	Positions human well-being as a development objective, shifting the emphasis from aggregate output to social outcomes, as reflected in alternative metrics such as the HDI.
SDG 4	Quality Education	Emphasises human capital formation as a long-term foundation of development, particularly within capability-based measures.

Source: Author's analysis based on the SDG framework (United Nations, 2025).

Ongoing United Nations initiatives in 2025–2026 to develop complementary indicators to GDP further reinforce the relevance of these metrics, aligning with the broader effort to evaluate progress across social, environmental, and economic dimensions.

5.1.1. Origins of GDP

To understand why GDP continues to function as the dominant benchmark of economic policy—despite its limitations as a measure of progress—it is necessary to trace its historical development and underlying assumptions.

Foundation of National Income Accounting

In the early 1930s, Simon Kuznets, an economist with the National Bureau of Economic Research (NBER), developed the first systematic national income estimates for the United States. His 1934 report to the US Congress, *National Income, 1929–1932*, provided one of the first quantitative assessments of the economic collapse during the Great Depression. These estimates were based on Gross National Product (GNP), the precursor to GDP, which later became the primary measure of national output.

Although Kuznets laid the foundations of national income accounting, he was cautious about interpreting these statistics as indicators of welfare. In that report, he warned that national income statistics were not intended to measure a nation's welfare, but rather its production and consumption capacity. As he famously observed, "the welfare of a nation can scarcely be inferred from a measurement of national income." He later emphasised that economic growth should not be treated as an end in itself, noting that "goals for more growth should specify more growth of what and for what." These early cautions foreshadow contemporary debates about the limits of GDP as a measure of progress and the need for broader indicators that incorporate social well-being and ecological sustainability.

Despite Kuznets's warning, GDP gained prominence in the decades following the Great Depression and World War II, when governments required reliable macroeconomic statistics to guide reconstruction and economic planning. Its legitimacy was formally institutionalised in 1953 with the introduction of the United Nations' *System of National Accounts* (SNA), which established internationally standardised guidelines for calculating GDP and ensured comparability across countries. GDP became the dominant global indicator of macroeconomic performance.

These historical foundations explain why GDP became the central indicator of modern macroeconomic analysis. Yet its original purpose as a measure of production rather than welfare also reveals its limitations when applied to contemporary challenges such as sustainability, inequality, and human well-being.

By the early 1970s, critiques of GDP had begun to emerge. A landmark intervention came in 1972, when the Club of Rome's report, *The Limits to Growth* (Meadows et al., 1972), warned that exponential growth in population and resource use could drive global systems beyond their limits—resulting in a sudden and uncontrollable decline in both population and industrial capacity.

Over time, economic growth came to be treated not merely as a technical measure of output but as a normative benchmark of progress. This transformation was reinforced by the rise of the neoliberal economic paradigm in the 1970s and 1980s, particularly through the influence of Milton Friedman and the growing emphasis on market-oriented policy frameworks. Within this context, the policy agenda known as the Washington Consensus—coined by John Williamson (1989) to describe a set of market-oriented policy prescriptions promoted by institutions such as the IMF, the World Bank, and the US Treasury—emphasised macroeconomic stabilization, trade liberalization, and privatisation. These policies were often grounded in the flawed assumption that economic growth would automatically translate into development.

This oversimplified conflation of GDP with development proved especially problematic for low- and middle-income countries. Structural adjustment programmes and growth-oriented loan conditions left many economies dependent on short-term capital inflows—often at the cost of increased macroeconomic volatility and rising income inequality.

Despite the emergence of numerous alternative metrics aimed at capturing social and environmental dimensions of progress, GDP remained the primary benchmark of economic progress throughout the late twentieth century. It continued to determine national priorities, guide development assistance, and set the global standard for measuring progress.

In response, a growing body of research and institutional initiatives has sought to develop alternative indicators capable of capturing the social, ecological, and intergenerational dimensions of development that GDP systematically overlooks. The emergence of these alternative metrics marks a shift towards more comprehensive approaches to measuring development.

5.1.2. Emergence of Alternative Metrics

By the late 1980s, scholars and institutions began developing alternative metrics in response to the recognised limitations of GDP, particularly regarding social welfare, environmental sustainability, and equity.

In 1989, Herman Daly and John B. Cobb developed the Index of Sustainable Economic Welfare (ISEW), which integrated income distribution, environmental degradation, and non-market activities into national accounting (Daly and Cobb, 1989).

In 1990, the United Nations Development Programme (UNDP) introduced the Human Development Index (HDI), a multidimensional measure of human development. It combines health (life expectancy at birth), education (mean years of schooling and expected years of schooling), and standard of living (GNI per capita, PPP-adjusted). Drawing on Amartya Sen's capabilities approach (Sen, 1999), the HDI emphasises the expansion of individual freedoms and opportunities. Since 2010, the HDI has been calculated using a geometric mean, ensuring that high scores in some dimensions do not offset low performance in others. This approach provides a more balanced and inclusive measure of well-being than GDP alone (Figure 5.1).

ıre 5.1: Components of the Human Development Index.

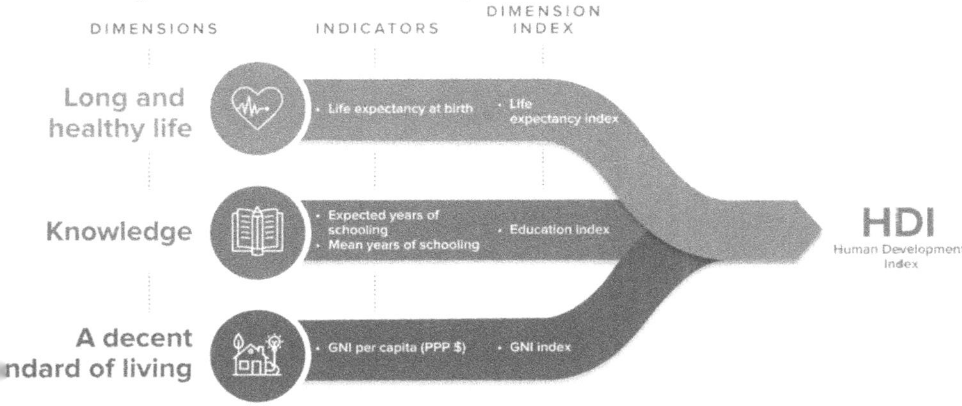

·ce: United Nations Development Programme (UNDP) (2025). *Human Development Report.* Eeprod·ıced attribution from official HDI materials.

In 1994, Clifford Cobb and collaborators introduced the Genuine Progress Indicator (GPI) as an extension of the Index of Sustainable Economic Welfare (ISEW). The GPI incorporates 26 indicators designed to measure genuine economic progress rather than market activity alone. Figure 5.2 categorises these indicators into three main domains—environmental, social, and economic—highlighting the need to adjust GDP for both negative externalities and non-market contributions. Environmental indicators include depletion of natural capital, greenhouse gas pollution, and solid waste pollution; social indicators include unpaid work, underemployment, and crime; and economic indicators include income inequality, consumer durable expenditures, and household investments. This structure renders the GPI a more comprehensive measure of long-term welfare than conventional output-based measures.

Figure 5.2: Genuine Progress Indicator (GPI).

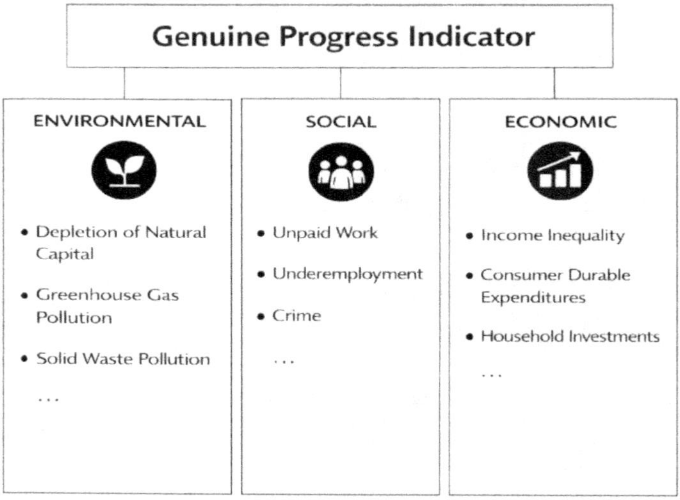

Source: Author's formulation based on Berik and Gaddis (2011).

In 2006, Nic Marks at the New Economics Foundation introduced the Happy Planet Index (HPI), a metric designed to measure resource efficiency and environmental sustainability.[76] The index is conceptually aligned with SDG indicators 9.4.1 (CO2 emissions per unit of GDP) and 12.2.1 (material footprint per unit of GDP). The HPI is calculated by multiplying life expectancy by self-reported well-being and adjusting the result by a country's per capita carbon footprint. This formulation reflects how long and satisfying lives can be achieved with minimal environmental impact.

Life expectancy data are sourced from the UN Population Division. Well-being is measured on a self-reported scale from 0 to 10. The carbon footprint is calculated using per-capita greenhouse gas emissions from datasets such as the Global Carbon Atlas and the EORA database. By linking subjective well-being to environmental impact, the HPI reframes progress as the ability to achieve long and satisfying lives with minimal ecological pressure.

In 2009, the Stiglitz–Sen–Fitoussi Report, commissioned by the French government and led by Joseph Stiglitz, Amartya Sen, and Jean-Paul Fitoussi, called for moving "Beyond GDP" by incorporating well-being, inequality, environmental sustainability, and non-market activities into official statistics. The report catalysed an international policy debate on redefining economic

[76] Hot or Cool Institute (2024).

performance and inspired the development of initiatives such as the OECD Better Life Index.

In 2011, the Organisation for Economic Co-operation and Development (OECD) introduced the Better Life Index (BLI), a multidimensional framework for comparing well-being across countries. Inspired by the recommendations of the Stiglitz–Sen–Fitoussi Report, the index broadens the assessment of economic progress beyond income by incorporating 11 dimensions, including housing, income, jobs, education, health, environment, and life satisfaction. On the OECD's interactive Better Life Index platform, users can assign different weights to each dimension according to their own priorities and values. This feature illustrates how well-being is shaped by cultural and social context, and how rankings shift depending on what aspects of life are considered most important.

In 2012, the Inclusive Wealth Index (IWI) was introduced by the United Nations Environment Programme (UNEP) and the United Nations University (UNU) to measure intergenerational well-being by combining three categories of capital: natural capital (such as forests, water, biodiversity, and ecosystems), human capital (knowledge, education, and skills), and produced capital (infrastructure, machinery, and physical assets). These assets are aggregated to assess whether a country's development path maintains or enhances its capacity to generate well-being across generations.

Together, these indicators embed ecological, social, and intergenerational dimensions into the measurement of development, reflecting a shift away from output-based metrics towards a more comprehensive understanding of well-being. In doing so, they establish the conceptual foundations for the post-GDP measurement agenda, which is further articulated through the Sustainable Development Goals.

SDGs and the Post-GDP Measurement Agenda

In 2015, the United Nations adopted the Sustainable Development Goals (SDGs)—a comprehensive framework that integrates economic, social, and environmental dimensions of development and redefines how progress towards these objectives is measured. Importantly, the SDGs explicitly recognise the need to complement conventional economic metrics with broader indicators of sustainable development. Specifically, Target 17.19 of SDG 17 calls on countries to "develop measurements of progress on sustainable development that complement GDP, and support statistical capacity-building in developing countries" (United Nations, 2015). This measurement agenda has prompted several high-level international initiatives. The UN's 2021 report *Valuing What Counts* outlined pathways for developing a post-GDP measurement system, grounded in political will, scientific integrity, and investment in data infrastructure. In parallel, the 2025 revision of the United Nations System of National Accounts (SNA)—adopted by the United Nations Statistical Commission in 2025—introduces important updates, including improved accounting for digitalisation, informal and unpaid labour, distributional outcomes (such as income inequality), and natural capital.

In addition to the composite indicators already discussed, a growing set of complementary frameworks expands the measurement of development beyond traditional macroeconomic tools. These include multidimensional approaches such as the Multidimensional Poverty Index (MPI) and broader analytical frameworks such as Doughnut Economics, developed by Kate Raworth. Gender-focused indices—including the Gender Development Index (GDI), Gender Inequality Index (GII), and Gender Equality Index (GEI)—provide further insight into structural disparities and social equity. Together, these approaches provide a more comprehensive basis for assessing sustainability and structural imbalances.

From Metrics to Institutional Frameworks

The increasing institutional recognition of comprehensive sustainability metrics—such as the Inclusive Wealth Index (IWI) and inequality-adjusted measures—is reinforced by emerging regulatory frameworks. These include the Sustainable Finance Disclosure Regulation (SFDR), introduced in Chapter 2, and the Corporate Sustainability Reporting Directive (CSRD), introduced in Chapter 4. Such frameworks embed sustainability metrics within corporate disclosure and investment processes, enabling them to function as practical instruments of accountability in both public and private governance.

Beyond their role as measurement tools, alternative indicators also serve a critical diagnostic function at the macroeconomic level. When GDP increases but broader indicators such as the HDI, GPI, or Inclusive Wealth Index (IWI) stagnate or decline, this reveals structural imbalances—often masked by traditional economic accounting. These imbalances typically reflect the erosion of natural capital, widening inequality, and declining prospects for intergenerational welfare. In this sense, the gap between GDP and broader sustainability indicators serves as an early warning signal of macroeconomic unsustainability and underscores the need for structural policy reforms.

One of the most significant structural imbalances revealed by these broader indicators concerns the distribution of economic outcomes, particularly the role of inequality as a key determinant of sustainable development trajectories.

5.2. The Inequality–Ecology–Climate Nexus

Contemporary economic systems are increasingly characterised by two interrelated crises: rising inequality and accelerating ecological degradation intensified by the global climate crisis.[77] These crises form a mutually reinforcing system in which economic disparities accelerate ecological degradation, including the depletion of natural capital, thereby deepening inequality. This feedback loop must be addressed through macroeconomic policy frameworks that respond to both crises in an integrated manner. This asymmetry between responsibility and exposure means that populations and countries least responsible for ecological harm are often the most exposed to its impacts.

This interdependence between inequality, ecological degradation, and climate vulnerability is reflected across several Sustainable Development Goals. The key Sustainable Development Goals (SDGs) associated with the inequality–ecology–climate nexus analysed in this section are presented in Table 5.2.

Table 5.2: SDGs associated with the Inequality–Ecology–Climate Nexus.

SDG	Goal Title	Relevance to Inequality–Ecology–Climate Nexus
SDG 10	Reduced Inequalities	Identifies inequality as a macroeconomic structural driver of economic divergence and unequal exposure to ecological and climate risks.
SDG 13	Climate Action	Reveals the unequal distribution of climate risks and adaptive capacity across countries and income groups.
SDG 12	Responsible Consumption and Production	Links unsustainable consumption and production patterns as key sources of ecological depletion.
SDG 15	Life on Land	Highlights the long-term erosion of natural capital and its disproportionate impacts on poorer countries.
SDG 6	Clean Water and Sanitation	Reveals scarcity, resource conflicts, and unequal access to safe water under ecological stress.
SDG 7	Affordable and Clean Energy	Exposes unequal access to clean energy and its role in reinforcing global inequality.
SDG 1	No Poverty	Shows unequal exposure to shocks from climate and ecological degradation.
SDG 2	Zero Hunger	Demonstrates how land and resource degradation contribute to food insecurity.
SDG 11	Sustainable Cities and Communities	Highlights unequal access to urban infrastructure, housing, and basic services in vulnerable communities.
SDG 8	Decent Work and Economic Growth	Identifies the tensions between GDP-driven growth, labour market fragility, and the challenges of achieving a just transition in vulnerable economies.

Source: Author's analysis based on the SDG framework (United Nations, 2025).

[77] UNEP, Inclusive Wealth Report (2023).

Inequality operates as the structural starting point of this nexus, shaping patterns of consumption, resource use, and ecological pressure, and ultimately influencing how climate vulnerability is distributed across societies. Recognising this feedback loop is essential for designing macroeconomic policies that reorient resource use towards sustainable outcomes while addressing distributional imbalances.

The following subsections explore this nexus in greater detail. Section 5.2.1 focuses on income and wealth inequality, while Section 5.2.2 examines how ecological degradation reinforces unequal development outcomes—highlighting the macro-distributional challenges at the heart of sustainability.

5.2.1. Piketty's Theory of Wealth Inequality

The r > g Model and its Policy Relevance

Piketty argues that when the rate of return on capital (r) exceeds the rate of economic growth (g), wealth inequality tends to widen over time. This dynamic concentrates income and wealth in the hands of the few, most notably the top 1–10%,[78] while the income and wealth of the bottom 50% stagnate or decline (Piketty, 2020). This is reflected, for example, in South Africa, where the bottom 50% receives just 5–6% of the national income, whereas in Nordic countries, this figure is around 20–25% (Piketty and Chancel, 2021). While the Nordic countries exhibit a more equal distribution due to robust welfare and taxation systems, the underlying dynamic of wealth concentration persists, as the rate of return on capital continues to exceed the rate of economic growth.

This dynamic leads to the concentration of wealth and may erode social cohesion while undermining trust in institutions.

According to Oxfam's 2026 report *Resisting the Rule of the Rich*, global billionaire wealth reached an all-time high of USD 18.3 trillion, growing three times faster than its average rate of increase since 2020. The 12 richest billionaires now hold more than the combined wealth of the poorest half of the world's population. Moreover, billionaires are estimated to be over 4,000 times more likely to hold political office compared to ordinary citizens—illustrating how extreme wealth translates into disproportionate political influence.

An earlier Oxfam report also highlighted that several African countries rank among the world's most unequal, with wealth increasingly concentrated among a narrow economic elite (Kamande and Hallum, 2025).

---

[78] Oxfam International (2024).

Climate Inequality and the Carbon Elite (Oxfam-SEI Evidence)

Oxfam's research with the Stockholm Environment Institute (SEI) highlights the disproportionate environmental and political impact of the global elite:

- As of 2019—the most recent year for which global emissions are disaggregated by income—the carbon emissions of the world's wealthiest 1% were equivalent to 66% of the total emissions generated by the poorest half of the global population. The top 10% accounted for half of all global emissions.
- The top 1% control 43% of global financial assets. Approximately 40% of billionaire wealth is invested in highly polluting industries, including oil, mining, cement, and shipping, thereby amplifying the environmental impact of their investment portfolios.
- The richest 1% are responsible for 50% of global aviation emissions, while benefiting from preferential tax treatment—such as a 2% tax rate on private jets[79] compared to 43% for economy-class passengers on similar routes (e.g., Paris-London).[80]
- This concentration of wealth translates into political influence. Members of the global economic elite frequently attend international climate summits (such as COP 29 in Baku, 2024), where lobbying activities have been reported to influence negotiations on climate regulation. Approximately one-third of the world's large media organisations are controlled by individual billionaires, further shaping public discourse.

The findings reviewed in this section highlight the structural relationship between wealth concentration and ecological degradation. Piketty's theory shows that when the return on capital consistently exceeds the rate of economic growth, inequality becomes self-reinforcing—favouring those who already own capital. The Oxfam-SEI evidence adds a critical ecological layer: the same elite groups that concentrate wealth also drive a disproportionate share of global emissions through their consumption patterns, investment portfolios, and policy influence. The high-emission patterns of the global economic elite undermine the prospects for climate action.

The next section turns to the other side of the spectrum, examining how environmental degradation reproduces inequality among low-income populations and in vulnerable regions.

---

[79] Armstrong, J. (2022); European Commission (2021).

[80] Watts, J. (2023).

5.2.2. Measuring Inequality: Gini, Atkinson, and IHDI

Measuring inequality is essential for diagnosing distributive imbalances and designing effective policy interventions. While the Gini coefficient remains the most widely used measure, other indices, such as the Atkinson Index and the Inequality-adjusted Human Development Index (IHDI), offer valuable complementary insights, especially when evaluating equity beyond income alone.[81]

1. Gini Coefficient

Developed by Italian statistician Corrado Gini (Gini, 1912), this index measures inequality in the distribution of income within a population on a scale from 0 (perfect equality) to 1 (perfect inequality). It is derived from the Lorenz Curve (Lorenz, 1905), which plots the cumulative share of income received by different segments of the population against a hypothetical line of perfect equality (the 45-degree line).

The Gini coefficient remains the most widely used measure of inequality, regularly reported by national governments and international institutions such as the World Bank and the United Nations. It allows for direct comparison across countries and over time. However, the index is less sensitive to changes at the extremes of the income distribution—both at the top and bottom—which limits its usefulness in capturing deep poverty or extreme wealth concentration. Moreover, countries with identical Gini values may exhibit very different income structures.

For example, in 2015, both Greece and Thailand reported a Gini index of 0.36. Yet in Greece, the richest 10% earned 13.8 times more than the poorest 10%, whereas in Thailand the ratio was 8.9 to 1—indicating a greater concentration of income at the top in Greece despite the two countries having identical Gini scores.

2. Atkinson Index

Introduced by economist Anthony Atkinson (Atkinson, 1970), the Atkinson Index was designed to address limitations of the Gini coefficient—particularly its limited sensitivity to changes at the lower end of the income distribution. The index incorporates an inequality-aversion parameter (ε) that reflects the weight society places on reducing disparities among the poor.

[81] United Nations, Department of Economic and Social Affairs (2020).

As the inequality aversion parameter increases, the index becomes more sensitive to changes within lower-income groups, placing greater weight on disparities at the lower end of the income distribution. This makes the Atkinson Index particularly appropriate for evaluating policies aimed at reducing poverty and income disparities, especially when priority is given to improvements for the most disadvantaged groups. For policymakers, it is particularly useful for targeting social spending and designing redistributive policies.

3. Inequality-Adjusted Human Development Index (IHDI)

Unlike the Gini and Atkinson indices, which measure income inequality directly, the Inequality-adjusted Human Development Index (IHDI) captures the loss in human development due to inequality in the distribution of health, education, and income.

The IHDI extends the Human Development Index (HDI) by incorporating inequality into each of its three core dimensions: health, education, and income.[82] It applies Atkinson-type inequality measures to these dimensions and reflects not only average achievements in human development but also how these achievements are distributed across the population.

The difference between a country's HDI and its IHDI represents the loss in potential human development due to inequality. In a perfectly equal society, the HDI and IHDI would be identical. The greater the gap, the more inequality erodes overall development outcomes.

The IHDI is increasingly used by governments and international agencies to identify inequality-related development losses, even when a country's average HDI appears high. It provides a valuable tool for integrating equity concerns into human development strategies and for revealing disparities that aggregate averages tend to obscure.

These differences are summarised in Table 5.3, which compares HDI and IHDI scores for G20 countries and quantifies the loss in human development due to inequality.

---

[82] United Nations Development Programme (UNDP) (2020).

Table 5.3: Human Development Losses due to Inequality — IHDI and HDI Scores of G20 Countries.

Rank	Country	IHDI	HDI	HDI due to inequality (%)
Very High Human Development				
10	Germany	0.87	0.95	8.20
11	Australia	0.87	0.94	8.20
16	United Kingdom and Northern Ireland	0.86	0.93	8.20
17	Canada	0.85	0.93	8.70
18	Japan	0.84	0.92	8.30
23	France	0.82	0.90	9.00
24	South Korea	0.82	0.92	11.00
28	United States	0.81	0.93	12.70
High Human Development				
34	Italy	0.78	0.89	12.20
42	Russian Federation	0.74	0.82	10.20
44	Argentina	0.73	0.85	13.70
Medium Human Development				
57	Türkiye	0.68	0.82	16.70
67	China	0.64	0.76	16.00
74	Mexico	0.61	0.78	21.30
81	Indonesia	0.59	0.72	17.80
88	Brazil	0.57	0.77	25.50
Low Human Development				
104	India	0.48	0.65	26.40
107	South Africa	0.47	0.71	34.00

Source: Author's compilation based on United Nations Development Programme (UNDP) (2020), *Human Development Report 2020.*

Several other measures of inequality exist, including the Hoover Index, the Theil Index, the General Entropy measures, the Decile Dispersion ratio, and the Palma ratio. Each offers additional insights depending on the context and focus of analysis. However, a detailed discussion of these metrics lies beyond the scope of this chapter.

5.2.3. Ecological Depletion and Inequality: A Reinforcing Loop

The relationship between ecological depletion and inequality is central to achieving the Sustainable Development Goals (SDGs), as it reveals how environmental degradation and economic disparities reinforce one another. However, current development models, heavily focused on GDP growth, often neglect the long-term costs of environmental degradation and widening inequality—particularly in low- and middle-income countries.

One of the key structural mechanisms underlying this dynamic is the unequal dependence on natural capital across countries, with the strongest effects observed in low-income economies.

Natural capital constitutes a disproportionately large share of the wealth of low-income countries, accounting for nearly one-third of their total wealth.[83] Unlike high-income countries, which rely more heavily on produced capital (infrastructure, machinery, built assets) and human capital (education, health, skills), low-income countries depend directly on natural capital (forests, water, agricultural land, biodiversity) for livelihoods, subsistence, and resilience. This structural dependence increases their vulnerability to ecological degradation, which in turn undermines livelihoods and reinforces existing economic inequalities.

Between 1990 and 2019, global natural capital declined by 28%—a loss that has disproportionately affected the world's poorest regions. This degradation has not only undermined ecological stability but also eroded economic opportunity, thereby widening development and income disparities across countries. Sustainable development depends on preserving the ecological foundations of prosperity; reversing this trend is therefore essential to achieving long-term equity and resilience under the 2030 Agenda.

Although GDP growth between 2000 and 2019 contributed to measurable improvements in development indicators—such as reductions in poverty (SDG 1), hunger (SDG 2), and increases in employment (SDG 8)—these gains have often come at the expense of environmental sustainability. In many low- and lower-middle-income countries, the pursuit of sustained high growth has led to overexploitation of natural resources, land degradation, and biodiversity loss. As a result, progress towards key environmental goals—SDG 13 (Climate Action), SDG 14 (Life Below Water), and SDG 15 (Life on Land)—has been slowed and, in some cases, reversed.

The distributive consequences of ecological degradation are examined in greater detail in the following section, which presents empirical evidence on the relationship between natural capital depletion and inequality.

5.2.4. Empirical Evidence on Natural Capital and Inequality

This section presents empirical findings from the *Inclusive Wealth Report 2023*, which systematically tracks changes in natural, human, and produced capital across 163 countries between 1990 and 2019. The data provide compelling evidence of ecological decline and its distributive consequences. Specifically, the report shows that 121 of 163 countries experienced an absolute decline in

[83] World Bank (2021).

natural capital, while 151 countries suffered net losses in wealth after adjusting for population growth—a trend that threatens the long-term development prospects of future generations.

Population Growth and Ecological Pressure: A Vicious Cycle

Empirical data reveal a critical feedback loop between population growth, rising consumption, and environmental degradation. As populations expand—particularly in low- and middle-income countries—there is often a parallel rise in human capital, a key driver of development. However, this demographic shift is often accompanied by rising aggregate and per capita consumption, placing unsustainable pressure on natural capital, including forests, water resources, and fisheries.[84] These dynamics therefore undermine the sustainability of production and consumption patterns, as highlighted in SDG 12 (Responsible Consumption and Production).

Inequality in the Distribution of Capital Assets: Global Gini Coefficient

The *Inclusive Wealth Report 2023* also highlights the growing inequality in the distribution of capital types—especially natural capital. While produced and human capital expanded in many high-income and emerging economies, the benefits were unevenly distributed, and natural capital declined disproportionately in low-income regions. Figure 5.3 illustrates the evolution of the global Gini coefficient for inclusive wealth and its three components—produced, human, and natural capital—each represented by a distinct line, allowing comparison of their trends over time. The figure shows that inequality in produced capital declined steadily, primarily due to its rapid accumulation in countries such as China and India. Human capital inequality remained high and relatively stable after 2000. In contrast, inequality in natural capital increased significantly: the Gini coefficient for natural capital rose from 0.67 in 1998 to 0.72 in 2019, indicating a deepening disparity in per capita ecological assets across countries.[85] This growing disparity reflects the interaction between ecological loss, unequal access to ecological assets, and unequal exposure to environmental risks, reinforcing the inequality–ecology–climate nexus at the heart of this chapter.

---

[84] Managi, S. et al. (2023).

[85] See Inclusive Wealth Report (2023), pp. 114-120 for a detailed exposition.

Figure 5.3: Global Gini Coefficient of Inclusive Wealth and its Components, 1990-2019.

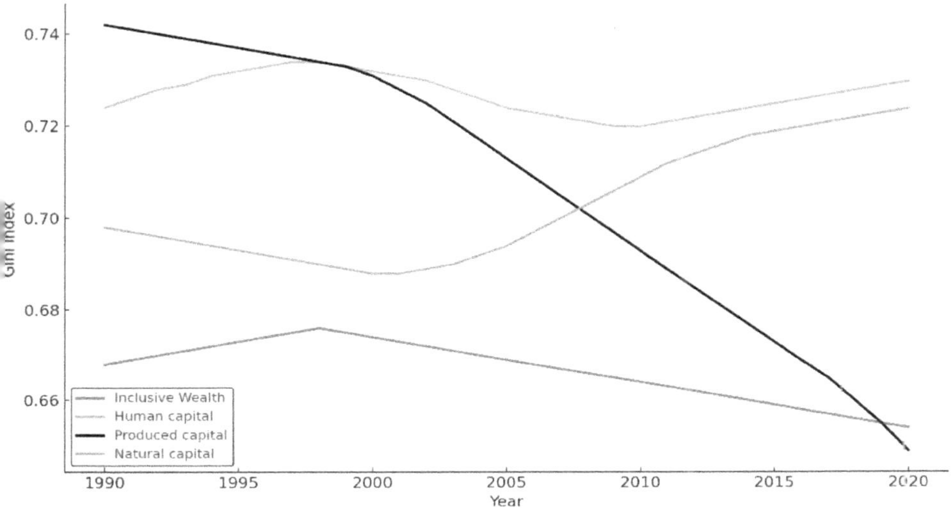

Source: Author's reconstruction based on data from United Nations Environment Programme (2023), *Inclusive Wealth Report 2023: Measuring Sustainability and Equity*. Values are approximated for visual representation; exact figures are reported in the text.

Total Factor Productivity (TFP) and Natural Capital: Divergent Growth Paths

Building on the previous discussion of capital inequality, this section introduces Total Factor Productivity (TFP) as a critical dimension of economic performance with profound implications for sustainability. TFP measures the efficiency with which inputs are converted into outputs and is often used as a proxy for technological progress. Within standard growth frameworks—such as the Cobb–Douglas production function and the Solow model discussed in Chapter 3—TFP captures residual productivity gains, typically without accounting for natural capital depletion. However, empirical work by Managi et al. (2024) shows that in many countries—particularly low- and middle-income ones—productivity gains have been accompanied by accelerated depletion of natural capital. In contrast, several high-income and G20 countries have achieved modest productivity growth while maintaining or even restoring natural capital stocks. This analysis complements the findings of the *Inclusive Wealth Report* by highlighting the role of production efficiency in shaping sustainability outcomes.

Figure 5.4 visualises this relationship, plotting average annual TFP growth (on the horizontal axis) against the rate of natural capital depletion (on the vertical axis) for the period 2010–2019. The lower-right quadrant—which represents countries with positive TFP growth and high rates of natural capital loss—comprises primarily low- and middle-income countries. These economies are achieving short-term efficiency gains at the cost of long-term ecological sustainability. In contrast, high-income and G20 countries are concentrated towards the upper-right quadrant, where productivity growth is more often aligned with slower or even negative rates of natural capital depletion. This distribution of countries reflects a deeper asymmetry in global development pathways: while high-income and G20 countries are improving productivity without further environmental degradation, many low- and middle-income countries continue to rely on resource-intensive growth strategies that erode their natural capital base—undermining long-term sustainability and intergenerational equity.

Figure 5.4: Relationship between Average Annual TFP Growth and Rates of Natural Capital Depletion (2010-2019).

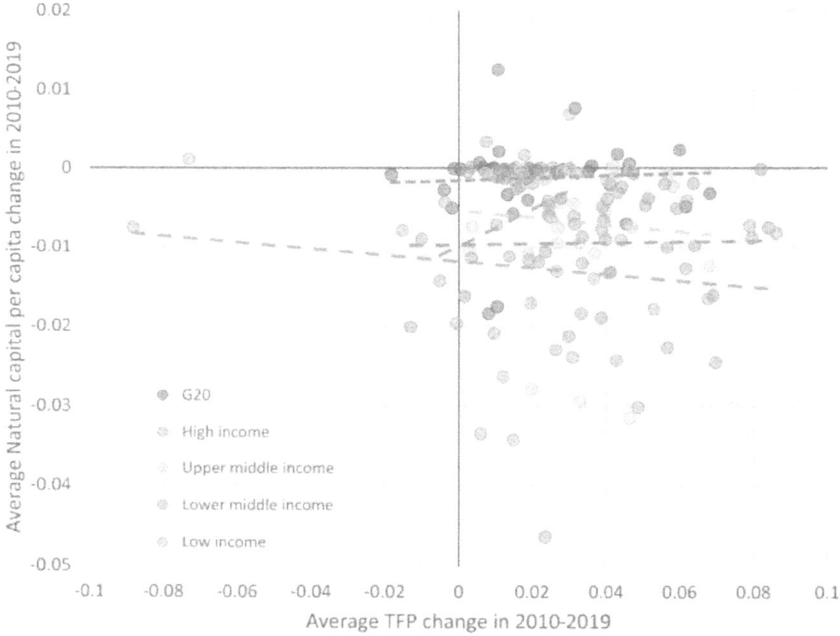

Source: Managi, S., Chen, S., Kumar, P. and Dasgupta, P. (2024), reproduced from an open access source.

The evidence presented in this section reinforces the chapter's central message: the depletion of natural capital and inequality are deeply interconnected globally. Many low- and middle-income countries continue to rely on resource-intensive growth strategies that erode their natural capital, while some high-income and G20 countries exhibit partial decoupling between productivity gains and environmental decline during 2010–2019. These patterns make it clear that macroeconomic approaches must respect environmental limits, reduce inequality, and build long-term resilience.

The next section explores how this could be pursued through a green macroeconomic agenda.

5.3. Green Keynesianism

The preceding chapters examined *sustainable investment* by analytically decomposing its core elements across different levels of analysis. Chapters 2 and 3 focused on how sustainable finance, materiality, carbon pricing, and uncertainty shape investment incentives, costs, and risk. Chapter 4 operationalised these elements at the micro level through life-cycle assessment, carbon accounting, and behavioural instruments. Building on this foundation, this section now integrates sustainable investment into a Keynesian macroeconomic framework, positioning it as the Investment (I) component in the Keynesian output equation, where total output (Y) is composed of consumption (C), investment (I), government expenditure (G), and net exports (X – M).

Embedding *sustainable investment* within this macroeconomic structure also enables observation of how macroeconomic conditions can reinforce or undermine sustainability-oriented capital allocation. In particular, placing sustainable investment inside the Investment (I) component highlights its interaction with government expenditure (G), including fiscal distortions such as fossil-fuel subsidies. While sustainable investment redirects capital towards low-carbon and productivity-enhancing activities, misaligned public spending offsets these effects by sustaining carbon-intensive structures. Sustainability, therefore, depends not only on investment decisions but also on the alignment of fiscal policy with long-term ecological goals.

Green Keynesianism extends the traditional Keynesian focus on demand management by shifting attention from the volume of economic activity to its qualitative composition. Rather than asking only how much to stimulate demand, it asks where demand should be directed and which types of investment should be prioritised. In this framework, public and private investment are deliberately steered towards low-carbon infrastructure, natural capital, human capital, and capacity building—areas that support long-term productivity while respecting planetary boundaries. This shift enables the Keynesian framework to capture not only the level of economic activity, but also its environmental and social composition.

As argued in earlier chapters, sustainability-driven investment reflects corrected price signals, cost structures, and uncertainty. When positioned within the Investment (I) component, sustainable investment connects firm-level flexibility and risk management to broader goals of long-term economic transformation, inclusive growth, and ecological balance. Building on this logic, the following section revisits the Keynesian output equation and examines how its components can be restructured to support a sustainability-oriented macroeconomic strategy.

The key Sustainable Development Goals (SDGs) associated with Green Keynesianism are presented in Table 5.4.

Table 5.4: SDGs associated with Green Keynesianism.

SDG	Goal Title	Relevance to Green Keynesianism
SDG 8	Decent Work and Economic Growth	Supports job creation and productivity through green investments and fiscal stimulus.
SDG 12	Responsible Consumption and Production	Integrates Target 12.c on fossil fuel subsidy reform and reorients aggregate demand away from carbon-intensive sectors.
SDG 7	Affordable and Clean Energy	Redirects fiscal policy towards clean energy and away from fossil fuel subsidies.
SDG 9	Industry, Innovation and Infrastructure	Strengthens clean technology, infrastructure upgrades, and industrial transformation.
SDG 13	Climate Action	Aligns macroeconomic policy with long-term climate goals and carbon-reduction imperatives.
SDG 10	Reduced Inequalities	Addresses the distributional effects of sustainability transitions and strengthens macroeconomic legitimacy.
SDG 11	Sustainable Cities and Communities	Invests in climate-resilient housing, green mobility, and sustainable urban planning.

Source: Author's analysis based on the SDG framework (United Nations, 2025).

To understand how fiscal policy can be repurposed as a lever for sustainability, it is therefore necessary to revisit the Keynesian output equation.

5.3.1. The Keynesian Equation for Output in the Context of Sustainability

From Keynes to Green Keynesianism

John Maynard Keynes famously advocated for active government intervention to stabilise economic cycles, primarily through fiscal instruments such as public expenditure and taxation. At the heart of his macroeconomic framework lies the Keynesian output equation (Keynes, 1936):

$$Y = C + I + G + (X - M) \tag{1}$$

where C denotes consumption, I investment, G government expenditure, X exports, and M imports.

In this framework, total output (Y) corresponds to aggregate demand, representing the total value of goods and services produced in an economy. This balance reflects a state where total planned spending by consumers, firms, governments, and foreign buyers aligns with the economy's productive capacity.

Keynesian output theory is typically understood as a demand-driven framework in which the level of production and income is determined by aggregate demand. This theoretical perspective emerged in response to the economic collapse of the Great Depression, when conventional economic thinking proved unable to explain prolonged unemployment and declining output. During this period (1929–1939), industrial output declined sharply across major industrial economies, prompting Keynes to advocate large-scale fiscal interventions—particularly through public investment—to stimulate aggregate demand and restore economic activity, a strategy he articulated in his landmark work, *The General Theory of Employment, Interest and Money* (1936).

While Keynes developed this framework to address cyclical instability and unemployment, contemporary sustainability challenges require a reinterpretation of its core components. In particular, the composition of aggregate demand—and especially the nature of investment and public expenditure—becomes central to aligning macroeconomic performance with ecological constraints and long-term social objectives.

Although ecological concerns were not central to Keynesian theory, Keynes himself recognised the intrinsic value of nature. In *Economic Possibilities for Our Grandchildren* (1930), he criticised the commodification of nature, writing:

> We destroy the beauty of the countryside because the unappropriated splendors of nature have no economic value. (Keynes, 1930, p. 331)

This insight aligns with contemporary critiques of conventional growth metrics—particularly GDP—and underscores the need to embed ecological value into economic measurement, pricing systems, and policy frameworks.

The Keynesian output equation provides a useful analytical framework that can be decomposed to examine how each component—consumption (C), investment (I), government expenditure (G), and net exports (X – M)—can be systematically reoriented to align macroeconomic performance with sustainability objectives.

Each component of the equation is therefore examined in turn, highlighting how its structure and composition can be reshaped to support a sustainability-oriented macroeconomic framework.

Consumption (C). Consumption patterns play a decisive role in shaping environmental outcomes, as they directly determine the level and composition of resource use and emissions. In conventional macroeconomic frameworks, consumption is treated primarily as a driver of aggregate demand. However, from a sustainability perspective, its qualitative composition becomes equally important. High-carbon and resource-intensive consumption patterns—often reinforced by distorted price signals and fossil fuel subsidies—contribute significantly to ecological degradation. Reorienting consumption, therefore, requires aligning price systems and incentives with environmental costs. Policy instruments such as carbon pricing, subsidy reform, and behavioural interventions can shift demand towards low-emission goods and services, more efficient resource use, and longer product lifecycles. In this way, consumption becomes not only a component of demand but also a key lever for reducing ecological pressure and supporting sustainable development over the long term.

Investment (I). Investment constitutes the most dynamic component of aggregate demand, as it shapes both current economic activity and future productive capacity. In conventional macroeconomic models, investment is primarily driven by expectations of profitability and cost of capital. However, from a sustainability perspective, the direction and composition of investment become critical. Capital allocation decisions determine whether economies become structurally embedded in carbon-intensive infrastructure or transition towards low-emission, resource-efficient systems. Sustainable investment, as developed in earlier chapters, reflects adjusted price signals, evolving cost structures, and uncertainty related to environmental risks and regulatory change. Redirecting investment towards renewable energy, sustainable infrastructure, natural capital, and human capital is therefore central to aligning economic growth with ecological constraints. Financial instruments such as green bonds, blended finance, and sustainability-linked incentives play a key role in facilitating this transition. In this framework, investment becomes a primary mechanism for structural transformation towards a sustainable economy.

Government Expenditure (G). Government spending serves as a central macroeconomic instrument for reorienting both the scale and direction of economic activity. Within a sustainability-oriented framework, its role extends beyond demand stabilisation to include the strategic allocation of public resources. Fiscal policy can either reinforce carbon-intensive economic structures—through mechanisms such as fossil fuel subsidies—or support the transition towards low-carbon and resilient systems. Redirecting public expenditure towards sustainability-related investments is therefore essential to align macroeconomic policy with long-term ecological and social objectives. Moreover, government spending plays a key role in coordinating large-scale transitions and reducing distributional inequalities associated with structural change. In this sense, public expenditure functions as a mechanism for guiding economic transformation.

Net Exports (X – M). Net exports represent the external dimension of economic activity, reflecting the balance between domestic production and international trade. In a sustainability context, trade patterns influence the global distribution of production, resource use, and emissions. Differences in environmental regulations, production standards, and energy systems can lead to the relocation of carbon-intensive activities across borders in response to differences in environmental regulations and cost structures. Aligning trade with sustainability objectives, therefore, requires integrating environmental considerations into trade policy and strengthening international coordination. Net exports thus become not only a measure of external balance, but also a channel through which sustainability considerations are embedded in the global economic system.

Green Keynesianism: Aligning Output with Ecological Imperatives

In the 21st century, with climate change and environmental degradation posing existential risks, a revised Keynesian approach—often referred to as Green Keynesianism—has emerged. This approach integrates traditional fiscal stimulus with ecological objectives, emphasising the role of public and private investment in supporting a transition towards low-carbon, resource-efficient, and resilient economic systems.

To operationalise this perspective within a coherent macroeconomic framework, the Keynesian output equation can be reinterpreted by examining how its components—consumption (C), investment (I), government expenditure (G), and net exports (X – M)—can be systematically reoriented towards sustainability objectives.

Specifically, the components C (consumption), I (investment), and G (government expenditure) can be subdivided into environmentally harmful and sustainable subcategories, whereas net exports (X – M) operate through external trade dynamics and are not directly decomposed.

Reclassifying Output Components

The proposed subcategories are as follows:

Consumption (C):

- Cg: Consumption of non-durable goods and energy-intensive services
- Cs: Consumption of human-capital-intensive services
- Cm: Consumption of durable goods (household investment in consumer durables)

Investment (I):

- Ime: Investment in energy-intensive manufactured capital
- Imc: Investment in energy-conserving manufactured capital
- In: Investment in natural capital
- Ih: Investment in human capital

Government Spending (G):

- Gg: Government consumption of non-durable and energy-intensive services
- Gs: Government consumption of human-capital-intensive services
- Gme: Government investment in energy-intensive manufactured capital
- Gmc: Government investment in energy-conserving manufactured capital
- Gn: Government investment in natural capital
- Gh: Government investment in human capital

This classification leads to an expanded version of the output equation:

$$Y = [Cg+Cs+Cm]+[Ime+Imc+In+Ih] \\ +[Gg+Gs+Gme+Gmc+Gn+Gh]+(X-M) \qquad \textbf{(2)}$$

We can further reorganise this to distinguish environmentally harmful from sustainable activities:

$$Y = (Cg+Ime+Gg+Gme)+(Cs+Cm+Imc+In+Ih+Gs+Gn+Gmc+Gh) \\ +(X-M) \qquad \textbf{(3)}$$

This reformulation enables policymakers to reduce components in the first bracket (associated with high emissions) and expand those in the second bracket (linked to sustainable development). By distinguishing between environmentally harmful and sustainability-enhancing forms of consumption, investment, and public expenditure, the output equation becomes an operational tool for designing fiscally active macroeconomic strategies aligned with ecological constraints and long-term development objectives.

This reconfiguration of the Keynesian framework highlights that sustainability is not only a matter of environmental policy, but also of how macroeconomic systems allocate resources and distribute income over the long term. It also underscores the need for coordinated fiscal and institutional approaches that align economic activity with ecological limits and social equity.

Correcting Distortions in the Investment (I) and Government Expenditure (G) Components

Despite increasing recognition of sustainability objectives in policy and finance, both private and public capital continue to be directed towards carbon-intensive activities, generating structural distortions in the Investment (I) and Government Expenditure (G) components of the output equation by misaligning capital allocation with ecological constraints.

Investment (I): Fossil Fuel Finance and Private Investment Distortions

Private financial flows play a central role in shaping the composition of the investment component of the output equation. Empirical evidence illustrates the persistence of fossil fuel financing within global banking systems. Data from the *Banking on Climate Chaos: Fossil Fuel Finance Report 2025* show that:

- In 2024, the 65 largest global banks committed USD 869 billion to fossil fuel-linked companies.
- In the same year, USD 429 billion of this total was directed to firms expanding fossil fuel extraction and infrastructure.
- In terms of individual institutions, the largest financiers were J.P. Morgan (USD 53.5 billion), Bank of America (USD 46 billion), and Citigroup (USD 44.7 billion).

These figures reveal a structural misalignment between sustainability objectives and actual capital allocation: despite increasing policy commitments to low-carbon transitions, financial flows continue to support carbon-intensive assets.

Government Expenditure (G): Fossil Fuel Subsidies and Public Spending Distortions

Fossil fuel subsidies remain one of the most entrenched barriers to sustainability, operating across both consumption (C) and government expenditure (G) channels. These subsidies weaken the effectiveness of climate policies, distort market signals in favour of carbon-intensive industries, and undermine carbon pricing mechanisms. As a result, they reinforce inefficient resource allocation while absorbing substantial fiscal resources that could otherwise support sustainable investment. Reforming or phasing out fossil fuel subsidies is therefore widely regarded as a critical intervention in the green transition, with the potential to enhance fiscal efficiency and redirect public spending towards long-term development objectives.

Addressing these public-sector distortions, alongside those embedded in private investment, is essential for Green Keynesianism to fulfil its transformative potential.

The following section examines the economic, political, and institutional challenges of fossil fuel subsidy reform as a central lever of sustainable macroeconomic policy.

5.3.1.1. Fossil Fuel Subsidy Reform: Implications for Government Expenditure (G) and Investment (I)

1. Introduction and Definitions

Fossil fuel subsidies remain one of the most entrenched obstacles to sustainable macroeconomic reform. Often justified on the grounds of energy affordability, poverty alleviation, or political stability—particularly in low- and middle-income countries—these subsidies generate significant structural distortions. By artificially lowering fossil energy prices, they encourage overconsumption, delay the transition to clean energy, and weaken the price signals needed to redirect investment towards sustainable alternatives. Within a Green Keynesian framework, they directly undermine efforts to realign government expenditure with ecological constraints and distributional objectives.

According to the International Energy Agency (IEA), energy subsidies are policy measures that reduce the cost of energy production or consumption. The World Trade Organization (WTO) defines a subsidy more broadly as a government financial contribution that confers a benefit. In this context, fossil fuel subsidies include tax breaks, direct transfers, price controls, and other mechanisms that lower the cost of fossil fuels used for transport, electricity, cooking, and heating.

The Sustainable Development Goals explicitly address this challenge in Target 12.c, which calls for the rationalisation of inefficient fossil fuel subsidies. As measured by Indicator 12.c.1, this target links fiscal reform to broader objectives for climate, equity, and sustainable consumption. Subsidy reform thus serves as a structural policy lever to align national budgets with sustainability priorities and the broader transition goals of the 2030 Agenda.

2. Fiscal and Economic Trade-Offs

The scale of fossil fuel subsidies underscores their significant implications for public finances and development priorities. Estimates from the International Energy Agency (IEA) and the International Monetary Fund (IMF) indicate that global fossil fuel subsidies exceeded USD 1.5 trillion in 2023—far surpassing total global official development assistance (ODA), which amounted to approximately USD 204 billion in the same period.[86] In several countries, these subsidies represent a substantial share of GDP, including Iran (10.5%), Indonesia (6.2%), Turkey (5.9%), Argentina (2.5%), and Nigeria (2.2%).

These figures highlight the opportunity costs associated with maintaining fossil fuel subsidies: fiscal resources that could be directed towards health,

[86] IEA (2023); IMF (2023).

education, clean energy, or climate-resilient infrastructure are instead used to sustain carbon-intensive energy consumption.

In addition, fossil fuel subsidies alter investment incentives by reducing the Net Present Value (NPV) of clean energy projects. This weakens carbon pricing mechanisms and discourages the long-term capital reallocation discussed in Chapter 2. As a result, subsidies distort the Government Expenditure (G) component by diverting public resources away from sustainability priorities, and the Investment (I) component by reducing incentives for private capital to shift towards clean technologies.

3. Political Economy of Reform

Despite widespread recognition of their economic inefficiency and environmental harm, fossil fuel subsidies remain exceptionally difficult to reform. This difficulty lies less in economic analysis than in entrenched political constraints. In many countries, subsidised energy prices serve as a de facto social policy, compensating for weak welfare systems or low public trust in government.

In low and middle-income countries, where energy affordability is closely tied to social stability, subsidy reforms have often triggered political backlash. The experience of Nigeria is illustrative. Repeated attempts to phase out fuel subsidies—notably in 2012 and again in 2023—provoked mass protests and policy reversals. In 2022, Nigeria's fuel subsidy expenditure exceeded four times its national health budget, underscoring the fiscal cost of maintaining social stability through broad-based energy price controls rather than delivering direct support to those most in need.

Similar patterns of unrest have emerged in other countries undertaking energy subsidy reform. In Mozambique, reductions in energy subsidies in 2010 led to widespread protests following sharp increases in bread and transport prices.[87] In Haiti and Lebanon, repeated fuel price adjustments throughout the 2010s and early 2020s triggered unrest amid broader economic instability and declining trust in public institutions.[88] In Kazakhstan, the removal of subsidies and the transition to market-based fuel pricing in early 2022 sparked mass protests and violent clashes, prompting the government to reverse course.[89] In these contexts, subsidy reform is often perceived not as an economic correction but as a direct threat to household welfare—particularly where trust in public institutions is already fragile.

[87] Hanlon, J. (2010).

[88] Belgioioso, M. and Newman, E. (2025).

[89] Al Jazeera (2022).

By contrast, high-income economies generally possess stronger administrative capacity and more comprehensive social protection systems, enabling them to manage the distributive impacts of reform more effectively. In France, for instance, the 2018–2019 "Gilets Jaunes" protests were triggered by a proposed increase in fuel taxes. However, the presence of fiscal buffers and institutional channels for dialogue helped contain the crisis—highlighting the role of state capacity in managing transition risks.

Subsidy reform cannot be pursued in isolation; it must be embedded in a broader macroeconomic strategy that reallocates fiscal savings towards visible and socially beneficial investments—such as healthcare, education, and access to clean energy. Without this redistributional dimension, subsidy reform risks reinforcing inequality rather than correcting it.

4. Strategic Reform Pathways

According to the Intergovernmental Panel on Climate Change (IPCC), eliminating fossil fuel subsidies could reduce global CO_2 emissions by 1–4% and total greenhouse gas (GHG) emissions by up to 10% by 2030. This potential highlights the environmental significance of subsidy reform. However, realising these gains depends critically on how reforms are designed and implemented. The following paragraphs examine four strategic dimensions: sequencing, institutional capacity, transparency, and redistribution.

First, effective reform depends on the pace and sequencing of subsidy removal. Abrupt eliminations—especially in economically or politically fragile contexts—can provoke strong social and political backlash. By contrast, gradual phase-outs, combined with targeted compensation mechanisms, such as cash transfers, energy vouchers, or visible social investments, can mitigate short-term shocks and strengthen public acceptance of reform.

Second, institutional capacity plays a central role in determining reform outcomes. In many countries, limited administrative capacity constrains the ability to identify vulnerable populations or distribute direct transfers effectively. Strengthening data systems, public financial management, and administrative delivery mechanisms is therefore essential to ensure that subsidy reforms are both efficient and socially equitable. International cooperation can support this process through technical assistance and capacity-building initiatives.

Third, transparency is essential for strengthening accountability and sustaining political support for reform. Publishing clear and accessible data on subsidy levels and fiscal savings—through national budgets, audit reports, or international reporting mechanisms—can reduce uncertainty, improve credibility, and limit political resistance. Mechanisms such as the WTO's Trade and Environmental Sustainability Structured Discussions (TESSD) and UNFCCC reporting frameworks also support international alignment and credibility in subsidy reform efforts.

Finally, subsidy reform must generate benefits that are visible and broadly shared. Redirecting fiscal savings towards climate-resilient infrastructure, expanded access to clean energy, education, or healthcare helps transform reform from a political liability into a tangible public benefit. This aligns directly with SDGs 7 (Affordable and Clean Energy), 12 (Responsible Consumption and Production), and 13 (Climate Action), while also addressing distributional outcomes associated with SDG 10 (Reduced Inequalities)—positioning subsidy reform as a lever for inclusive and sustainability-oriented development.

Taken together, these four dimensions show that subsidy reform is a politically sensitive and strategically complex process—one that must be grounded in equity, credible policy design, and institutional trust to succeed.

5.3.1.2. Carbon Border Adjustment Mechanism (CBAM) and Net Exports (X–M)

While fossil fuel subsidy reform addresses domestic distortions in consumption and government spending, it is insufficient in an open economy where carbon-intensive production can be relocated across borders. In such contexts, carbon leakage—where emissions-intensive production shifts to jurisdictions with weaker environmental regulation—becomes a central concern. Within the Keynesian framework, this dynamic appears through the net exports component (X–M), as emissions embedded in imports undermine domestic decarbonisation efforts.

This section introduces a regionally significant policy mechanism to illustrate how trade policy influences climate outcomes: the European Union's Carbon Border Adjustment Mechanism (CBAM), which entered into force in January 2026. CBAM provides a timely example of how cross-border carbon pricing can affect decarbonisation trajectories and the international distribution of costs and responsibilities.

CBAM applies a carbon adjustment to imported goods based on their embedded emissions, aligned with the carbon price established under the EU Emissions Trading System (ETS). In effect, it ensures comparable carbon cost conditions between EU producers, who are subject to the EU Emissions Trading System (ETS), and foreign producers not bound by similar carbon pricing. It is initially applied to sectors such as cement, aluminium, steel, fertilisers, and electricity.

From a macroeconomic perspective, CBAM affects both investment (I) and net exports (X–M) in the Keynesian output equation. It incentivises foreign firms to decarbonise their production processes to maintain market access, while reinforcing the competitiveness of domestic producers already subject to the EU Emissions Trading System (ETS). At the same time, it may create tensions in global trade relations, particularly for developing countries that export high-emission goods but lack the financial and technological capacity to transition rapidly. These dynamics position CBAM as a key instrument linking SDG 13 (Climate Action), SDG 12 (Responsible Consumption and Production), and SDG 17 (Partnerships for the Goals). Its distributional effects raise significant concerns for SDG 10 (Reduced Inequalities) and SDG 8 (Decent Work), particularly in low-income exporting countries.

CBAM also reinforces the institutional development of "Beyond GDP" metrics and climate-aligned governance frameworks. It complements sustainability disclosure regimes—such as the EU's Corporate Sustainability Reporting Directive (CSRD) and the Sustainable Finance Disclosure Regulation (SFDR)—by creating demand-side incentives for cleaner production and enhanced transparency in supply chains. At the international level, CBAM has intensified policy debates at the World Trade Organization (WTO), particularly within the Agreement on Subsidies and Countervailing Measures (ASCM) and the Trade and Environment Sustainability Structured Discussions (TESSD) in Geneva. These fora seek to harmonise trade rules with climate commitments and to improve transparency in environmental subsidies and standards.

The legitimacy of CBAM depends not only on its environmental effectiveness but also on how it is designed and implemented across countries with differing historical responsibilities and development capacities. Such measures may constrain the trade and development opportunities of lower-income countries that lack the financial and technological capacity to decarbonise rapidly. These concerns are grounded in the principle of Common but Differentiated Responsibilities (CBDR), first articulated in the 1992 Rio Declaration and enshrined in the UNFCCC. CBDR recognises that all countries share responsibility for addressing climate change, but those with greater historical emissions and financial and technological capacity should take the lead while supporting others.

In the context of CBAM, the CBDR principle requires differentiated implementation across countries. In practice, this means that CBAM should incorporate: Transitional exemptions or delayed enforcement for least-developed countries;

- Revenue recycling, whereby a portion of CBAM proceeds is invested in climate adaptation and green industrial upgrading in exporting nations;
- Technology transfer and financial support to help developing countries decarbonise key sectors.

Without these equity-oriented mechanisms, CBAM risks undermining SDG 10 (Reduced Inequalities), slowing progress on SDG 8 (Decent Work and

Economic Growth) in the Global South, and eroding trust in multilateral institutions such as the WTO.

In this light, CBAM should not be viewed solely as a carbon pricing instrument. Rather, it constitutes a litmus test of whether climate-aligned trade policy can simultaneously achieve efficiency, enforceability, and equity—linking national decarbonisation efforts to a more inclusive and coordinated international transition.

Key Insights – Chapter 5: Sustainability at the Macro Level

1. GDP Provides an Incomplete Measure of Sustainable Development. GDP focuses only on the market value of output and excludes ecological degradation, social inequality, and human well-being, treating them as external rather than binding constraints. This creates a mismatch between what is measured and the multidimensional objectives of the SDGs. As a result, GDP-based evaluation frameworks prioritise output expansion over ecological constraints and social inclusion, leading to the systematic mispricing of ecological and social costs.

2. Alternative Metrics Redefine Progress. Alternative metrics redefine economic progress by integrating ecological, social, and intergenerational dimensions alongside economic output. They provide a more comprehensive framework for evaluating sustainable development by capturing dimensions that conventional GDP-based measures overlook, thereby supporting the multidimensional objectives of the SDGs.

3. Measurement Structures Economic Priorities. Economic metrics influence how economies define progress and allocate resources. They structure investment decisions, institutional priorities, and policy outcomes. When ecological and social dimensions are excluded from core metrics, they are systematically marginalised in economic decision-making. Redefining measurement is therefore a structural transformation of the economic system. As a result, what is measured becomes what is valued.

4. Inequality Constrains Sustainable Development. Economic inequality concentrates income and wealth, limiting access to resources and investment, which in turn constrains sustainable development.

5. Inequality, Ecological Degradation, and Climate Risk Are Structurally Linked. Inequality and ecological degradation form a structural feedback loop. Concentrated wealth drives higher emissions and resource use, while the impacts of ecological degradation and climate change fall disproportionately on lower-income populations. This feedback loop reinforces inequality and ecological degradation, constraining sustainable development.

6. Green Keynesianism Aligns Investment and Fiscal Policy. At the core of this chapter, Green Keynesianism places sustainable investment within the Investment (I) component of the Keynesian output equation and shows that its effectiveness depends on alignment with Government expenditure (G). This positions sustainability as a macroeconomic coordination problem: while sustainable investment redirects capital towards low-carbon activities, misaligned public spending—especially fossil-fuel subsidies—can offset these effects by sustaining carbon-intensive structures. Green Keynesianism shifts macroeconomic analysis from the volume of demand to its composition, asking where demand is directed and which investments are prioritised.

7. Trade Influences the Effectiveness of Sustainability Policies. Finally, the trade dimension completes the macroeconomic framework by considering how cross-border flows affect sustainability outcomes. In an interconnected economy, emissions embedded in imports can undermine domestic decarbonisation efforts. Trade mechanisms such as carbon border adjustments link carbon pricing to international competitiveness and extend sustainability policies beyond national borders. However, differences in development levels and capacities create challenges for aligning climate objectives across countries.

In Simple Words — Chapter 5: Sustainability at the Macro Level

Economic thinking has traditionally focused on growth as a measure of progress. The performance of an economy is still measured by its output, using indicators such as Gross Domestic Product (GDP). This approach treats economic progress as exclusively quantitative, without fully considering its effects on the environment and society.

When a forest is destroyed, this activity is recorded as an increase in GDP, even though it depletes natural capital. This reflects a fundamental accounting failure: GDP records all forms of economic activity as added value without considering their sources or impacts, thereby ignoring environmental degradation and its effects on human well-being.

In response to this limitation, new ways of measuring progress have emerged. These approaches aim to capture not only economic output, but also its ecological and social consequences. The Sustainable Development Goals reflect this broader understanding by defining progress as a combination of environmental, social, and economic objectives, rather than output alone.

At the same time, economic inequality and environmental degradation are closely connected. Higher-income groups tend to consume more resources and generate more emissions, while lower-income populations are more exposed to the consequences of these emissions, including environmental damage and climate risks. This creates a reinforcing dynamic in which inequality and ecological pressure increase together.

These dynamics also change how macroeconomic policy is understood. The question is no longer only how much to increase activity, but where investment is directed. Sustainable investment plays a central role, but its impact also depends on the direction of public spending, as both must be aligned. When public spending supports carbon-intensive structures—for example, through fossil fuel subsidies—it can offset the benefits of sustainable investment.

Finally, economic activity is also shaped by exchanges across borders. When goods are imported, the emissions linked to their production can undermine domestic efforts to reduce emissions. Some regional initiatives, such as carbon border measures, aim to address this challenge by linking trade to climate objectives. However, differences in development levels and capacities make it difficult to apply these policies uniformly across countries.

Chapter 6
Conclusion

6.1. A Misaligned Global Pricing System

The central conclusion of this book is straightforward and decisive: the global pricing system is structurally misaligned with sustainability imperatives and most ecological and social distortions stem from this structural failure. Environmental degradation and rising social disparities are predictable outcomes of a system in which market prices systematically fail to reflect ecological limits, social costs, and intergenerational consequences.

This failure stems from the way market systems treat ecosystems as costless, carbon emissions as external, and social conditions as peripheral. As a result, prices cease to convey reliable signals about long-term welfare. This leads to a persistent divergence between private returns and collective outcomes. Growth continues, but it is increasingly financed through the depletion of natural capital, rising inequality, social fragmentation, and the transfer of risk to future generations.

This book demonstrates that as long as prices remain misaligned with ecological and social realities, markets will continue to reward depletion rather than preservation, short-term extraction rather than long-term resilience. Aligning prices with ecological and social realities is therefore the economic precondition for sustainable development, as originally defined in the 1987 Brundtland Report and reinterpreted in this study.

6.2. From Cobb–Douglas to Nordhaus: Models that Exclude and Include Nature as a Constraint

The misalignment of the global pricing system has deep historical roots. For much of the twentieth century, economic models—by design, abstractions of reality—focused on output as a function of labour and capital, omitting environmental constraints. The Cobb–Douglas production function is a well-known example of this approach.

These models were subsequently interpreted within policy and institutional contexts as broadly representative of real-world market dynamics. As a result, ecosystems were systematically excluded from the logic of value creation and were not treated as constraints in the design of economic policy and investment decisions.

The neoliberal turn in the 1970s—led intellectually by Milton Friedman—reinforced this disconnection. His doctrine, which held that the sole social responsibility of business is to maximise shareholder value, narrowed the definition of economic rationality and encouraged the exclusion of ecological and social concerns from pricing and policy frameworks. In this way, a technical modelling simplification hardened into an ideological norm: nature was treated as economically invisible.

A decisive shift began with the work of William Nordhaus, whose Dynamic Integrated Climate-Economy (DICE) model explicitly linked economic output to emissions, climate dynamics, and long-term damages. In a systematic way, nature was incorporated into the formal structure of economic reasoning as a binding constraint. Nordhaus's integrated assessment models (IAMs) laid the groundwork for a new generation of research, policy tools, and global governance structures.

The Intergovernmental Panel on Climate Change (IPCC), established in 1988, extended this modelling approach—integrating biophysical data, economic scenarios, and risk analysis to provide the scientific foundation for global climate policy. Its assessments are largely based on IAMs. The Conference of the Parties (COP) process—particularly the Paris Agreement and its temperature-based targets—represents the institutional expression of this transformation, anchoring international climate negotiations in IPCC-led research and scenario analysis. Climate–economy integration thus emerged as a global framework for aligning development with ecological thresholds.

Yet despite this progress, the shift remains incomplete. Scientific understanding and IAMs have advanced—and the adoption of carbon pricing mechanisms in parts of the global economy is encouraging—but in the vast majority of cases, mispricing remains. Nature is still treated as external to production, short-term profitability remains prioritised, and long-term ecological and social costs continue to be excluded from economic signals.

The implication is clear: achieving sustainable development requires more than recognising environmental limits in theory. It demands that those limits be fully internalised into the frameworks that govern pricing, investment, and economic decision-making.

6.3. Sustainable Investment as the Transmission Mechanism

Correcting prices and updating economic models are necessary steps, but they remain incomplete unless they translate into capital allocation. Sustainable investment is the primary economic mechanism through which sustainability becomes operational.

Sustainability fundamentally transforms firms' cost structures. The internalisation of externalities—through, for example, carbon pricing—introduces additional, uncertain costs into production and investment decisions. These costs are dynamic rather than static: they evolve with climate policy, market expectations, technological change, and carbon price volatility.

As a result, firms face not only higher costs but also heightened uncertainty, making investment irreversibility a critical concern. This transformation renders traditional, static appraisal methods—such as Net Present Value (NPV)—increasingly inadequate. It calls for more adaptive approaches. Tools such as real options analysis enable firms to incorporate flexibility into decision-making by valuing the option to delay, scale, or adjust investments. Flexibility thus becomes a central source of economic value.

Sustainable investment is a structured transmission mechanism for aligning capital allocation with long-term environmental and social goals. Building on the framework presented in Table 1.2, the core dimensions of sustainable investment are:

- *Sustainable objectives and SDG alignment*
- *Exclusions and governance*
- *Double materiality (financial and impact)*
- *Irreversibility and flexibility tools*
- *Impact measurement*
- *Long-term and intergenerational orientation*
- *Regulatory and standards alignment*
- *ESG integration*

Together, these elements define sustainable investment as the mechanism through which sustainability enters financial systems and reshapes economic reasoning. This synthesis constitutes the book's working definition, developed and applied across Chapters 1–4.

Within this broader transmission framework, Ecological Footprint accounting provides a meso-level perspective linking investment decisions to planetary boundaries. By assessing whether aggregated resource demand remains within Earth's biocapacity, it reveals how local and sectoral decisions scale into global ecological pressure. As shown in Chapter 4, it serves as a diagnostic bridge between micro-level operational sustainability and the macro-level framework examined in Chapter 5.

6.4. Coordinating Private Investment and Public Spending: A Green Keynesian Framework

While private investment is central to operationalising sustainability, government expenditure plays a parallel and reinforcing role in allocating economic resources. If private capital is to shift towards low-carbon, inclusive, and resilient systems, public spending must be reoriented away from supporting carbon-intensive, resource-depleting activities. In this context, fossil fuel subsidies constitute a macroeconomic contradiction.

Chapters 2 through 4 established the core components of sustainable investment—from sustainable finance and materiality to carbon pricing and life-cycle analysis. Chapter 5 reintegrates these insights at the macroeconomic level.

This integration embeds sustainable investment within a Green Keynesian framework, in which the Investment (I) term is no longer treated as a homogeneous aggregate. Instead, it is disaggregated into two divergent paths: one that reinforces carbon-intensive, resource-depleting structures and the other that builds long-term productive capacity compatible with ecological constraints and intergenerational equity. Sustainable investment redirects capital towards low-carbon infrastructure, natural capital preservation, human capital formation, and institutional capacity building. This redefinition of the I component shows that sustainability-oriented investment may alter the composition of aggregate demand, leading to structural transformation.

At the same time, government spending plays a critical role. Misaligned fiscal policies—particularly fossil fuel subsidies—distort market signals and constrain sustainability-aligned investment. They sustain carbon-intensive structures and weaken the institutional credibility of climate and development goals.

Thus, sustainable development requires more than reallocating private capital: it demands that public finance be redirected away from harmful subsidies and towards long-term investments that reinforce social equity and ecological stability. A coherent macroeconomic strategy requires this alignment between private investment and public spending, ensuring that the sustainability transmission mechanism remains intact on both sides of the output equation.

Sustainable development is further constrained by a structural nexus linking inequality, ecological degradation, and the climate crisis. Inequality and ecological depletion reinforce one another, while the climate crisis intensifies this dynamic by amplifying ecological stress and disproportionately affecting vulnerable populations. This asymmetry between responsibility and exposure creates a self-reinforcing cycle that must be addressed within macroeconomic policy frameworks.

Yet macroeconomic coherence also depends on how progress is measured. GDP fails to capture the structural risks and inequalities generated by environmental degradation. Climate change exacerbates inequality by exposing vulnerable populations to livelihood losses, displacement, and rising living costs—none of which are captured by GDP. Similarly, the depletion of natural capital widens the gap between and within countries, deepening global disparities.

The study emphasises the use of alternative metrics—such as the Inclusive Wealth Index (IWI), Genuine Progress Indicator (GPI), and Inequality-adjusted Human Development Index (IHDI)—which offer a more comprehensive view of sustainability and equity. These constitute essential components of any fiscal or investment strategy that supports the SDGs within a Green Keynesian framework.

Together, these metrics reinforce the argument that economic reasoning must be restructured not only through investment and fiscal policy, but also through how we define progress itself. Only then can capital flows, public budgets, and development goals be meaningfully aligned with ecological and social realities.

6.5. Development as a Human Right: Global Culture and Intergenerational Well-Being

> All human beings are born free and equal in dignity and rights.

This is the opening sentence of the Universal Declaration of Human Rights (UDHR). Yet a large share of the global population cannot enjoy the rights to which they are entitled under this first article.

It is like living in an invisible prison, whose walls are unseen but deeply felt—each time people are unable to access food, shelter, education, or healthcare. These walls reflect structural and economic constraints, created by systems that exclude rather than enable, and maintained by a development model that fails to deliver dignity.

That is why sustainable development is, first of all, a human rights question. The Sustainable Development Goals (SDGs) provide a framework to support the enjoyment of these rights by current generations.

This responsibility extends beyond the present generation. The 1987 Brundtland Report (*Our Common Future*) defined sustainable development as:

> Development that meets the needs of the present without compromising the ability of future generations to meet their own needs.

This definition makes clear that development must serve not only the living, but also those who are not yet born and whose well-being depends on the systems we create today.

Caring for future generations means asking what kind of civilisation we are part of. It is a question of identity. If our actions knowingly undermine the ability of future generations to live with dignity, can we truly be proud to belong to such a civilisation?

In this sense, sustainability can be understood as a global culture. It is expressed through those who recognise themselves in it, regardless of their nationality or ethnic origin, and act accordingly. In this way, the intergenerational dimension of sustainable development, as articulated in the Brundtland Report, can become a lived reality.

Key Insights — Chapter 6: Conclusion

1. The Global Pricing System is Structurally Misaligned with Sustainability Imperatives. Market prices systematically fail to reflect ecological limits and social costs, resulting in a persistent divergence between private returns and collective well-being. As long as this misalignment persists, economic activity continues to incentivise resource depletion and social inequality. Aligning prices with ecological and social realities is therefore the fundamental economic condition for achieving sustainable development.

2. The Misalignment of Pricing Systems is Rooted in the Evolution of Economic Thought. Traditional economic models—designed as abstractions of reality—omitted environmental costs. Over time, policymakers and institutions treated these models as representative of real-world market dynamics, leading to a systematic exclusion of ecological constraints from pricing and decision-making. Although more recent approaches have incorporated environmental externalities into economic models, this shift remains incomplete, and, in the vast majority of cases globally, pricing systems continue to reflect earlier paradigms.

3. Sustainable Investment Functions as the Transmission Mechanism Through Which Sustainability Becomes Operational within the Economic System. The internalisation of environmental externalities and social costs transforms firms' cost structures by introducing dynamic and uncertain constraints, restructuring investment behaviour. As a result, traditional static decision-making frameworks become inadequate, and flexibility becomes a central component of economic value. Through this process, sustainability becomes embedded within financial systems, aligning private capital allocation with long-term environmental and social objectives.

4. **Sustainable Development is a Macroeconomic Coordination Problem Requiring Alignment Between Private Investment, Public Spending, and Measurement Frameworks.** Within a Green Keynesian framework, sustainability depends on redirecting capital and fiscal policy away from carbon-intensive structures toward long-term investments compatible with ecological constraints and social equity. This coordination occurs within a structural nexus linking inequality, ecological degradation, and the climate crisis, thereby reinforcing systemic imbalances. Achieving macroeconomic coherence, therefore, requires not only aligning the Investment (I) and Government (G) components of the output equation but also redefining progress through alternative metrics that integrate ecological limits, distributional outcomes, and intergenerational well-being.

5. **Sustainable Development is, first of all, a Human Rights Question.** The Sustainable Development Goals (SDGs) enable all human beings to enjoy their basic rights affirmed in the first article of the Universal Declaration of Human Rights. Within this framework, sustainability can be understood as a global culture. It is expressed through individuals who recognise themselves in it and act accordingly.

In Simple Words — Chapter 6: Conclusion

In today's global economy, many prices do not reflect the true costs of what we produce and consume. Environmental damage and social impacts are often left out. As a result, activities that harm the environment or increase inequality can still appear profitable.

Prices should include these environmental and social costs. When they do not, they send the wrong signals, encouraging businesses and investors to focus on short-term gains, even if this leads to long-term environmental damage or social problems.

The problem of misaligned prices has deep historical roots. For much of the twentieth century, economic models focused mainly on capital and labour, leaving nature outside the analysis. These simplified models were often treated as if they fully described how the real economy works. As a result, environmental limits were largely ignored in policy and business decisions. Over time, this way of thinking turned into an economic mindset. In particular, the idea that businesses should focus only on maximising profits reinforced the exclusion of environmental and social concerns from economic decision-making.

A shift began when economists started to include nature directly in their models. The basic idea is simple: the economy depends on the environment and must operate within its limits. New approaches linked economic activity to emissions, climate change, and long-term damages, helping policymakers better evaluate the consequences of economic growth. This shift also influenced global policy. Scientific institutions and international agreements now use these models to guide climate action and set environmental targets. However, the transition is still incomplete. In many cases, economic decisions continue to prioritise short-term profits, while environmental and social costs remain only partially reflected. Achieving sustainable development, therefore, requires that environmental limits are fully taken into account in economic thinking and decision-making.

Correcting prices and improving economic models are important steps, but what ultimately matters is where money goes. In simple terms, capital needs to flow towards activities that support long-term environmental and social sustainability. This is the role of sustainable investment, which is the main way sustainability becomes part of the economic system. In practice, this changes how companies make decisions. Taking environmental costs into account often makes investments more expensive and more uncertain. Because of this uncertainty, companies need to remain flexible. Instead of making fixed decisions upfront, they must be able to adjust, delay, or scale their investments as new information becomes available. Flexibility becomes an important source of value in a changing world. Sustainable investment provides a structured way to guide these decisions, ensuring that financial flows support long-term goals.

But this is not enough on its own. Government spending also plays a key role in structuring how resources are used. Private investment and public policy need to move in the same direction. If governments continue to support activities that harm the environment, it becomes much harder for sustainable investment to succeed. In today's economy, this alignment is often missing. Public spending can still support carbon-intensive activities, thereby weakening the impact of sustainability efforts and slowing the transition to a low-carbon, more inclusive system. This challenge is further complicated by a deeper problem. Inequality, environmental degradation, and the climate crisis are closely linked and reinforce each other. Those who contribute least to environmental damage are often the most affected by its consequences, creating a cycle in which social and environmental problems grow together.

Another important issue is how we measure progress. Traditional indicators like GDP focus on economic output but do not capture environmental damage or social inequality. As a result, they can give a misleading picture of development. For this reason, alternative measures are needed. Indicators that include environmental and social factors provide a more complete understanding of progress and help guide better decisions. Together, these elements show that achieving sustainable development requires a coordinated approach—where investment, public policy, and the way we measure progress are all aligned with long-term environmental and social realities.

Ultimately, however, the discussion extends beyond economics. Sustainable development is, first of all, a question of human rights. The basic idea is simple: the first article of the Universal Declaration of Human Rights states that every human being has the right to access essential needs such as food, shelter, education, and healthcare, and to live with dignity. However, to enjoy these rights, societies must reach a certain level of development. When this is not the case, people remain unable to enjoy the rights to which they are entitled. For those affected, it can feel like living in an invisible prison—where the walls are not seen, but are experienced every day through limited access to opportunities and basic needs. These constraints are created by systems that exclude rather than support people.

Sustainable development also concerns future generations. It means meeting people's needs today without reducing the ability of future generations to meet their own needs. This raises a question about identity: can we truly be proud of ourselves if we act otherwise?

In this sense, sustainability can be understood as a global culture. It is expressed by those who feel they belong to it and recognise themselves in it—across countries, societies, and generations. You may be from Nigeria, China, Australia, Brazil, or anywhere else. What matters is not where you are from, but whether you feel part of this global culture. This culture is not an abstraction of reality—it exists concretely in the daily lives of those who live it, grounded in shared mental models.

Annex: Real Options - Evaluating Sustainable Investment Projects

Sustainable investments are characterised by high uncertainty, significant irreversibility, and the need for strategic flexibility—features that traditional evaluation tools, such as Net Present Value (NPV), fail to capture adequately. In contrast, the Real Options Approach (ROA) offers a dynamic and adaptive framework that accounts for the value of managerial flexibility under uncertainty, making it particularly suitable for sustainability-driven projects.

Conceptual Foundation of Real Options

The foundational concept of real options was introduced by Stewart Myers (1977), who described them as "opportunities to purchase real assets on possibly favourable terms." Drawing an analogy from financial options, real options give managers the right—but not the obligation-to undertake specific actions (such as deferring, expanding, or abandoning a project) based on how future uncertainties unfold.

In the context of capital budgeting, real options represent the strategic choices available to decision-makers over time, allowing them to revise or stage investments in response to evolving information. Unlike the traditional NPV method, which evaluates projects through a static, all-or-nothing lens, real options incorporate sequential decision-making under uncertainty, enhancing both the precision and robustness of investment appraisals.

This distinction is especially relevant for sustainable investment projects, where the irreversible nature of many capital expenditures compounds long-term environmental, regulatory, and technological uncertainties. Real options theory enables more realistic project valuation, reflecting their inherent flexibility and responsiveness to complex, dynamic conditions.

Types of Real Options in Sustainable Investment

Real options offer a structured approach to valuing flexibility in capital-intensive, long-term projects under uncertainty. Below are the key types of real options particularly relevant to sustainable investment contexts:

1. **Option to Delay (Timing Flexibility)**
   This option allows decision-makers to defer investment until more information becomes available or uncertainty is reduced—such as awaiting

regulatory clarity, policy shifts, or technological breakthroughs. It is especially valuable in volatile or policy-sensitive markets, such as carbon pricing or renewable energy sectors.

2. **Option to Stage (Sequential or Phased Investment)**
   Projects can be structured as a series of contingent stages. Investment in one phase proceeds only if the outcomes of the previous phase are satisfactory. This staged approach is particularly suited to research and development (R&D), clean technology deployment, or infrastructure rollouts, where learning in early stages informs future decisions.

3. **Option to Scale (Expand or Contract Capacity)**
   This option allows for adjustments in the scale of operations in response to market signals. A firm may expand capacity under favourable market conditions or contract in adverse scenarios. Such operational flexibility is highly beneficial for sustainable production facilities or circular economy models.

4. **Option to Abandon (Exit Strategy)**
   Under adverse conditions—such as cost overruns, technological failure, or regulatory reversals—the abandonment option allows for early project termination to minimise sunk costs. This helps safeguard capital and reallocate resources more efficiently, particularly in high-risk sustainability ventures.

5. **Option to Switch Inputs or Outputs (Flexibility in Operations)**
   This option enables technological or market adaptation—switching between input sources (e.g., renewable vs. conventional fuels) or product outputs (e.g., biofuels vs. electricity). This is particularly relevant in dynamic environments affected by resource availability, policy incentives, or consumer preferences.

Valuing Flexibility in Sustainable Investment

The Real Options Approach (ROA) introduces strategic flexibility into investment valuation, allowing decision-makers to adapt to evolving circumstances. By incorporating models borrowed from financial option theory—most notably the Black–Scholes framework—ROA quantifies the value of managerial flexibility in uncertain environments. This is particularly relevant for sustainable investments, where uncertainty is both high and multidimensional.

Unlike traditional Net Present Value (NPV) methods, which produce static, binary decisions (invest or not invest), real options embed a time-sensitive decision-making layer. This framework enables investors to:

- **Defer commitments** until more information becomes available,
- **Adjust to dynamic policy or market conditions**, such as carbon pricing mechanisms or subsidy regimes,
- **Limit downside risk** while retaining exposure to upside potential, enhancing capital efficiency in volatile contexts.

Strategic Application in Sustainability

Real options are particularly well-suited for sustainability-related projects, which are typically characterised by:

- **High uncertainty** in outcomes (e.g., regulatory frameworks, climate volatility, long-term environmental impact),
- **Partial or full irreversibility** of investment (e.g., infrastructure for green energy, ecosystem restoration),
- **Gradual technology adoption** and market uptake, such as electric mobility or green hydrogen.

In such settings, the flexibility to defer, scale, stage, or abandon an investment provides a decisive strategic advantage and improves capital allocation efficiency.

NPV and Real Options: A Conceptual Illustration

The difference between NPV and ROA is illustrated in Figure A.1 below as follows[90]:

- In the NPV framework, the decision rule is binary: if the present value of expected benefits (V) exceeds the investment cost (I), proceed with the project; otherwise, abandon it. This model assumes a now-or-never decision under certainty.
- In contrast, ROA introduces the option value (C). Even if $V < I$ today, the option to invest may be valuable. The decision becomes: invest now if $V - I > C$, otherwise, wait. This added flexibility is particularly advantageous in sustainability investments, where waiting for policy clarity or market readiness can significantly improve outcomes.

---

[90] Cassimon, D. Engelen, P.J. and Van Liedekerke, L. (2014).

Figure A.1: NPV and Real Options Approach (ROA).

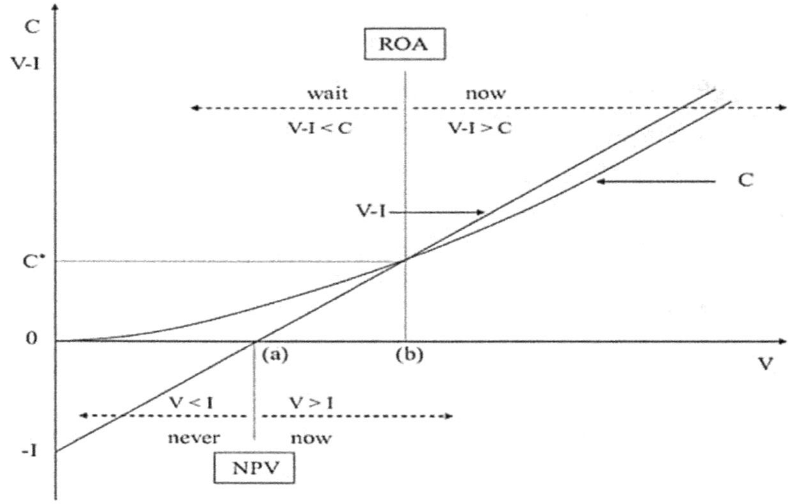

Source: Cassimon, D., Engelen, P.J., and Van Liedekerke, L. (2014). Reproduced with permission from the authors.

To conclude, the Real Options Approach offers a robust framework for assessing sustainable investment projects in contexts characterised by deep uncertainty, irreversibility, and long-term horizons. By explicitly valuing strategic flexibility, ROA enables decision-makers to optimise the timing, scale, and sequencing of investments—key considerations in dynamic policy and market environments. This is particularly critical in emerging sectors such as renewable energy, green hydrogen, and carbon capture, where the trajectory of returns is contingent on evolving regulatory landscapes, technological breakthroughs, and alignment with global climate commitments. As such, ROA not only enhances financial decision-making but also supports more adaptive and resilient strategies aligned with sustainability goals.

Bibliography

Note: Online sources, including those cited as n.d. (no date), are listed in full in the Web References section below.

Aït-Sahalia, Y., Hansen, L. P. and Scheinkman, J. A. (2024) 'When uncertainty and volatility are disconnected: implications for asset pricing and portfolio performance', *Journal of Econometrics*, 241, pp. 105–132.

Allcott, H. and Rogers, T. (2014) 'The short-run and long-run effects of behavioural interventions: experimental evidence from energy conservation', *American Economic Review*, 104(10), pp. 3003–3037. https://doi.org/10.1257/aer.104.10.3003

Annan, K. (2005). *In Larger Freedom: Towards Development, Security and Human Rights for All.* Report of the Secretary-General. New York: United Nations.

Armstrong, J. (2022) *Climate impacts of exemptions to the EU's shipping proposals.* Brussels: Transport & Environment.

Atkinson, A. B. (1970) 'On the measurement of inequality', *Journal of Economic Theory*, 2(3), pp. 244–263. https://doi.org/10.1016/0022-0531(70)90039-6

Ayres, R. U. and Warr, B. (2005) *Accounting for growth: the role of physical work.* Cheltenham: Edward Elgar. https://doi.org/10.1016/j.strueco.2003.10.003

Belgioioso, M. and Newman, E. (2025) 'Fossil fuel subsidy reform, distributive justice and civil unrest', *Energy Research & Social Science*, 119, pp. 1–10. Available at: https://doi.org/10.1016/j.erss.2023.103115 (Accessed: 2 February 2026).

Benartzi, S. and Thaler, R. H. (2013) 'Behavioural economics and the retirement savings crisis', *Science*, 339(6124), pp. 1152–1153. https://doi.org/10.1126/science.1231320

Benes, J. and Devarajan, S. (2000) 'Modelling the environment in economic growth models', *World Bank Economic Review*, 14(1), pp. 1–25.

Benz, E. and Trück, S. (2009) 'Modelling the price dynamics of CO_2 emission allowances', *Energy Economics*, 31(1), pp. 4–15. Available at: https://doi.org/10.1016/j.eneco.2008.07.003

Berik, G. and Gaddis, E. (2011) *The Utah Genuine Progress Indicator (GPI), 1990–2007: a report to the people of Utah.* Salt Lake City: Utah Population and Environment Council.

Berr, E. (2008) *Whither sustainable development? A Keynesian perspective.* Paper presented at the 10th Conference of the Association for Heterodox Economics (AHE), Anglia Ruskin University, Cambridge, UK.

Böhm, C., Sourdeval, O., Mülmenstädt, J., Quaas, J. and Crewell, S. (2019) 'Cloud base height retrieval from multi-angle satellite data', *Atmospheric Measurement Techniques*, 12, pp. 1841–1860. Available at: https://doi.org/10.5194/amt-12-1841-2019

Bretschger, L. and Smulders, S. (2006) *Sustainability and substitution of exhaustible natural resources.* CER-ETH Working Paper No. 03/26, ETH Zurich. Available at: https://ethz.ch/content/dam/ethz/special-interest/mtec/cer-eth/cer-eth-dam/documents/working-papers/wp_03_26.pdf (Accessed 7 February 2026).

Brunner, F. and Bakhshi, A. (2022) *Deep real options: neural network-based decision-making for multi-stage infrastructure investments under uncertainty. arXiv preprint.* Available at: https://arxiv.org/abs/2204.05267

Camilleri, A. and Larrick, R. P. (2015) 'Choice architecture', in Scott, R. A. and Kosslyn, S. M. (eds.) *Emerging Trends in the Social and Behavioural Sciences.* Hoboken, NJ: John Wiley & Sons, pp. 1–14. https://doi.org/10.1002/9781118900772.etrds0039

Canadian Climate Institute (2022) *Closing the carbon pricing certainty gap.* Ottawa: Canadian Climate Institute.

Capelli, L. *et al.* (2022) 'Is buying local food a sustainable practice? A scoping review of consumers' preferences for local food', *Sustainability,* 14, Article 772. Available at: https://doi.org/10.3390/su14020772

Cassimon, D., Engelen, P. J. and Van Liedekerke, L. (2014) 'When do firms invest in corporate social responsibility? A real options framework', *Journal of Business Ethics,* 125(1), pp. 15–29. Available at: https://doi.org/10.1007/s10551-013-1907-5

Chevallier, J. (2011) 'A model of carbon price interactions with macroeconomic and energy dynamics', *Energy Economics,* 33(6), pp. 1295–1312. Available at: https://doi.org/10.1016/j.eneco.2011.07.012

City of Copenhagen (2013) *Carbon neutral by 2025: Copenhagen climate plan.* Copenhagen: City of Copenhagen.

City of Geneva (2022) *Climate strategy: Ville de Genève.* Geneva: City of Geneva.

Cobb, C. W. and Douglas, P. H. (1928) 'A theory of production', *American Economic Review,* 18(1), pp. 139–165.

Comert, M. (2019) 'Revival of Keynesian economics or greening capitalism: green Keynesianism', *Sosyoekonomi,* 27(42), pp. 129–144.

Cui, Q. and Zhou, Y. (2025) 'Protocol to calculate the climate effects of the global aviation industry using the Aviation FAIR model', *STAR Protocols,* 6(1), Article 103656. Available at: https://doi.org/10.1016/j.xpro.2024.103656

Daly, H. E. (1996) *Beyond growth: the economics of sustainable development.* Boston: Beacon Press.

Daly, H. E. and Cobb, J. B. (1989) *For the common good: redirecting the economy toward community, the environment, and a sustainable future.* Boston, MA: Beacon Press.

Daly, H. E. and Farley, J. (2011) *Ecological economics: principles and applications.* 2nd ed. Washington, DC: Island Press.

Delgado-Ceballos, J., Ortiz-de-Mandojana, N., Antolín-López, R. and Montiel, I. (2023) 'Connecting the Sustainable Development Goals to firm-level sustainability and ESG factors: the need for double materiality', *BRQ Business Research Quarterly.* Available at: https://journals.sagepub.com/doi/full/10.1177/23409444231156415 (Accessed: 15 November 2025).

DeMartino, G. (2024) 'Economics for an uncertain world', *World Development,* 173. https://doi.org/10.1016/j.worlddev.2023.106426

Denzau, A. T. and North, D. C. (1994) 'Shared mental models: ideologies and institutions', *Kyklos*, 47(1), pp. 3–31. Available at: https://doi.org/10.1111/j.1467-6435.1994.tb02246.x

Diesendorf, M., Wiedmann, T., Lenzen, M. and Ward, J. (2024) 'Sustainability scientists' critique of neoclassical economics'. *Global Sustainability*, 7, e33. Available at: https://doi.org/10.1017/sus.2024.27

Dixit, A. K. and Pindyck, R.S. (1994) *Investment under uncertainty*. Princeton, NJ: Princeton University Press. https://doi.org/10.1515/9781400830176

Dyllick, T. and Muff, K. (2015) 'Clarifying the meaning of sustainable business: introducing a typology from business-as-usual to true business sustainability', *Organization & Environment*, 28(2), pp. 156–174. https://doi.org/10.1177/1086026615575176

Eich, S. (2024) *Antinomies of Green Keynesianism: Keynes's Faustian bargain and the politics of green growth*. Unpublished manuscript.

Espinosa, R. M. E. and Koh, S. C. L. (2024) 'Forecasting the ecological footprint of G20 countries in the next 30 years', *Scientific Reports*, 14, article 8298. https://doi.org/10.1038/s41598-024-57994-z

European Commission (2019) *Guidelines on non-financial reporting: supplement on reporting climate-related information (2019/C 209/01)*. Official Journal of the European Union, C 209, 20 June 2019, pp. 1–30. Available at: https://eur-lex.europa.eu/legal-content/EN/TXT/?uri=CELEX:52019XC0620(01) (Accessed: 26 April 2025).

European Commission (2020) *A hydrogen strategy for a climate-neutral Europe*. Brussels: European Commission. Available at: https://eur-lex.europa.eu/legal-content/EN/TXT/?uri=CELEX:52020DC0301 (Accessed: 26 April 2025).

European Commission (2021) *Fit for 55: delivering the EU's 2030 climate target on the way to climate neutrality*. COM(2021) 550 final. Brussels: European Commission.

European Commission, Joint Research Centre (JRC) (2023) *Weitzman meets Taylor: EU allowances futures price drivers and carbon cap rules*. Luxembourg: Publications Office of the European Union.

European Union (2014) *Directive 2014/95/EU of the European Parliament and of the Council of 22 October 2014 amending Directive 2013/34/EU as regards disclosure of non-financial and diversity information by certain large undertakings and groups, Official Journal of the European Union*. Available at: https://eur-lex.europa.eu/legal-content/EN/TXT/?uri=CELEX:32014L0095 (Accessed: 22 February 2026).

European Union (2019) *Regulation (EU) 2019/2088 of the European Parliament and of the Council of 27 November 2019 on sustainability-related disclosures in the financial services sector, Official Journal of the European Union*. Available at: https://eur-lex.europa.eu/legal-content/EN/TXT/?uri=CELEX:32019R2088 (Accessed: 26 April 2025).

European Union (2022) *Directive (EU) 2022/2464 of the European Parliament and of the Council of 14 December 2022 amending Regulation (EU) No 537/2014 and Directives 2004/109/EC, 2006/43/EC and 2013/34/EU, as regards corporate sustainability reporting, Official Journal of the European Union*. Available at: https://eur-lex.europa.eu/legal-content/EN/TXT/?uri=CELEX:32022L2464 (Accessed: 26 April 2025).

Evola, R. S., Peira, G., Varese, E., Bonadonna, A. and Vesce, E. (2022) 'Short food supply chains in Europe: scientific research directions', *Sustainability*, 14, 3602. Available at: https://doi.org/10.3390/su14063602

Evola, R. S., Caracciolo, F., Cembalo, L. and Lombardi, A. (2022) 'Local and short food supply chains in sustainable food system transitions: a review of definitions, benefits, and limitations', *Sustainability*, 14(4), 2292. Available at: https://doi.org/10.3390/su14042292

Friedman, M. (1970) 'A Friedman doctrine: the social responsibility of business is to increase its profits', *The New York Times Magazine*, 13 September. Available at: https://www.nytimes.com/1970/09/13/archives/a-friedman-doctrine-the-social-responsibility-of-business-is-to.html (Accessed: 26 April 2025).

Fuchs, M. et al. (2024) *Carbon VIX: Carbon price uncertainty and decarbonization investments*, Working Paper, Copenhagen Business School, NYU Stern School of Business and National Bureau of Economic Research (NBER). https://doi.org/10.3386/w32937

Gachechiladze, M. (2022) 'Application of machine learning in real options analysis', *Business and Academic Research Project*, 1(3), pp. 47–60. Available at: https://barp.openjournals.ge/index.php/barp/article/view/6047 (Accessed: 26 April 2025).

Ghisellini, P. et al. (2021) 'Revisiting Keynes in the light of the transition to circular economy', *Circular Economy and Sustainability*, 1, pp. 143–171. Available at: https://doi.org/10.1007/s43615-021-00033-6

Gillingham, K. et al. (2018) *Modelling uncertainty in integrated assessment of climate change: a multi-model comparison*. Unpublished manuscript.

Gini, C. (1912) *Variabilità e mutabilità: contributo allo studio delle distribuzioni e delle relazioni statistiche*. Bologna: Tipografia di Paolo Cuppini.

Gollier, C. (2024) *The cost-efficiency carbon pricing puzzle*, Toulouse School of Economics Working Paper No. 952. https://doi.org/10.1016/j.jeem.2024.103062

González-Muñoz, R., Molina-Muñoz, J., Mora-Valencia, A. and Perote, J. (2024) 'Real options volatility surface for valuing renewable energy projects', *Energies*, 17(5), Article 1225. Available at: https://doi.org/10.3390/en17051225 (Accessed: 26 April 2025).

Haasnoot, M., Kwakkel, J. H., Walker, W. E. and ter Maat, J. (2013) 'Dynamic adaptive policy pathways: a method for crafting robust decisions for a deeply uncertain world', *Global Environmental Change*, 23(2), pp. 485–498. Available at: https://doi.org/10.1016/j.gloenvcha.2012.12.006

Hardesty, L. (2017) 'Explained: neural networks', *MIT News*, 14 April. Available at: https://news.mit.edu/2017/explained-neural-networks-deep-learning-0414 (Accessed: 26 April 2025).

Harper, S. (2018) *Demography*. Oxford: Oxford University Press.

Harris, J. M. (2013) *Green Keynesianism: beyond standard growth paradigms, Global Development and Environment Institute Working Paper* No. 13-02. https://doi.org/10.14321/j.ctt7zt76x.9

Hot or Cool Institute (2024) *The 2024 Happy Planet Index*. Berlin: Hot or Cool Institute. Available at: https://hotorcool.org/hpi (Accessed 26 April 2025).

Intergovernmental Panel on Climate Change (IPCC) (2022) 'Annex II: glossary', in Pörtner, H.-O. et al. (eds.) *Climate change 2022: impacts, adaptation and vulnerability.* Contribution of Working Group II to the Sixth Assessment Report of the IPCC. Cambridge and New York: Cambridge University Press, pp. 2897–2930.

International Energy Agency (IEA) (2006) *Carrots and sticks: taxing and subsidising energy.* Paris: OECD/IEA. Available at: https://www.iea.org/reports/carrots-and-sticks-taxing-and-subsidising-energy (Accessed: 26 April 2025).

International Organization for Standardization (ISO) (2006) *Environmental management — life cycle assessment — Principles and framework (ISO 14040:2006).* Geneva: ISO.

International Organization for Standardization (ISO) (2006) *Environmental management — life cycle assessment — Requirements and guidelines (ISO 14044:2006).* Geneva: ISO.

Kahneman, D. (2011) *Thinking, fast and slow.* New York: Farrar, Straus and Giroux.

Kahneman, D. and Tversky, A. (1979) 'Prospect theory: an analysis of decision under risk'. *Econometrica,* 47(2), pp. 263–291. https://doi.org/10.2307/1914185

Kamande, A. and Hallum, C. (2025) *Africa's inequality crisis and the rise of the super-rich.* Oxford: Oxfam International. https://doi.org/10.21201/2025.000078

Kaushiva, A. (2017) 'Nobel laureate Richard Thaler's contribution to behavioural economics: a brief review', *International Journal of Research in Economics and Social Sciences,* 7(12), pp. 1–10.

Kemala, P. N. and Hakam, D. F. (2025) 'Optimizing final investment decision with real options valuation: a case study of offshore natural gas development project in Indonesia', *Energy,* 316, 134363. Available at: https://doi.org/10.1016/j.energy.2025.134363 (Accessed: 26 April 2025).

Keynes, J. M. (1921) *A treatise on probability.* In Moggridge, D. E. and Johnson, E. S. (eds.) *The collected writings of John Maynard Keynes,* Vol. VIII. London: Macmillan.

Keynes, J. M. (1930) 'Economic possibilities for our grandchildren', in Moggridge, D. E. (ed.) *The collected writings of John Maynard Keynes, Vol. IX: essays in persuasion.* London: Macmillan, pp. 321–332. https://doi.org/10.1007/978-1-349-59072-8_25

Keynes, J. M. (1936) *The general theory of employment, interest and money.* London: Macmillan.

Keynes, J. M. (1937) 'The general theory of employment', *Quarterly Journal of Economics,* 51(2), pp. 209–223. https://doi.org/10.2307/1882087

Keynes, J. M. (1971–1989) *The collected writings of John Maynard Keynes.* 30 vols. Edited by Moggridge, D. E. and Johnson, E. S. London: Macmillan; New York: Cambridge University Press for the Royal Economic Society.

Kirchherr, J., Reike, D. and Hekkert, M. (2017) 'Conceptualizing the circular economy: an analysis of 114 definitions', *Resources, Conservation and Recycling,* 127, pp. 221–232. https://doi.org/10.1016/j.resconrec.2017.09.005

Klöpffer, W. (2008) 'Life cycle sustainability assessment of products', *The International Journal of Life Cycle Assessment,* 13(2), pp. 89–95. https://doi.org/10.1065/lca2008.02.376

Legiedz, T. (2022) 'The ecological boundaries of green Keynesianism', *International Journal of Public Administration, Management and Economic Development*, pp. 150–171. https://doi.org/10.60026/ijpamed.v8i2.114

Lee, G. G. and Ham, S.-W. (2023) 'A comprehensive review of real options analysis with deep learning applications for infrastructure investment', *Energies*, 16(17), p. 6333. Available at: https://doi.org/10.3390/en16176333.

Lempert, R. J., Lawrence, J., Kopp, R. E., Haasnoot, M., Reisinger, A., Grubb, M. and Pasqualino, R. (2024) 'The use of decision making under deep uncertainty in the IPCC', *Frontiers in Climate*, 6, 1380054. Available at: https://doi.org/10.3389/fclim.2024.1380054 (Accessed: 26 April 2025).

Life Cycle Initiative (n.d.) *Towards a life cycle sustainability assessment.* Paris: United Nations Environment Programme (UNEP), Sustainable Consumption and Production Branch (UNEP DTIE).

Liu, S., Eriksson, A., Holmberg, H. and Jönsson, L. (2025) *Electric aviation as alternative to fossil-based jet fuel.* Policy brief. Linköping: Linköping University. Available at: https://liu.se/dfsmedia/dd35e243dfb7406993c1815aaf88a675/115507-source/policy-brief-electric-aviation-2025-09-25 (Accessed: 26 April 2025).

Lorenz, M. O. (1905) 'Methods of measuring the concentration of wealth', *Publications of the American Statistical Association*, 9(70), pp. 209–219. https://doi.org/10.1080/15225437.1905.10503443

Malthus, T. R. (1798) *An essay on the principle of population as it affects the future improvement of society.* London: J. Johnson.

Managi, S., Chen, S., Kumar, P. and Dasgupta, P. (2024) 'Sustainable matrix beyond GDP: investment for inclusive growth', *Humanities and Social Sciences Communications*, 11(1), Article 185. Available at: https://doi.org/10.1057/s41599-024-02659-5

Meadows, D. H. (1972) *The limits to growth.* Hanover, NH: Dartmouth College. Available at: https://collections.dartmouth.edu/teitexts/meadows/diplomatic/meadows_ltg-diplomatic.html (Accessed: 26 April 2025).

Meadows, D. H., Randers, J. and Meadows, D. L. (2004) *A synopsis: limits to growth – the 30-year update.* Available at: https://donellameadows.org/archives/a-synopsis-limits-to-growth-the-30-year-update/ (Accessed: 26 April 2025).

Migliorelli, M. (2021) 'What do we mean by sustainable finance? Assessing existing frameworks and policy risks', *Sustainability*, 13(2), Article 975. https://doi.org/10.3390/su13020975

Monkelbaan, J. and Steenblik, R. (2021) Fossil fuel subsidy reform: what role for the World Trade Organization?, *Trade and Environmental Sustainability Series*, Working Paper No. 3.

Montano, B. and Garcia-Lopez, M. (2020) 'Malthusianism of the 21st century', *Environmental and Sustainability Indicators*, 6, Article 100040. https://doi.org/10.1016/j.indic.2020.100032

Myers, S. C. (1977) 'Determinants of corporate borrowing', *Journal of Financial Economics*, 5(2), pp. 147–175. https://doi.org/10.1016/0304-405X(77)90015-0

Naik, H. J., Maundeni, C., Hamilton, A. G. and Kuncic, A. (2024) *Behavioural science and nudge interventions database for SDG acceleration.* UN RCO KSA Working Paper.

Nelen, D., Manshoven, S., Peeters, J., Van der Meersch, D. and Van Acker, K. (2013) 'Life cycle thinking as a decision tool for waste management policy', *Metallurgical Research and Technology,* 110(4), pp. 467–478. Available at: https://www.cambridge.org/core/journals/metallurgical-research-and-technology/article/abs/life-cycle-thinking-as-a-decision-tool-for-waste-managementpolicy/F65D61EE2DFD96098D0B4945462CED4E (Accessed: 26 April 2025).

Nobel Foundation (2007) *The Nobel Peace Prize for 2007.* Available at: https://www.nobelprize.org/prizes/peace/2007/summary (Accessed: 7 Feb 2026).

Nordhaus, W. D. (1991) 'To slow or not to slow: the economics of the greenhouse effect'. *The Economic Journal,* 101(407), pp. 920–937. https://doi.org/10.2307/2233864

Nordhaus, W. D. (1992) 'An optimal transition path for controlling greenhouse gases', *Science,* 258(5086), pp. 1315–1319. https://doi.org/10.1126/science.258.5086.1315

Nordhaus, W. D. (1993) 'Rolling the "DICE": an optimal transition path for controlling greenhouse gases'. *Resource and Energy Economics,* 15(1), pp. 27–50. https://doi.org/10.1016/0928-7655(93)90017-O

Nordhaus, W. D. (1994) *Managing the global commons: the economics of climate change.* Cambridge, MA: MIT Press.

Nordhaus, W. D. (2007) 'A review of the Stern Review on the Economics of Climate Change'. *Journal of Economic Literature,* 45(3), pp. 686–702. https://doi.org/10.1257/jel.45.3.686

Nordhaus, W. D. (2017) 'Integrated assessment models of climate change', *NBER Reporter,* No. 3.

Nordhaus, W. D. (2017) 'Revisiting the social cost of carbon', *Proceedings of the National Academy of Sciences,* 114(7), pp. 1518–1523. https://doi.org/10.1073/pnas.1609244114

North, D. C. (1990) *Institutions, institutional change and economic performance.* Cambridge: Cambridge University Press. https://doi.org/10.1017/CBO9780511808678

OECD (2017) *Behavioural insights and public policy: lessons from around the world.* Paris: OECD Publishing.

OECD (2018) *OECD due diligence guidance for responsible business conduct.* Paris: OECD Publishing.

Oxfam International (2024) *Carbon inequality kills: why curbing the excessive emissions of an elite few can create a sustainable planet for all.* Oxford: Oxfam GB.

Pareto, V. (1906) *Manuale di economia politica: con un'introduzione alla scienza sociale.* Milano: Giard & Brière.

Parry, I., Black, S. and Vernon, N. (2023) *Still not getting energy prices right: an update on global fossil fuel subsidies.* Washington, DC: International Monetary Fund. Available at: https://www.imf.org/en/Publications/WP/Issues/2023/08/24/Still-Not-Getting-Energy-Prices-Right-An-Update-on-Global-Fossil-Fuel-Subsidies-537269 (Accessed: 2 February 2026).

Parvathy, P., Koellner, T. and Finkbeiner, M. (2024) 'Mainstreaming life cycle thinking in EU circular economy policies', *Journal of Cleaner Production*, 429, 139989. Available at: https://doi.org/10.1016/j.jclepro.2023.139989

Parvathy, R., Kumar, S., Nair, A. and Menon, R. (2024) 'Integrating sustainable development goals into life cycle thinking: a multidimensional approach for advancing sustainability', *Environment, Development and Sustainability*. https://doi.org/10.1007/s10668-024-05810-z

Paolella, M. S. and Taschini, L. (2008) 'An econometric analysis of emission allowance prices', *Journal of Banking & Finance*, 32(10), pp. 2022–2032. Available at: https://doi.org/10.1016/j.jbankfin.2007.09.024

Pech, W. and Milan, M. (2009) 'Behavioural economics and economics of Keynes', *The Journal of Socio-Economics*, pp. 1–10.

Pigou, A. C. (1920) *The economics of welfare*. London: Macmillan.

Piketty, T. (2020) *Capital and ideology*. Cambridge, MA: Harvard University Press.

Piketty, T. and Chancel, L. (2021) 'Global income inequality, 1820–2020: the persistence and mutation of extreme inequality', *Journal of the European Economic Association*, 19(6), pp. 3025–3062. https://doi.org/10.1093/jeea/jvab047

Reuver, M., Sørensen, C., Basole, R. C. and Gawer, A. (2020) 'Digital platforms and responsible innovation: expanding value sensitive design to overcome ontological uncertainty', *Ethics and Information Technology*, 22, pp. 223–236. Available at: https://doi.org/10.1007/s10676-020-09537-z

Rigamonti, L. and Mancini, E. (2021) 'Life cycle assessment and circularity indicators', *The International Journal of Life Cycle Assessment*, 26, pp. 1937–1942. https://doi.org/10.1007/s11367-021-01966-2

Robbins, L. (1932) *An essay on the nature and significance of economic science*. London: Macmillan.

Rockström, J. et al. (2009) 'A safe operating space for humanity'. *Nature*, 461(7263), pp. 472–475. https://doi.org/10.1038/461472a

Rockström, J. et al. (2009) 'Planetary boundaries: exploring the safe operating space for humanity', *Ecology and Society*, 14(2), article 32.

Romer, P. M. (1990) 'Endogenous technological change', *Journal of Political Economy*, 98(5), Part 2, pp. S71–S102. Available at: https://web.stanford.edu/~klenow/Romer_1990.pdf (Accessed: 26 April 2025).

Royal Swedish Academy of Sciences (2018) *Economic growth, technological change, and climate change: scientific background on the Sveriges Riksbank Prize in Economic Sciences in Memory of Alfred Nobel 2018*. Stockholm: Nobel Prize Committee. Available at: https://www.nobelprize.org/prizes/economic-sciences/2018/summary/ (Accessed: 26 April 2025)

Sachs, J. D., Schmidt-Traub, G., Mazzucato, M. and Messner, D. (2019) 'Six transformations to achieve the Sustainable Development Goals', *Nature Sustainability*, 2, pp. 805–814. https://doi.org/10.1038/s41893-019-0352-9

Schoenmaker, D. and Schramade, W. (2019) *Principles of sustainable finance*. Oxford: Oxford University Press.

Schubert, C. (2017) 'Green nudges: Do they work? Are they ethical?', *Ecological Economics*, 132, pp. 329–342. https://doi.org/10.1016/j.ecolecon.2016.11.009

Sen, A. (1999) *Development as freedom*. Oxford: Oxford University Press.

Simon, H. A. (1955) 'A behavioural model of rational choice'. *Quarterly Journal of Economics*, 69(1), 99–118. https://doi.org/10.2307/1884852

Simon, H. A. (1957) *Models of man: social and rational mathematical essays on rational human behaviour in a social setting*. New York: John Wiley & Sons.

Smith, A. (1759) *The theory of moral sentiments*. Edited by D. D. Raphael and A. L. Macfie. Oxford: Oxford University Press. https://doi.org/10.1093/oseo/instance.00042831

Smith, A. (1776) *An inquiry into the nature and causes of the wealth of nations*. Edited by R. H. Campbell, A. S. Skinner and W. B. Todd. Oxford: Oxford University Press.

Solow, R. M. (1956) 'A contribution to the theory of economic growth,' *Quarterly Journal of Economics*, 70(1), pp. 65–94. Available at: https://doi.org/10.2307/1884513

Solow, R. M. (1957) 'Technical change and the aggregate production function', *Review of Economics and Statistics*, 39(3), pp. 312–320. https://doi.org/10.2307/1926047.

Steffen, W. et al. (2015) 'Planetary boundaries: guiding human development on a changing planet', *Science*, 347(6223), 1259855. Available at: https://doi.org/10.1126/science.1259855

Sunstein, C. R. (2014) *Why nudge? The politics of libertarian paternalism*. New Haven, CT: Yale University Press.

Thaler, R. H. and Sunstein, C. R. (2003) 'Libertarian paternalism', *American Economic Review*, 93(2), pp. 175–179. https://doi.org/10.1257/000282803321947001

Thaler, R. H. and Sunstein, C. R. (2008) *Nudge: improving decisions about health, wealth, and happiness*. New Haven, CT: Yale University Press.

The Rodney and Otamatea Times (1912) 'Science notes and news: coal consumption affecting climate', *Waietama and Kaipara Gazette*, 14 August.

Thompson, S. (2025) *Green and sustainable finance: principles and practice in banking, investment and insurance*. London: Kogan Page.

United Nations (n.d.) *Inequality-adjusted Human Development Index (IHDI): frequently asked questions*. Available at: https://data.un.org/_Docs/FAQs_2011_IHDI.pdf (Accessed: 26 April 2025).

United Nations (1997). *Kyoto Protocol to the United Nations Framework Convention on Climate Change*. Kyoto.

United Nations (2015) *Paris Agreement*. Adopted at the 21st Conference of the Parties (COP21), Paris, 12 December 2015. New York: United Nations Available at: https://unfccc.int/process-and-meetings/the-paris-agreement/the-paris-agreement (Accessed: 26 April 2025).

United Nations (1987) *Report of the World Commission on Environment and Development: our common future*. New York: United Nations. Available at: https://sustainabledevelopment.un.org/content/documents/5987our-common-future.pdf (Accessed: 26 April 2025).

United Nations (2015). *Transforming our world: the 2030 Agenda for Sustainable Development*. Resolution adopted by the General Assembly on 25 September

2015, A/RES/70/1. New York: United Nations. Available at: https://sdgs.un.org/2030agenda (Accessed: 26 April 2025).

United Nations Department of Economic and Social Affairs (UN DESA) (n.d.) *Development Issues No. 2: Inequality Measurement.* Available at: https:// www.un.org/development/desa/dpad/wp-content/uploads/sites/45/publication/dsp_policy_02.pdf (Accessed: 26 April 2025).

United Nations (1992) *Rio declaration on environment and development.* United Nations Conference on Environment and Development, Rio de Janeiro. Available at: https://www.un.org/en/development/desa/population/migration/generalassembly/docs/globalcompact/A_CONF.151_26_Vol.I_Declaration.pdf

United Nations (2021) *Secretary-General's guidance on behavioural science.* Available at: https://www.un.org/en/content/behaviouralscience/assets/pdf/UN%20Secretary-General's%20Guidance%20on%20Behavioural%20Science.pdf (Accessed: 13 January 2026).

United Nations, Department of Economic and Social Affairs (2020) *World social report 2020: inequality in a rapidly changing world.* New York: United Nations.

United Nations Development Programme (UNDP) (2020) *Human development report 2020: the next frontier – human development and the Anthropocene.* New York: UNDP.

United Nations Development Programme (UNDP) (2025) *Human development report 2025: a matter of choice – people and possibilities in the age of AI.* New York: UNDP Human Development Report Office.

United Nations Industrial Development Organization (UNIDO) (n.d.) *Material flow analysis: textbook 3.* Vienna: UNIDO. Available at: https://www.unido.org (Accessed: 26 April 2025).

United Nations Environment Programme (UNEP) (2023) *Inclusive wealth report 2023: measuring sustainability and equity.* Available at: https://www.unep.org/resources/report/inclusive-wealth-report-2023-measuring-sustainability-and-equity (Accessed: 26 April 2025).

van Assche, H. and Compernolle, T. (2022) 'Using real options thinking to value investment flexibility in carbon capture and utilization projects (CCU): a review', *Sustainability,* 14(4), Article 2098. Available at: https://www.mdpi.com/2071-1050/14/4/2098 (Accessed: 26 April 2025).

van der Ploeg, F. (2021) 'Carbon pricing under uncertainty', *International Tax and Public Finance,* 28, pp. 1122–1142. https://doi.org/10.1007/s10797-021-09686-x

Yang, Z. R. and Yang, Z. (2014) *Comprehensive biomedical physics.* Oxford: Elsevier.

Wackernagel, M. and Rees, W. (1996) *Our ecological footprint: reducing human impact on the Earth. Gabriola Island,* BC: New Society Publishers.

Weinmann, M., Schneider, C. and vom Brocke, J. (2016) 'Digital nudging', *Business and Information Systems Engineering,* 58(6), pp. 433–436. https://doi.org/10.1007/s12599-016-0453-1

Williamson, J. (1989) '*What Washington means by policy reform*'. in Williamson, J. (ed.), *Latin American adjustment: how much has happened?* Washington, DC: Institute for International Economics.

Wolf, A. (2025) 'Public support for the roll-out of renewable hydrogen in Europe: a real options perspective', *International Journal of Hydrogen Energy*, 97, pp. 1440–1452. https://doi.org/10.1016/j.ijhydene.2024.11.471

World Bank (2023) *State and trends of carbon pricing 2023.* Washington, DC: World Bank Group. Available at: https://www.worldbank.org (Accessed: 26 April 2025).

World Bank (2021) *The changing wealth of nations 2021: managing assets for the future.* Washington, DC: World Bank.

World Bank (2024) *Guidance note on shadow price of carbon in economic analysis.* Washington, DC: World Bank Group.

World Bank Research Observer (2023) 'Measuring total carbon pricing', *World Bank Research Observer.*

World Meteorological Organization (WMO) (2025) *WMO confirms 2024 warmest year on record, about 1.55°C above pre-industrial level.* Geneva: World Meteorological Organization. Available at: https://wmo.int/news/media-centre/wmo-confirms-2024-warmest-year-record-about-155degc-above-pre-industrial-level (Accessed: 26 April 2025).

World Resources Institute (WRI) and World Business Council for Sustainable Development (WBCSD) (2004). *The Greenhouse Gas Protocol: A Corporate Accounting and Reporting Standard (Revised Edition).* Washington, DC.

World Trade Organization (WTO) (n.d.) *Agreement on Subsidies and Countervailing Measures.* WTO Legal Texts. Available at: https://www.wto.org/english/docs_e/legal_e/scm_e.htm (Accessed: July 2025).

Zhou, M., Zhang, D., Zhou, D. and Sun, H. (2019) 'Carbon price forecasting with a hybrid model based on ensemble empirical mode decomposition and long short-term memory neural network', *Journal of Cleaner Production*, 226, pp. 884–893. Available at: https://doi.org/10.1016/j.jclepro.2019.04.119

Web References

Acciona (n.d.) *Sustainability for all.* Available at: https://www.activesustainability.com/sustainable-development/do-you-know-when-sustainability-first-appeared/ (Accessed: 26 April 2025).

Al Jazeera (2022) 'Kazakhstan unrest highlights tricky terrain of fuel subsidy cuts'. *Al Jazeera*, 13 January. Available at: https://www.aljazeera.com/economy/2022/1/13/kazahstan-unrest-highlights-tricky-terrain-of-fuel-subsidy-cuts (Accessed: 2 February 2026).

Armstrong, C. (2023) 'Megayachts are environmentally indefensible. The world must ban them', *The Guardian*, 11 December. Available at: https://www.theguardian.com/commentisfree/2023/dec/11/megayachts-environment-carbon-emissions-ban (Accessed: 15 June 2025).

Banking on Climate Chaos (2025) *Fossil fuel finance report 2025.* Available at: https://www.bankingonclimatechaos.org (Accessed: 26 April 2025).

Cambridge Institute for Sustainability Leadership (n.d.) *What is COP?* Available at: https://www.cisl.cam.ac.uk/cop-climate-change-conference (Accessed: 26 April 2025).

CEPR (Centre for Economic Policy Research) VOX EU (2025) 'Efficient carbon pricing under uncertainty', *VoxEU*. Available at: https://cepr.org/voxeu/columns/efficient-carbon-pricing-under-uncertainty (Accessed: 26 April 2025).

Cherwell Collective (n.d.) *Carbon-costed menu pricing*. Available at: https://cherwellcollective.com/carbon-cost-menu-pricing/ (Accessed: 26 April 2025).

Climate Council (2025) *Carbon metrics explained*. Available at: https://www.climatecouncil.org.au/what-is-the-difference-between-absolute-emissions-and-emissions-intensity/ (Accessed: 26 April 2025).

Copernicus/ECMWF (2025) *Global climate highlights 2024: Hottest year on record*. Copernicus Climate Change Service / European Centre for Medium-Range Weather Forecasts. Available at: https://climate.copernicus.eu (Accessed: 14 November 2025).

Ellen MacArthur Foundation (2021) *Material circularity indicator – methodology*. Available at: https://ellenmacarthurfoundation.org/material-circularity-indicator (Accessed: 26 April 2025).

Emission Trading from the Cap and Trade System (n.d.) *Climate policy info hub*. Available at: https://www.climatepolicyinfohub.eu (Accessed: 26 April 2025).

Encyclopaedia Britannica (2025) 'Keeling Curve – atmospheric CO concentration at Mauna Loa Observatory', *Encyclopaedia Britannica*. Available at: https://www.britannica.com/science/Keeling-Curve (Accessed: 26 April 2025).

European Commission (2022) *Proposal for a regulation on ecodesign for sustainable products*. Available at: https://eur-lex.europa.eu/legal-content/EN/TXT/?uri=COM:2022:142:FIN (Accessed: 7 January 2026).

European Commission (2025) 'EU Emissions Trading System – emissions cap and allowance reduction schedule', *European Commission*. Available at: https://climate.ec.europa.eu/eu-action/carbon-markets/eu-emissions-trading-system-eu-ets/eu-ets-emissions-cap_en (Accessed: 26 April 2025).

European Commission (n.d.) 'Ecodesign for sustainable products regulation', European Commission. Available at: https://commission.europa.eu/energy-climate-change-environment/standards-tools-and-labels/products-labelling-rules-and-requirements/ecodesign-sustainable-products-regulation_en (Accessed: 26 April 2025).

European Commission (n.d.) 'EU Ecolabel – about the EU ecolabel', *European Commission*. Available at: https://environment.ec.europa.eu/topics/circular-economy/eu-ecolabel/about-eu-ecolabel_en (Accessed: 26 April 2025).

European Commission (n.d.) European hydrogen bank. *European Commission*. Available at: https://energy.ec.europa.eu/topics/eus-energy-system/hydrogen/european-hydrogen-bank_en (Accessed: 26 April 2025).

European Commission (n.d.) Hydrogen – EU energy system. *European Commission*. Available at: https://energy.ec.europa.eu/topics/eus-energy-system/hydrogen_en (Accessed: 26 April 2025).

European Commission Joint Research Centre (n.d.) Raw materials information system – circular economy indicators, tools and methods. *European Commission Joint Research Centre*. Available at: https://rmis.jrc.ec.europa.eu/CE (Accessed: 26 April 2025).

European Union (2019) *Regulation (EU) 2019/2088 on sustainability-related disclosures in the financial services sector (SFDR). Official Journal of the*

European Union. Available at: https://eur-lex.europa.eu/legal-content/EN/TXT/?uri=CELEX:32019R2088 (Accessed: 26 April 2025).

European Commission (2008) *Sustainable consumption and production and sustainable industrial policy action plan.* Available at: https://eur-lex.europa.eu/legal-content/EN/TXT/?uri=CELEX%3A52008DC0397 (Accessed: 7 January 2026).

European Commission (n.d.) *EU Emissions Trading System – emissions cap.* European Commission. Available at: https://climate.ec.europa.eu/eu-action/eu-emissions-trading-system-eu-ets/eu-ets-emissions-cap_en (Accessed: 26 April 2025).

European Parliament and Council (2008) *Directive 2008/98/EC on waste (Waste Framework Directive).* Available at: https://eur-lex.europa.eu/legal-content/EN/TXT/?uri=CELEX%3A32008L0098 (Accessed: January 2026).

European Parliament and Council (2010) *Regulation (EC) No 66/2010 of the European Parliament and of the Council of 25 November 2009 on the EU Ecolabel.* Available at: https://eur-lex.europa.eu/legal-content/EN/TXT/?uri=CELEX%3A32010R0066 (Accessed: 7 January 2026).

Federal Reserve Bank of St. Louis (2025) *Assets: total assets (less eliminations from consolidation), weekly level. FRED, Federal Reserve Economic Data.* Available at: https://fred.stlouisfed.org/series/WALCL (Accessed: 15 November 2025).

Friedman, M. (1970) 'The social responsibility of business is to increase its profits', *The New York Times Magazine,* 13 September. Available at: https://www.nytimes.com/1970/09/13/archives/a-friedman-doctrine-the-social-responsibility-of-business-is-to.html (Accessed: 26 April 2025).

Geneva Environment Network (n.d.) *History of environment in Geneva.* Available at: https://www.genevaenvironmentnetwork.org/environment-geneva/history/ (Accessed: 26 April 2025).

Global Footprint Network (2024) *Earth Overshoot Day 2024 – humanity consumes nature's budget by 1 August.* Oakland, CA: Global Footprint Network. Available at: https://www.footprintnetwork.org/2024/07/21/earth_overshoot_day_2024/ (Accessed: 17 November 2025).

Global Investors for Sustainable Development Alliance (GISD) (2020) *Definition of sustainable development investing (SDI).* Available at: https://www.gisdalliance.org/sites/default/files/2020-08/SDI%20Definition%20-%20Final%202020%2006%2004.pdf (Accessed: 26 April 2025).

Global Reporting Initiative (GRI) (n.d.) *GRI Standards: sustainability reporting standards.* Available at: https://www.globalreporting.org/how-to-use-the-gri-standards/gri-standards-english-language/ (Accessed: 26 April 2025).

Global Reporting Initiative (GRI) (2021) *The double materiality concept: application and issues.* Available at: https://www.globalreporting.org/how-to-use-the-gri-standards/gri-standards-english-language/ (Accessed: 26 April 2025).

Global Reporting Initiative (GRI) (n.d.) *GRI 1: foundation 2021.* Available at https://www.globalreporting.org/how-to-use-the-gri-standards/gri-standards-english-language/ (Accessed: 26 April 2025).

Global Reporting Initiative (GRI) (n.d.) *GRI 3: material topics 2021.* Available at: https://www.globalreporting.org/how-to-use-the-gri-standards/gri-standards-english-language/ (Accessed: 26 April 2025).

Global Reporting Initiative (GRI) (n.d.) *About GRI.* Available at: https://www.globalreporting.org/about-gri/ (Accessed: 26 April 2025).

Hanlon, J. (2010) 'Mozambique: fuel price riots — the true story'. *Pambazuka News,* 9 September. Available at: https://www.pambazuka.org/governance/fuel-price-riots-true-story (Accessed: 2 February 2026).

Harvard Business School Online (2023) *What is sustainable investing?* Available at: https://online.hbs.edu/blog/post/sustainable-investing (Accessed: 26 April 2025).

IEA (2023) *World Energy Outlook 2023.* Paris: IEA. Available at: https://www.iea.org/reports/world-energy-outlook-2023 (Accessed: 2 February 2026).

International Organization for Standardization (ISO) (n.d.) *ISO 14040: Life cycle assessment — principles and framework.* Available at: https://www.iso.org/standard/37456.html (Accessed: 26 April 2025).

Lausanne Région (2025) *Ça bouge, je consomme local – local campaign for sustainable consumption.* Available at: https://www.lausanneregion.ch/ (Accessed: 15 September 2025).

Lausanne Région (n.d.) *Lausanne Région – regional economic development.* Available at: https://www.lausanneregion.ch (Accessed: 26 April 2025).

Life Cycle Initiative (2025) *What is life cycle thinking?* Available at: https://www.lifecycleinitiative.org/activities/what-is-life-cycle-thinking/ (Accessed: 26 April 2025).

Magic Tomato (2025) *Sustainable local food delivery in Geneva.* Available at: https://geneve.magictomato.ch/en/ (Accessed: 26 April 2025).

MLG Cambridge (2025) *Atmospheric carbon dioxide growth rate.* Available at: https://mlg.eng.cam.ac.uk/carl/climate/CO2growth.html (Accessed: 26 April 2025).

NASA Goddard Institute for Space Studies (NASA GISTEMP) (2025) *Global surface temperature data.* Available at: https://data.giss.nasa.gov/gistemp/ (Accessed: 26 April 2025).

National Oceanic and Atmospheric Administration (NOAA) (2025) *Global climate report 2024.* National Centers for Environmental Information. Available at: https://www.ncei.noaa.gov (Accessed: 26 April 2025).

NOAA Global Monitoring Laboratory (2025) *Global monthly mean CO_2 concentration – trends in atmospheric carbon dioxide.* Available at: https://gml.noaa.gov/ccgg/trends/gl_trend.html (Accessed: 5 February 2026).

Our World in Data (n.d.) *Fertility rate.* Available at: https://ourworldindata.org/grapher/children-per-woman-un (Accessed: 26 April 2025).

Planetary Health Check (2024) *Planetary health check 2024: a scientific assessment of the state of the planet.* Potsdam Institute for Climate Impact Research. Available at: https://www.planetaryhealthcheck.org (Accessed: 5 February 2026).

Potsdam Institute for Climate Impact Research (2025) *Planetary boundaries infographic, version 3.1.* Available at: https://www.pik-potsdam.de/en/output/planetary-boundaries (Accessed: 5 February 2026).

Robeco (n.d.) *Definitions of sustainability.* Available at: https://www.robeco.com/en-us/glossary/sustainable-investing/definitions-of-sustainability (Accessed: 10 July 2025).

Sandbag (2025) *EU ETS carbon price viewer.* Available at: https://sandbag.be/carbon-price-viewer/ (Accessed: April 2025).

Scripps Institution of Oceanography (n.d.) *Keeling Curve.* Available at: https://keelingcurve.ucsd.edu/ (Accessed: 26 April 2025).

Thaler, R. H. (2018) *Behavioural economics: past, present, and future.* The Ryerson Lecture. [Video] Available at: https://www.youtube.com/watch?v=A1M9VSgsSW4 (Accessed: 26 April 2025).

The American Presidency Project (n.d.) *Ronald Reagan inaugural address.* Available at: https://www.presidency.ucsb.edu/documents/inaugural-address-10 (Accessed: 26 April 2025).

TheCityUK (n.d.) *Sustainable finance data: carbon pricing schemes and the price of carbon.* Available at: https://www.thecityuk.com/news/sustainable-finance-data-carbon-pricing-schemes-and-the-price-of-carbon/ (Accessed: 26 April 2025).

United Nations (n.d.) *Conferences on environment and sustainable development.* Available at: https://www.un.org/en/conferences/environment (Accessed: 26 April 2025).

United Nations Development Programme (UNDP) (2020) *Inequality-adjusted Human Development Index (IHDI).* Available at: https://hdr.undp.org/en/content/inequality-adjusted-human-development-index-ihdi (Accessed: 30 January 2026).

United Nations Framework Convention on Climate Change (UNFCCC) (n.d.) *Emissions trading under the Kyoto Protocol.* Available at: https://unfccc.int/process/the-kyoto protocol/mechanisms/emissions-trading (Accessed: 26 April 2025).

United Nations Framework Convention on Climate Change (UNFCCC) (n.d.) *Mechanisms under the Kyoto Protocol.* Available at: https://unfccc.int/process/the-kyoto-protocol/mechanisms (Accessed: 26 April 2025).

United Nations Framework Convention on Climate Change (UNFCCC) (n.d.) *Conference of the Parties (COP).* Available at: https://unfccc.int/process/bodies/supreme-bodies/conference-of-the-parties-cop (Accessed: 26 April 2025).

United Nations Global Compact (n.d.) *Sustainable finance explained: why it matters and how your business can lead. United Nations Global Compact.* Available at: https://unglobalcompact.org/journal/sustainable-finance-explained-why-it-matters-and-how-your-business-can-lead (Accessed: 26 April 2025).

United Nations (n.d.) *Sustainable consumption and production and sustainable industrial policy action plan.* Available at: https://sdgs.un.org/partnerships/sustainable-consumption-and-production-and-sustainable-industrial-policy-scpsip-action (Accessed: 26 April 2025).

United Nations (2025) *Sustainable Development Goals.* Available at: https://sdgs.un.org/goals (Accessed: 26 April 2025).

UNPRI (2023) *What are the Principles for Responsible Investment? United Nations–supported Principles for Responsible Investment.* Available at: https://www.unpri.org/about-us/what-are-the-principles-for-responsible-investment (Accessed: 26 April 2025).

Watts, J. (2023) 'Richest 1% account for more carbon emissions than poorest 66%, report says', *The Guardian,* 19 November. Available at: https://www.theguardian.com/environment/2023/nov/20/richest-1-account-for-more-carbon-emissions-than-poorest-66-report-says (Accessed: 15 June 2025).

Whitehead, J. (2008) 'Carbon taxes vs. cap-and-trade'. *Economists' View.* Available at: https://economistsview.typepad.com/economistsview/2008/06/carbon-taxes-vs.html (Accessed: 26 April 2025).

World Bank (2025) *World Development Indicators – fertility rate (total births per woman).* Available at: https://data.worldbank.org/indicator/SP.DYN.TFRT.IN (Accessed: 5 February 2026).

World Bank (2025) *Carbon dioxide (CO_2) emissions excluding LULUCF per capita (tCO_2e/capita).* World Development Indicators. Available at: https://data.worldbank.org/indicator/EN.GHG.CO2.PC.CE.AR5 (Accessed: 26 April 2025).

World Bank (2025) *World Development Indicators – CO_2 emissions (metric tons per capita).* Available at: https://data.worldbank.org/indicator/EN.ATM.CO2E.PC (Accessed: 5 February 2026).

Worldometer (n.d.) *CO_2 emissions per capita.* Available at: https://www.worldometers.info/co2-emissions/co2-emissions-per-capita/ (Accessed: 26 April 2025).

Author's Bio

Haluk Haksal is an economist specialised in green macroeconomics. He holds a graduate degree in Economics from the University of Florence, a Master's degree in Banking and Finance from HEC Lausanne, and a PhD in Economics from the University of Geneva.

He has extensive professional experience within the United Nations system, having served at FAO, UNCTAD, and ILO. He is active within the international sustainability community and teaches at the graduate level at academic institutions in Switzerland.

His research focuses on green macroeconomics, particularly on the political economy of sustainable investment and on operationalising the Sustainable Development Goals (SDGs). He has a particular interest in the role of sustainable investment in aligning economic systems, financial markets, and public policy within ecological limits.

Index

VERNON PRESS

Other Distinguished Titles from "Series in Economics":

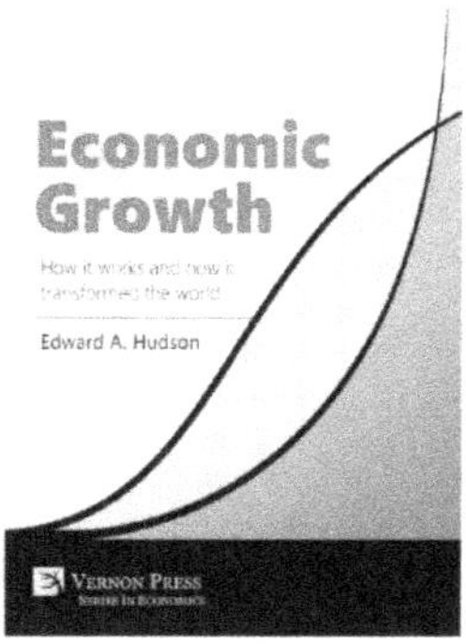

Economic Growth

How it works and how it transformed the world

Edward A. Hudson

Economic Growth explores how nations achieve sustained growth, combining 2000 years of historical analysis with a new industry-level theory that places demand at the center. Clear, comprehensive, and practical, it's essential reading for economists, policymakers, and anyone curious about how economies truly thrive.

$80 | €70 | £55
Subjects: Economics, History.
ISBN: 978-1-62273-021-6 | Hardback | 424 pp | 1/2015
Also available in Paperback and E-book.
vernonpress.com/book/36

Economics of Economy Pricing

Marin Muzhani

This book introduces the concept of the "Economy Pricing System" to explain a new phase in advanced economies, where mass-produced goods are frequently sold at discounted prices. Challenging traditional micro and macro theories, it explores how globalization, tech, and consumer behavior reshape economic models and real-world outcomes.

$77 | €70 | £62
Subjects: Economics, Business and Finance.
ISBN: 978-1-64889-670-5 | Hardback | 279 pp | 8/2023
Also available in Paperback and E-book.
vernonpress.com/book/1750

Reimagining Capitalism

Applying Negative Dialectics for a Better Future

David M. Atkinson

Reimagining Capitalism offers a bold, critical examination of capitalism in crisis. Through applied negative dialectics, Atkinson challenges systemic power and proposes new ways to rethink and reform our socio-economic future. A must-read for those seeking real change beyond surface reform.

$82 | €77 | £65
Subjects: Economics, Philosophy, Political Science.
ISBN: 978-1-64889-595-1 | Hardback | 455 pp | 4/2023
Also available in Paperback and E-book.
vernonpress.com/book/1673

Vernon Press is accepting proposals for monographs or multi-author volumes in this series.

For more information, visit https://vernonpress.com/publish-with-us or contact us directly at submissions@vernonpress.com

www.ingramcontent.com/pod-product-compliance
Lightning Source LLC
LaVergne TN
LVHW020414220926
848484LV00018B/2572/J